D1110605

THE
WORK AND WORDS
OF JESUS

REVISED EDITION

BOOKS BY ARCHIBALD M. HUNTER
PUBLISHED BY THE WESTMINSTER PRESS

The Work and Words of Jesus, *Revised Edition*
Introducing the New Testament, *Third Revised Edition*
The Parables Then and Now
Bible and Gospel
According to John: The New Look at the Fourth Gospel
The Gospel According to St Paul
(*A revised edition of* Interpreting Paul's Gospel)
A Pattern for Life (*Revised Edition*)
Teaching and Preaching the New Testament
Paul and His Predecessors
Interpreting the Parables
Introducing New Testament Theology
Interpreting the New Testament, 1900–1950
The Message of the New Testament

THE
WORK AND WORDS
OF JESUS

REVISED EDITION

by
ARCHIBALD M. HUNTER

THE WESTMINSTER PRESS
PHILADELPHIA

© SCM PRESS LTD. 1950, 1973

Scripture quotations from the Revised Standard Version of the Bible are copyright, 1946 and 1952, by the Division of Christian Education of the National Council of Churches, and are used by permission.

PUBLISHED BY THE WESTMINSTER PRESS ®

PHILADELPHIA, PENNSYLVANIA

PRINTED IN THE UNITED STATES OF AMERICA

Library of Congress Cataloging in Publication Data

Hunter, Archibald Macbride.
  The work and words of Jesus.

  Includes bibliographical references.
  1. Jesus Christ—Teachings. 2. Jesus Christ—Person and offices. I. Title.
BS2415.H77 1973   232   73–7559
ISBN 0–664–24976–0

CONTENTS

PREFACE

More than twenty years have passed since this book was first published. Originally, it was designed to provide divinity students with a sketch of the ministry of Jesus which made serious use of the sources—Mark, Q, M and L—which scholars had shown to underlie the synoptic gospels.

Since the book appeared a lot has been happening in the field of New Testament studies, so that I readily accepted the SCM Press's invitation to revise it thoroughly. In revising it, I have rewritten most of the chapters, sometimes enlarging them to include new material, and sometimes correcting deficiencies in the early edition. Three changes fall to be mentioned. First, I have omitted the opening chapter in it, 'The Quest of the Historical Jesus', because there are now available several good books on the theme, besides Schweitzer's famous one bearing this title. Second, for quotations from the gospels I have substituted the RSV for the RV, while on occasion using the NEB where its version seemed better. (In the appendices at the end, however, the RV text of the gospel sources, Q, M and L, has been retained, in order to cut down expense.) Third, since 1950 a 'new look' has been coming over the Fourth Gospel, which is now admitted by a great many scholars to be independent of the first three and to preserve a good deal of early tradition. The reader will therefore find in the new edition fairly extensive reliance on the testimony of St John, notably in the account of the post-Galilean phase of Jesus' work.

It is my hope that this radically-revised edition will provide the student of theology with an account of the works and words of Jesus which, while not ignoring the contribution of German critics, reflects that less radical (but, in my opinion, much sounder) approach to gospel criticism to be found in the writings of such British scholars as C. H. Dodd and Vincent Taylor, T. W. Manson and C. F. D. Moule, H. E. W. Turner and G. B. Caird.

It remains for me again to express my warm gratitude to my friend and neighbour the Rev. David Gray for helping me to remove many inconcinnities from my manuscript.

Ayr, 1973   A. M. HUNTER

INTRODUCTION

Everything in the Christian faith goes back to the story of Jesus recounted in the gospels. As any true Christian ethic is based on the moral teaching of Jesus, so all sound Christian doctrine must rest back on the person and work of Jesus as they are presented in the gospels. Theologians must therefore found their teaching about Christ on the truest portrait of him in 'the days of his flesh' which biblical scholars can paint. Moreover, if they do not like that portrait, they must not retouch it, or they may find themselves correcting 'the wisdom of God' by the wisdom of man.

There is another equally important point. Any critical account of Jesus and his mission which leaves an unbridgeable gap between the Jesus of history and the faith of the early church (as reflected in their 'preached gospel' or *kērygma*) is alike inadequate and uncritical: inadequate, because it fails to explain the origin of the church; uncritical, because a critical study of the New Testament points to the life, death and resurrection of Jesus as the sole ground of such faith.

How then should we view the work and words of Jesus *vis-à-vis* the preaching and teaching of the apostolic men? If they may not be separated, they are not on the same footing; rather they stand to each other as call and response. The life, deeds and death of Jesus, the man who addressed God as Abba; who with divine authority invited sinners to his table; and who, as God's Servant, went finally to the cross to 'ransom the many', is the call of God. The early church's proclamation of faith, the Spirit-led chorus of a thousand tongues to be heard in Paul, John, Hebrews and the book of Revelation, is the response to that call of God.

Here is the plan of the book.

First, sources and chronology.

Next, the background: geographical, historical, religious.

In 'Before the Ministry' we shall study the birth and early years, the Baptist's mission, the baptism and temptation of Jesus.

The main section of the book sketches the ministry of Jesus up to the transfiguration. There we pause to study the miracles, the disciples, and Jesus' teaching about the kingdom of God, his own person, his death and the future. Then picking up the narrative again we tell the story of the journey to Jerusalem and the events which led to the passion and the resurrection.

Part One

I

DOCUMENTS AND DATES

What are our sources of information about Jesus? The New Testament apart, they amount to no more than a few references in the Talmud and the Jewish historian Josephus plus some sentences in three Latin writers.

Non-Christian sources

The allusions to Jesus in the Talmud are mostly late, slanderous and untrustworthy. Where its tradition can be traced back to the first two centuries of our era, some true history may be preserved. The sum of it is that Jesus practised sorcery, ridiculed the wise men, led the people astray and was hanged on Passover eve. His disciples, five in number, cured sick people in their master's name. The statement that Jesus was 'hanged on Passover eve' may well be right: it has the support of both John's gospel and the tradition of the church in Asia. For the rest, what these references prove is that there is no reason to doubt the existence of Jesus. Men, as a rule, do not vehemently slander myths.

Two passages in Josephus's *Antiquities* (AD 93) mention Jesus. One, probably genuine, records the stoning of 'James, the brother of Jesus who was called the Christ'. The other says: 'Jesus, a wise man, if indeed we should call him a man, for he was a doer of miracles and a master of men who receive the truth with joy . . . he was the Christ.' Would a Jew like Josephus have written thus about Jesus? It looks as if what he wrote has been touched up by a Christian hand.

The three Latin writers are Pliny the Younger, Tacitus and Suetonius.

Pliny, governor of Bithynia, writing about AD 112 to his emperor Trajan, reports that the Christians there are wont 'on a fixed day to assemble before daylight and sing by turns hymns to Christ as a god'.

In his *Annals* (*c*. AD 115) Tacitus tells how the great fire which
devastated Rome in AD 64 was blamed on the Christians, and adds:
'Christ, from whom they derive their name, was put to death in the
reign of Tiberius by the procurator[1] Pontius Pilate.'

Lastly, Suetonius, the contemporary of Tacitus, states that the
emperor Claudius 'banished the Jews from Rome when they made
a constant rioting at the instigation of Chrestus'. 'Chrestus' is doubtless a corruption of 'Christus'. The reference is to the event of AD 49
mentioned in Acts 18.2.

Such is our information from non-Christian sources. Its smallness
is surprising till we remember that what we now see to be the most
pregnant fact in history must have struck contemporary pagans as
simply another oriental superstition.

The Christian sources

This means, for all practical purposes, the New Testament. Little
for our purpose is to be found in the apocryphal gospels written in
the first two or three Christian centuries to gratify popular curiosity
about the early years of Jesus or the wonders accompanying his
death and resurrection. Here and there they may preserve a slender
tithe of history, but it is mostly smothered beneath a veneer of legend
and fantasy.[2] Perhaps a dozen authentic sayings may be found in
what are known as the *agrapha*, those 'uncanonical' words of Jesus
found either in the early church fathers or recovered from papyrus
documents found in the last seventy years in the sands of Egypt.

In the New Testament, Paul's letters, written roughly between
AD 50 and 62, are our earliest source. Paul did not set out in them
to recount 'all that Jesus began to do and to teach'. (For him, 'the
life of Jesus', as Rom. 5.10 shows, was primarily the life that followed
the crucifixion and resurrection.) Yet a careful study of his letters
shows that he was not ignorant about the ministry, character and
teaching of Jesus in the days of his earthly life.[3] Slightly later in date
are the allusions to 'the days of his flesh' in Hebrews (5.7ff.; 13.12).
To these we may add the apostolic speeches in Acts (2.14–39; 3.12–
26; 10.34–43), where sometimes an Aramaic original seems to glim-
mer through the Greek and point to early tradition.

---

[1] An inscription found at Caesarea in 1961 suggests that Pilate's proper title was
'prefect', not 'procurator'.

[2] See M. R. James, *The Apocryphal New Testament*, Oxford University Press 1929.

[3] See my *Gospel according to Paul*, SCM Press 1966, pp. 56–60.

But our main documents are the four gospels. How do modern scholars evaluate them? The literary analysis of the synoptic gospels (Mark, Matthew and Luke) which began more than a century ago and may be said to have culminated in B. H. Streeter's *The Four Gospels* (1925), finds four sources underlying them.

First comes Mark's gospel written in Rome about AD 65–67. Its author, John Mark, a Jerusalemite, must have learned much about Jesus from his friend Peter, as he undoubtedly had access to many stories about Jesus circulating in the Christian circles in which he moved. The writer of the best modern commentary on his book, Vincent Taylor,[1] judges Mark 'an authority of the first rank for our knowledge of the Story of Jesus'. We do not wonder that both Matthew and Luke used his work as a primary source when they in turn composed gospels. But Mark was not their only source.

Matthew and Luke also used what scholars call 'Q' (German *Quelle*, 'source'): a collection of Jesus' sayings, now lost (though it can be roughly reconstructed). Probably compiled in Antioch about AD 50, it was meant to serve as a dominical pattern for living for all who had become Christians.

L, the symbol commonly used for the matter peculiar to Luke (or, more specifically, Luke 3–24), is probably the fruit of Luke's personal research in Caesarea round about AD 57–59. It is very valuable for the many parables of Jesus which it preserves, as also for its account of the passion.

The least valuable source is M, the matter peculiar to Matthew. It consists of both narrative and teaching. Some of Matthew's narratives sound like Jerusalem gossip (e.g. Matt. 27.51–53), others show embellishment bordering on the apocryphal (e.g. Matt. 14.28–33). But very important is the teaching material which the evangelist has masterfully gathered into five great discourses.[2]

What of John's gospel? Not so long ago it was usual when attempting to write a 'Life' of Jesus to set this gospel aside as theology without much real rootage in history. Thanks to 'the new look' which has recently been coming over this gospel,[3] this cavalier dismissal is no longer permissible. Now critics—and it is 'a majority opinion' even in Germany—increasingly recognize that John's gospel is independent of the synoptics, and recent research shows that it rests back on

[1] *The Gospel according to Mark*, Macmillan 1957, p. 148.

[2] English texts of Q, L and M are printed at the end of this book.

[3] See C. H. Dodd, *Historical Tradition in the Fourth Gospel*, Cambridge University Press 1963, and my *According to John*, SCM Press 1968.

ancient Palestinian tradition about Jesus which amplifies, illumi-
nates and sometimes corrects the synoptic tradition. If, more
profoundly than the first three evangelists, St John brings out the
ultimate meaning of Christ's coming among men:

> Word of the Father
> Now in flesh appearing,

he also sheds light at the beginning, the middle and the end of
Jesus' ministry. Many examples of this will appear later.

The sum of all this is that we have five sources of gospel tradition
—Mark, Q, L and M, plus John's special tradition.

Thus far we have been summarizing the verdicts of what is called
'source criticism'; and though they have not all gone unchallenged,
they seem to be basically right and sound. But since 1920, especially
in Germany, interest has turned from source criticism to what is
called form criticism,[1] i.e. the study of the oral tradition about
Jesus and the 'forms' it took before it was written down in our
gospels. Radical practitioners of it, notably Bultmann, have raised
afresh the question of the historical value of the gospels. Because
(they say) the gospels, written after the resurrection, were written by
believers in order to make believers, what they contain is not 'bare
facts' but 'facts plus interpretations', viz. the faith of the early
church. This faith, they assert, has gravely obscured the facts. The
suggestion is that the evangelists did not distinguish between the
pre-resurrection situation and the post-resurrection one. The gospels
are therefore palimpsests in which the beliefs of the early church are
so heavily written over the tradition about Jesus that, in Bultmann's
words, 'we can now know almost nothing concerning the life and
personality of Jesus'.[2]

Here is historical scepticism with a vengeance, well deserving
T. W. Manson's astringent comment:[3] 'It is not Higher Criticism
but the Higher Credulity which boggles at a verse in Mark and
swallows without a qualm pages of pure conjecture about the primitive
Christians' psychology and its workings on the pre-literary tradition.'

The interested reader will find a powerful rebuttal of this extreme
radical position in *Vindications*, ed. A. T. Hanson, SCM Press 1966.
Here we content ourselves with three observations.

---

[1] The best English account of form criticism is Vincent Taylor's *The Formation
of the Gospel Tradition*, Macmillan 1933.

[2] *Jesus and the Word*, Fontana Books 1958, p. 14.

[3] *The Expository Times*, May 1942, p. 249.

First: the gospels, so far from being merely written 'from faith to faith', are basically expanded *kērygma*, i.e. proclamation of the 'good news' to interested outsiders, telling them how it all began. Luke, for example, in his preface (Luke 1.1–4) dedicated to Theophilus and men like him, aims to give them 'authentic knowledge' about Christian origins.

Second: the evangelists were well aware of the difference between the pre-resurrection situation and the post-resurrection one. If the radical critics were right, why is Mark's gospel not much more *credal* than it is? Why is it not shot through with the Christian doctrine which Paul, in writing *Romans*, could assume was shared by his readers in Rome? Why does Mark not enlarge on how Christ might be appropriated by dying and rising with him in baptism, being incorporated into his body the church, and receiving the power of the Holy Spirit?

Third: of course what we have in the gospels is facts plus interpretation. There never was such a thing as a 'bare fact'—if it existed, it would be 'a rock in the sky', a blank unintelligibility. Nowadays, the dream of nineteenth-century historians—that they could strip off the interpretation and find themselves with a bare residue of fact—is seen to be a chimaera. On the contrary, as secular historians now freely admit, the meaning which an event had for those who first experienced it is part of the event itself.

If the evangelists aimed to tell 'how it all started', they sought also (in John Marsh's[1] apt phrase) to tell 'what was going on in what was taking place'. Now this is quite another matter from saying that, to suit their own purpose, they falsified the record of events. True, they were writing on the far side of the resurrection; but it is common knowledge that hindsight has a way of illuminating events not always clear to those who took part in them. Moreover, such was the nature of the story they had to tell that sometimes, as in the tale of Jesus' baptism, they found themselves confronted by incidents where plain prose would not serve and they had to fall back on their stock of Jewish images and symbols. What happened to Jesus as he rose from the water of Jordan? Nothing, to be sure, that could have been photographed or recorded on tape—supposing such inventions to have been available. Yet, as we shall see, something very important did happen to him—it was a crucial event in that traffic between two worlds which formed the deepest secret of Jesus' own spiritual life.

[1] *Saint John*, Penguin Books 1968, p. 52.

So much by way of criticism of the extreme form critics. But it is only fair to add that the modern successors of Bultmann in Germany have realized how untenable this extreme scepticism is, and one of the best of them, Bornkamm,[1] has even declared that the gospels are 'brimful of history'.

What has been said will show that the viewpoint of this book is the 'common-sense' approach of British scholarship to the problem of history in the gospels. Nowadays critics fall roughly into two schools—the 'radicals' mostly in Germany and the 'conservatives' in this country. The radicals tend to regard any incident or saying in the gospels as inauthentic until proved otherwise. The conservatives accept the incident or saying as authentic until convincing reasons are given that it is not.

It is an axiom of British law that a man is innocent until proved guilty. This study of the work and words of Jesus stands unashamedly in that 'conservative but open' position. It holds that a gospel passage is to be regarded as 'innocent', i.e. historical, until clearly shown to be 'guilty', i.e. unhistorical. It is the inauthenticity, not the authenticity, of the gospel episode or saying that needs to be demonstrated. The burden of proof rests on those who would deny the historical truth of what is recorded.

There are, we believe, three solid reasons for affirming the substantial historicity of the gospels.

First: The early Christians had a care for the faithful tradition of their Lord's words and works. To us 'tradition' suggests something floating, unfixed, unreliable. But for the Jews 'tradition' was *the* means of preserving the words and deeds of their great teachers or leaders, and there was nothing unreliable about it, because they had been trained to remember accurately, as we, who rely so much on print, are not.

Now the first Christians were Jews, and, as passages in Paul's letters show, were concerned about the careful transmission of what Jesus had said and done. For example, very early in Christian history —well before AD 50—they had put together a connected account of the events that led up to the cross and its sequel. Their task of preserving the sayings of Jesus was made easier by two factors:

(*a*) Jesus himself had cast much of his teaching (e.g. in the Sermon

[1] *Jesus of Nazareth*, Hodder and Stoughton 1960, p. 24. The gospels, he says, bring most vividly before our eyes the historical person of Jesus in a way not effaced by the church's Easter faith.

on the Mount) in the form of Semitic poetry which made it easy
to memorize; and

(b) one third of his teaching was in parables, those wonderful short
stories which have a way of sticking in the memory.

(We might forget a sermon on the grace of God; but who that heard
it could forget Jesus' story about the father and his two so different
sons?) Here we are in direct contact with the mind of Jesus. All this
is not to assert that from the earliest days the tradition about Jesus
was fixed and guarded; but it is to claim that in essentials it goes
back to Jesus and was handed down by trustworthy persons.

Second: The evangelists were in a position to know the main facts
about Jesus. Mark, friend of Peter and of Paul, moved, as we might
say, in the best apostolic circles where, if anywhere, the truth about
Jesus was to be known. From the 'epistle dedicatory' to his gospel
(Luke 1.1–4) it is clear that Luke knew a tradition handed on by
'original eye-witnesses' and written narratives based on it. Matthew
may have been the compiler of the collection of Jesus' sayings we
call Q. The Fourth Gospel rests back on ancient Palestinian tradition, and behind it may well stand the authority of the apostle John.

Third: Through the gospels shines one fundamental picture of
Jesus, whose authenticity forces itself on any unprejudiced reader.
In order to receive this impression we do not need to be experts in
biblical criticism. The impression is pre-scientific, and can be felt by
the layman no less than by the professional.

What are the chief features in this picture? Jesus' deep humility
before God and, conjoined with it, his claim to divinely-given
authority; his complete self-dedication to the purpose of his heavenly
Father and, in like manner, complete self-dedication to the service
of men; his unerring judgments on the secrets of men's hearts—and
his limitless forgiveness of the guilty; his passionate concern for all
the needy, the poor, the underprivileged, the sinful; his unshakable
conviction that for them the hour of God's salvation had struck, that
he himself was God's chosen agent in it, and that men's destiny
depended on their relation to himself.

In fine, through all the gospels runs the conviction that Jesus was
a unique person who did things that passed men's understanding,
that his whole ministry was full of the presence and power of God,
and that it did not end with death. To put it otherwise: scientific
study of the gospels does not lead to the conclusion that the original
story was about the life and death of an ordinary man and that this

story was later given a supernatural twist by sophisticating theologians like Paul and John. The writers of our gospels believed they were witnesses to the life of the Son of God on earth, to his death on a cross for men's sins, and to his victory over 'the last enemy'. On this assumption they tell their story in their different ways, and on this assumption it makes sense.

Are they right in their assumption? Historical criticism can help us to understand the story of Jesus better. It can disengage the kernel from the husk, save time so often lost in the defence of outposts, and enable us to discard obsolete weapons and superfluous baggage. Thus it can clear the ground for the erection of a house of doctrine in which the component parts can be chosen according to their real strength. But of itself it cannot answer the ultimate question. What the gospels do is to leave us face to face with the question, 'What think ye of Christ? Whose son is he?' At this point it is 'over to us'. How we answer is a matter of personal decision.

Chronology[1]

The evangelists, who were not much interested in chronology, have left us few data. Yet in an age which loves to probe the answers we can give them:

> When was Jesus born?
> How long did his ministry last?
> In what year was he crucified?

The date of the birth. According to Matt. 2.1, Jesus was born 'in Bethlehem of Judea in the days of Herod the king'. Herod died in 4 BC. Accordingly, Jesus must have been born at least five years before the year we call *Annus Domini*. According to Luke 2.1, he was born during a census carried out in Syria by the Roman governor Quirinius. Now the only census conducted by Quirinius of which we can be certain took place in AD 6. Luke *may* have got the governor's name wrong. Yet we need not question his statement that Jesus' birth coincided with the taking of a census. Tertullian records the taking of such a census in Judea while Saturninus, the penultimate predecessor of Quirinius, was governor, i.e. between 9 and 6 BC. If

---

[1] On the whole subject see G. B. Caird's article on New Testament chronology in *The Interpreter's Dictionary of the Bible*, Abingdon Press, Nashville 1962, Vol. I, pp. 599–607.

this was the nativity census, a date about 6 or 7 BC would suit the evidence of Matthew and Luke.

The length of the ministry. Here we may exclude Matthew, who gives us no chronological help. Luke is a little more helpful. If, as seems likely, in Luke 3.1 he is reckoning the reign of Tiberius in Jewish (not Roman) fashion, the fifteenth year of that emperor's reign, when the Baptist began his mission, would be AD 27. (But Luke 4.19, 'the acceptable year of the Lord', being a quotation from Isa. 61.2, provides no solid basis for the old theory of a one year's ministry.)

Mark implies a ministry of at least two years. Thus Mark 2.23 describes a time when the grain was ripe—April or May. Since, in Mark 6.39, we learn that the grass was 'green' when Jesus fed the multitude, we infer that a year has elapsed. The events recorded in Mark 6.45—10.52, which include much journeying, imply the passage of another year between the feeding and the fatal Passover (Mark 14.1).

It is one of the signs of 'the new look' coming over John's gospel that we are again taking seriously many of his chronological references. Now John mentions three Passovers (2.13; 6.4; and 12.1). In other words, he represents Jesus' ministry as lasting at least two years—roughly the same time as Mark suggests. The answer to the question, How long did Jesus' ministry last?, would seem to be 'Two years plus'.

The date of the crucifixion. Jesus was crucified on a Friday during the Passover season. But was that Friday 15 Nisan (the first month of the Jewish year), as Mark 14.12 implies, or Nisan 14, as John 19.28 and 19.14 imply? If Mark is right, the Last Supper was the official Passover; and Jesus was arrested, condemned, crucified and buried on 15 Nisan. If John is right, the official Passover was eaten on the Friday evening (i.e. 15 Nisan)[1] *after* the crucifixion, which occurred on Nisan 14. This agrees with the Talmud's statement that 'they hanged Jesus of Nazareth on the eve of the Passover'.

At this point we call in the astronomers, whose researches, based on the appearance of the new moon, help us to reconstruct the Jewish calendar in the time of Jesus. What they tell us suggests that John and the Talmud are likely to be right. The Friday of the

[1] The Jewish day began about 6 a.m. and ended about 6 p.m.

crucifixion was 14 Nisan, and the precise day and year either 7 April AD 30 or 3 April AD 33.[1]

AD 33 seems unlikely because it commits us to a ministry of over three years and because it complicates the problem of the chronology of the apostolic age (which suggests that Paul was converted in AD 33). On the other hand, AD 30, tallying with John 2.20 (which refers to the Passover of AD 28), agrees with the idea of a two years' ministry, and has astronomical support.

We conclude that Jesus was born about 6 or 7 BC, that his ministry lasted at least two years, and that he was probably crucified in the April of AD 30.

[1] J. Jeremias, *The Eucharistic Words of Jesus*, SCM Press 1966, p. 41.

2

THE BACKGROUND

Geography

Palestine, situated at the western end of the Fertile Crescent, is about the size of Wales and had in Jesus' day a population of about half a million. It is bounded on the west by the Mediterranean; on the east by the Jordan; on the north by Lebanon and Hermon; and on the south by the hills of Judea which slope away into the Negeb and the desert. Its length 'from Dan to Beersheba' is roughly one hundred and fifty miles, its average breadth barely fifty. It is a mountainous land, and he who would understand it must often 'lift up his eyes to the hills'. It is a land with surprising climatic contrasts, from the temperate airs of Jerusalem to the tropical heats of Jericho, 'the city of palms', only fifteen miles away. It is a colourful land—a land whose most famous features are the blue Lake of Galilee, the vivid green of the Jordan valley, and the gleaming snows of Mount Hermon.

The geography of Palestine is best explained in terms of four parallel bands running north and south. The outermost is the coastal plain, a strip of low-lying land along the shores of the Mediterranean, forming a highway from Egypt along which have marched many conquerors. The second band is the central range of limestone hills, running, like a great backbone, through Galilee, Samaria and Judea. The third band is the deep cleft of the Jordan valley: there the river, after rising at Hermon's base, winds its serpentine way down through Lake Huleh and the Lake of Galilee, to end in the deep-dug grave of the Dead Sea. The fourth band is the highlands of Transjordan, a barricade of hills east of Jordan running from north to south.

Galilee

Galilee is the garden of Palestine, well-watered and fertile. In Jesus' day it was thickly populated and had many good roads. If Judea was on the road to nowhere, Galilee was covered with roads to everywhere. Chief of these was the great highway which connected Damascus and the Mediterranean and crossed Galilee, touching Capernaum where once Levi sat at its custom-house (Mark 2.14). In Christ's day Galilee was wide open to Greek influences. 'Galilee of the Gentiles', as the prophet had called it (Isa. 9.1), contained many who had non-Jewish blood in their veins. The Galileans were a hardy and gallant race, 'inured,' said Josephus, 'to war from infancy'; and from Galilee sprang most of the Zealots, eager to drive out the Romans at the sword-point. They were also a religious people, though the Jews of the south doubted their orthodoxy and despised their 'north country' accent (cf. Matt. 26.73).

The Lake of Galilee is pear-shaped and measures thirteen miles in length and eight at its broadest: a sheet of fresh water lying 685 ft below sea-level, surrounded by low brown hills and notorious for sudden storms (Mark 4.37). In the time of Jesus it supported a large fishing industry, and its western shore was studded with sizeable towns. Of these Chorazin and Capernaum (the modern *Tell Hum*) were scenes of Christ's ministry (Luke 10.13–15 Q); but there is no evidence that he visited Tiberias, the Greek city further south on the lake shore which Herod Antipas had built as his capital. If we travel north-east round the lake past the place where the Jordan enters it, we reach Bethsaida Julias (Mark 6.45). Bethsaida, which means 'Fishermen's town', owes its second name to the tetrarch Philip who rebuilt and renamed it after the daughter of the Emperor Augustus. Near Bethsaida was 'the desert place' where Jesus fed the multitude.

Twenty-odd miles to the north, near the foot of Mount Hermon (9,100 ft), are the ruins of Caesarea Philippi (Mark 8.27). It had been rebuilt by Philip and renamed 'Philip's Caesarea', to distinguish it from Caesarea on the coast where the Roman governor resided.

Nazareth, 'his home town' (Mark 6.1), lies high on a sharp slope of the Galilean hills a dozen miles south-west of the lake, and commands from its northern hilltops splendid views of the whole surrounding terrain. Not so secluded or small a town as we commonly suppose, for from its hills the boy Jesus would look down on the great trade-routes carrying travellers and caravans from many parts of the civilized world.

Samaria, the Decapolis, Perea

South of Galilee lies Samaria, a land of fat valleys diversified by hills: in area, a territory of twenty miles from north to south and thirty from east to west. Its inhabitants were the descendants of Assyrian colonists who had intermarried with the Jewish remnant left behind after the fall of Samaria in 722 BC. They claimed, as they still claim, to be the true representatives of Israel. But 'the Jews have no dealings with the Samaritans' (John 4.9). True then, it is true still. So the Samaritans had set up a rival temple and priesthood; their holy place was Mount Gerizim (the 'this mountain' of John 4.20); their holy book the Pentateuch, and their holy city not Samaria (which was Greek), but Shechem at the pass between Mounts Gerizim and Ebal.

A Galilean pilgrim trekking south for the Passover would normally cross the Jordan before reaching inhospitable Samaria, and travel down the east bank of the river before re-crossing it at the ford near Jericho. On this eastern side he would touch the fringe of the Decapolis (Mark 5.20; 7.31), a federation of ten Greek towns, and then pass through Perea (which means 'Transjordan'). If the men of 'the Ten Towns' were Gentiles, the Pereans were predominantly Jews. Though the name never occurs in the gospels, we know that Jesus 'came into the regions of Judea and Transjordan', i.e. Perea (Mark 10.1; John 10.40) and taught there before making his last march on Jerusalem. Moreover, a strong case can be made out[1] that Perea was the main centre of John the Baptist's work, as it was the Perean fortress of Machaerus in which he finally met his death.

Judea

Judea is a high table-land cleft by deep gullies running east and west: altogether, a small territory fifty-five miles long by thirty broad, in area about the size of Aberdeenshire. The country was divided into five regions: the coastal plain, the Shephelah (or lowlands near the coast), the Negeb (or southland), the hill country and the wilderness. Only the last two concern us here. The hill country is a rough stony land cut by deep ravines and rising 2,500 ft to the bare plateau on which Jerusalem stands. The wilderness is the bleak, barren region where the eastern Judean mountains slope down 4,000 ft to the lowest part of the earth's surface, the Dead Sea (1,275 ft below sea-level), on whose north-western shore, at Qumran, the Essene sectarians who wrote the Dead Sea Scrolls had established their monastic community.

[1] T. W. Manson, *The Servant Messiah*, Cambridge University Press 1953, pp. 40f.

The population of Judea was purely Jewish. Crowning the rocky plateau stood the grey city of Jerusalem with its splendid temple (not yet completed) on Mount Zion. 'He who has not seen Jerusalem in its beauty,' said the rabbis proudly, 'has not seen a beautiful great city in his whole life, and he who has not seen the Second Temple has not seen a handsome building in his life.' Due west of the temple was the gilt palace built by King Herod. Adjoining the temple on its north-western side was the fortress of Antonia with its garrison of Roman auxiliary troops. Here probably during the Passover when Jesus was crucified, Pilate, the Roman governor, had his residence.

History

Herods and Romans seem always to be somewhere in the background of the gospel story, so that we must have some knowledge of the rulers of Palestine in the time of Christ.

If we erect the historical fences at 63 BC (when Pompey captured Jerusalem) and at AD 70 (when Jerusalem again fell to Roman arms), we must briefly glance back at the fortunes of the Jews after their return from the exile. At the battle of Issus in 333 BC, Alexander of Macedon overthrew their Persian overlords, and after his death Palestine became a bone of contention between Egyptian Ptolemies and Syrian Seleucids. When the Seleucids prevailed they spread Greek civilization over the land. But the attempt of Antiochus Epiphanes, the Seleucid king, to stamp out Judaism broke down before the heroic resistance of the Maccabees, and for some eighty years (143–63 BC) the Jews enjoyed a precarious independence under their priest-kings of the Hasmonean line. At length, in 63 BC the Roman Pompey took Jerusalem, and the Jews became subject to Rome.

Troubled years followed till in 37 BC the Idumean Herod, with Rome's help, had himself made 'king of the Jews'. A Jew by religion, Herod was a Greek by sympathy, and a Roman by allegiance. From the beginning the Jews hated him. 'He stole along to his throne like a fox,' it has been picturesquely put, 'he ruled like a tiger, and he died like a dog.' Yet, for all his brutality, he was an able and adroit ruler. His passion was for building, and with money extorted from the Jews by taxation, he gratified it to the full. It was he who in 20 BC began the rebuilding of the temple (John 2.20). For the rest, he outwardly respected the Jews' religion in Jerusalem, and elsewhere zealously promoted Greek culture, to the disgust of the Jews whom he restrained by a strong mercenary army. Before he died in 4 BC, he arranged with Rome that three of his sons should divide his dominions. Archelaus got Judea, Samaria and Idumea; Antipas, Galilee and Perea (Transjordan); and Philip, the north-east regions. Archelaus did not, however, inherit his father's title of king: he was styled 'ethnarch', and his brothers 'tetrarchs'.

In cruelty at least Archelaus was a true son of his father and earned the cordial hatred of the Jews. For ten years the Romans tolerated his misrule, but at last, in AD 6, they deposed him, and set a Roman governor in his stead.

The new *régime* pleased the Jews no better. Under the governor the high priest and the Sanhedrin (or supreme Jewish ecclesiastical court) had the semblance of autonomy; but no grave decision—such as the passing of the death sentence (John 18.31)—could be taken without the procurator's approval. Of these procurators Pilate (AD 26 – 36) was the fifth. In his contempt for the Jews he typified the baser sort of Roman governor, and, as Luke 13.1 shows, had no scruple about spilling blood to preserve the *Pax Romana*. At last, the wanton massacre of some Samaritans led to his deposition in AD 36.

Meanwhile, Antipas (4 BC–AD 39), the Herod who figures mostly in the gospels, ruled over Galilee and Perea, maintaining his position by means of an army of his own, in which doubtless the centurion of Capernaum served. In his subtlety, love of women and passion for building, he too resembled his father. Of his subtlety Jesus' 'that fox' (Luke 13.32 L) is evidence; to his love of women his liaison with Herodias (Mark 6.17) bears testimony; and of his passion for building, Tiberias is the monument.

Philip (4 BC–AD 34), who ruled over the country north-east of Galilee, seems to have been the best of Herod's sons. Salome, daughter of Herodias, was his wife. He too went in for building, with Caesarea Philippi (Mark 8.27) and Bethsaida Julias (Luke 9.10; John 1.44) his chief monuments.

Altogether, these were troubled times with much misery and bloodshed. The Jews groaned under the Roman yoke, or that of their satellites, the Herods. Jew did not understand Roman, or Roman Jew. Two classes of men this suffering bred among the Jews: on the one hand, fanatical freedom-fighters like the Zealots; on the other hand, quietists who fed their souls with apocalyptic hopes and dreamed of supernatural deliverance.

Important, also, to remember is the economic malaise of the time, of which the root-cause was the twofold taxation. When the Jews, tired of the Herods, invited the Romans to take over the government, they got more than they bargained for. Rome imposed a fresh burden of taxation in the shape of a poll-tax, plus other land and cattle dues. These taxes the Romans collected through their *publicani*; though we must note that the tax-collectors in the gospels were only the underlings of their Roman superiors, the small fry of the bureaucracy. The whole system, being honeycombed with graft, exasperated the Jews. When on top of the taxes 'due to God' were piled these new taxes 'due to Caesar'—and the double taxation must have exceeded 40p in the £1—not surprisingly there were riots and a smouldering unrest ultimately destined to blaze out in open rebellion.

Another cause of unrest was increasing over-population causing food shortage. And a third cause was the introduction of slave-labour which threw many smallholders out of business and drove desperate men to brigandage.

In short, the times were out of joint and there seemed to be only one remedy:

They all were looking for a King
To slay their foes and lift them high.

If you had asked the average Jew of the time what he was hoping and praying for in the good time coming, his answer might well have been like that of the good old priest Zachariah: 'rescue from enemy hands' (i.e. Rome) and freedom to worship God, with Torah in temple and synagogue, his whole life long (Luke 1.73–75).

Religion

In first-century Judaism there were three main religious parties: Essenes, Sadducees and Pharisees.

The Essenes, though Philo, Josephus and the elder Pliny refer to them, find no mention in the gospels. Not long ago anybody who linked Jesus with the Essenes could be dismissed as a crank. The discovery of the Dead Sea Scrolls and the remains of an Essene settlement at Qumran has made us think again. We now know that down on the north-western shores of the Dead Sea there lived in Jesus' time a community of sectarian Jews who regarded themselves as the true Israel. Despairing of the world and of the Jerusalem hierarchy, they had withdrawn to the Judean wilderness and formed a monastic order, with priests and laymen in it observing a strict discipline. They led celibate lives, interpreted the Law in their own fashion, took ritual baths, held sacred meals, and all in preparation for the coming Day of the Lord and the final conflict between 'the children of light' and 'the children of darkness'.

If no direct connection has been proved, John the Baptist and Jesus must have known about the Essenes. Jesus, who was certainly no ascetic, did not share their views, but the Baptist may have been influenced by them. His 'headquarters' were near Qumran; he was an ascetic; he baptized; he saw his vocation, as the Essenes did, in Isa. 40.3 ('to prepare the way of the Lord'); and like them, he expected an imminent *Dies Irae*.

Very different from these Dead Sea monastics were the priestly party called the Sadducees, with their centre in Jerusalem and their stronghold in the temple. The common view is that they derived their name from Zadok, the high-priest under Solomon (I Kings 2.35). T. W. Manson[1] thought their name a corruption of 'syndics', a group of civic officials called first the *gerousia* and later the Sanhedrin, whose job was to give legal advice to the Jews, look after fiscal interests, and deal with the Roman authorities. Not many in number and including lay aristocrats besides priests, the Sadducees were rich and haughty and had a name for harsh judgment and brusque speech. During Jesus' ministry they included not only the reigning high priest Caiaphas, but, lurking formidably in the background, his father-in-law Annas, whom the Romans had deposed from the high priesthood. In politics the Sadducees were defenders of the *status quo*, fearful of falling out with Rome (cf. John 11.50). In religion, they were ultra conservatives. By 'scripture' they meant the written Law of Moses. Not for them 'the tradition', or mass of casuistical elucidations, with which the scribes had hedged the Law, or the Pharisees' new-fangled doctrine of resurrection (Mark 12.18; Acts 23.8) and 'unbiblical' interest in angels and demons.

If the Sadducees were the conservatives in Judaism, the Pharisees were the progressives. Numbering about six thousand, they were 'the practising Jews' and had (says Josephus) 'the multitude on their side'. For their origin we have to go back to the Hasidim, or Pious, who in Maccabean times fought for the Law by the side of Judas but, with their object achieved, withdrew from the campaign.

[1] *The Servant Messiah*, pp. 11–20.

Conceivably this action earned them their name—'the separatists' or 'seceders'.

In contrast with the Sadducees, for the Pharisees the Law meant the written Torah plus the oral tradition, or scribal interpretations of the Law, designed to apply it in detail to such matters as ritual cleanness, tithing, sabbath-keeping, divorce, duty to parents, etc. Most of the scribes were in fact Pharisees and served as professional theologians to the party. Too often in Christian speech 'Pharisee' has become a synonym for 'hypocrite'. If we reckon the Pharisees misguided, we must remember that the party included such great and good men as Hillel and Gamaliel, and that they were men in earnest about their religion. With a firm faith in God's purpose in history, they cherished the hope of a Messiah of David's line who would overthrow their oppressors, and they believed in a resurrection from the dead.

It was not so much their belief as their observance that was at fault. They were not wrong, with the help of their scribes, to try to revivify the ancient Law by making it relevant to the needs of daily life. What they got wrong (as Christians so often do) was their practice and their priorities. Jesus charged them with saying one thing and doing another; he accused them of putting casuistry before love, and the tithing of garden herbs before justice. Pharisaism in fact led to a fastidious scrupulosity ('straining out a gnat and swallowing a camel'), to a stress on the outward at the expense of the inward ('cleaning the outside of the cup' and forgetting the dirt inside), to a holiness that easily became a 'holier-than-thou-ness', and to the belief that a man could save himself by 'works of law'. The end-result was a self-righteous legalism which, instead of bringing men nearer, took them further away from God.

Not all Pharisees, however, believed their whole duty to lie in keeping the Law. On the left wing of the party stood the Zealots who, as Klausner says, 'were simply active and extremist Pharisees'. Fonder of the sword than of the phylactery and 'sworn to invincible liberty and to God as their only Leader and Lord' (Josephus), they believed that the deliverance of Israel from the Roman yoke lay in the power of their own right arms; and when at last, in AD 66, the great revolt burst into flame, they fought with savage cruelty and superb heroism. Among Jesus' chosen twelve was one of them, Simon the Cananaean, or, as Luke calls him, 'the Zealot'.

Essenes, Sadducees, Pharisees—add them all together, and their

number can hardly have exceeded 10 per cent of the total population of Palestine. This means that about 90 per cent of the Jews
owed no formal allegiance to any of the three parties. Among these
must have been these known as 'the quiet in the land'—humble,
pious folk like Simeon and Anna described in Luke 2.25–38, who
stood aloof from the hurly-burly of religion and politics and waited
for the salvation of the Lord. If the motto of the Zealots might have
been 'God helps those who help themselves', that of these 'quietists'
might have been, 'In God's good time'. In some such circles, 'the
special seed-plot of Christianity' (as William Sanday called it), Jesus
must have been born.

What has been said must have suggested the general religious
background of the time. The keystone of Judaism was a noble monotheism—belief in one living God, transcendent, righteous, holy—
but a national monotheism, for the only God was pre-eminently the
God of the Jews, his chosen people. Between God and his people
stood the Torah, God's revealed will for men, at once the law of the
nation and the private law of the individual, in keeping of which
there was great reward. If in Jerusalem the temple cult of ritual and
sacrifice still flourished, elsewhere the synagogue, a sort of chapel-
cum-school, was the rallying place of Judaism.

Thus far the religion of the Torah and the temple. But we err if
we suppose that the religious aspiration of the time found full satis-
faction in the punctilious keeping of the Law and annual attendance
at the great festivals in Jerusalem (Passover, Pentecost and Tabernacles). When the times are out of joint and a God-fearing people
contrast the ideal with the actual—the glorious future promised by
God through his prophets with their present miseries—they inevi-
tably seek comfort in apocalypses of one kind or another. They
dream of a divine vindication and a heaven-sent saviour. Thus did
many Jews in Jesus' day. For the present evil seemed to be in the
ascendant, clouds and thick darkness were about God's throne, and
his people groaned under an alien yoke. But the living God was
merely biding his time: yet a little while, and he would decisively
manifest his reign in the world, the powers of evil would be vanquished, and the faithful find salvation. Then as one apocalyptic
writer[1] put it,

> God's Kingdom will be manifest in all his creation
> And then the Devil will have an end

[1] *The Assumption of Moses*. ch. 10, probably written when Jesus was a youth.

And with him sorrow will be removed.

This would be the final coming of God's rule—the beginning of the new age which was part of God's reserved purpose. Some looked for God to interpose directly, without help of intermediary. Others expected the advent of God's great vice-gerent, the Messiah, who should be the bearer of God's rule to the world. Many and various were the dream-pictures which they painted of the kingdom and the Messiah. Yet, however they differed, all save the Sadducees yearned for the decisive intervention of God. When that blessed day dawned, they would say 'Lo, this is our God; we have waited for him; we will be glad and rejoice in his salvation' (Isa. 25.9).

Part Two

BEFORE THE MINISTRY

3

BIRTH AND EARLY YEARS

The birth

According to Matt. 2.1 and Luke 2.1–7, Bethlehem was the birth-place of Jesus. Both evangelists say he was born of Mary, while still a virgin, through the special action of the Holy Spirit.

These are the only direct references in the New Testament to the virginal conception, though Mark 6.3 may well be an indirect one. The tradition did not figure in the apostolic preaching. On the other hand, there is no warrant for regarding the passages in Matthew and Luke as interpolations. It is possible that in the first Christian generation the tradition was current only in limited circles.

Is it fact or fiction? Matthew (1.23) supports his account with a quotation, in the LXX version, of Isa. 7.14: 'A virgin (*parthenos*— the Hebrew means simply 'young woman') will conceive and bear a son.' Since no Messianic interpretation of this passage has been found, it is unlikely that Matthew invented the doctrine to agree with scripture. The strongly Jewish atmosphere of Luke's birth story tells against the view that we have here the pagan idea of divine generation through a human parent. Both evangelists evidently accepted the virginal conception as fact, and some have surmised that Luke's information may go back ultimately to Mary herself. One argument in its favour is therefore the difficulty of accounting for the belief except on the assumption of its truth.

Here we should note that the evangelists' interest is not scientific. They are concerned not with the possibility of virginal conception in general but with the virginal conception of Jesus Christ. All discussion of 'parthenogenesis' is therefore irrelevant. We may also dismiss the notion that the virginal conception is an attempt to explain the sinlessness of Jesus, since it would still leave him connected with sinful human nature on one side of his person.

What conclusion are we then to draw? It has been well said that

33

the virginal conception is not so much an explanation as an affirmation of mystery—an affirmation that God is here at work. If the two evangelists speak of a physical miracle, the theological truth they are expressing is that *God sent Jesus* (cf. Matt. 1.18 with Luke 1.35). Now this truth may be interpreted in two different ways. Those who find in the birth stories primarily poetry and symbol should not try to drain away the vigour of the truth which Matthew and Luke are declaring. Those who, to preserve the divine initiative, accept literally that Jesus had no human father, must hold fast the New Testament conviction that Jesus was a real man who lived a truly human life.

The New Testament nowhere suggests that belief in the virginal conception is required for salvation. If a Christian rejects it, he will probably justify himself by saying, 'The historical evidence for it is inadequate, and—if a theological reason must be added—belief in a true incarnation must mean that Jesus was born in the same way as other men are.' On the other hand, if a Christian accepts it, he will probably say, 'I cannot account for the tradition on any other assumption than its truth, and—if you ask me for a theological reason—the spiritual stature of Jesus in the gospels, especially his claim to be the only Son of God, makes it credible, as it forms a fitting preface to a life which was crowned by resurrection from the dead.'

Early years

Except for a few facts to be gleaned from the gospels, we know little directly about the early years of Jesus. This is the sum of it. He grew up in Nazareth as the son of Joseph and Mary; besides sisters he had four brothers (Mark 6.3); he worked as a carpenter, and at the age of twelve visited Jerusalem at Passover and became a *bar mitzvah*, a son of the Law, ready now to accept for himself the obligations to which his parents had committed him at circumcision.

And yet from scattered hints in the gospels we can picture the Nazareth home and the kind of education he must have received. If we visit Nazareth, we can still see the well where Mary drew water. From the Nazareth hill-tops we can command the magnificent prospects of Galilee and beyond on which the youthful eyes of Jesus must have rested. Across the foot of those hills ran a branch of the great trade route, and from the hill-top Jesus must have seen all

sorts and conditions of men posting along the highways—imperial
digr'taries, Midianite caravans, princes with their retinues, the
gleaming eagles of the Roman legionaries and 'all the great ones of
the Gentiles'. News of the wider world must have found its way to
Nazareth—the scandals of the Herods, the latest decrees of the
Prefect of Judea, and even rumours of Augustus in distant Rome.
All this should remind us that it was in no place far from the dusty
ways of men that Jesus grew up, but in surroundings where he must
have felt the pressure and the problems of the wider world.

Sayings in the gospels enable us to picture the Nazareth home
where *Abba* and *Imma*[1] must have been among the first words Jesus
learnt. We are to think of a clay-built, flat-roofed, one-roomed house
whose owner when disturbed by a midnight caller does not need to
rise in order to talk with a man outside the door (Luke 11.5ff. L). The
furniture is simple: the saucer-shaped lamp of clay, the bed—a light,
low frame on which a mat was stretched—the bushel, or meal-tub,
which could be put over the lamp's smoking wick at bed-time. Something of what went on by day we can also guess: Mary his mother
baking for the family's needs and hiding the yeast in a batch of
flour—a process that was later to become a parable of God's reign
(Luke 13.20f.; Matt. 13.33 Q). Not a rich house, but one in which
the finding of a lost shilling was a matter for rejoicing (Luke 15.8–
10 L). And where, if not in the Nazareth home, did Jesus learn that
'an old coat' will not tolerate 'a new patch of unshrunk cloth'—a
bit of domestic knowledge which was later to symbolize the incom-
patibility of God's new order with the old one (Mark 2.21)?

Other sayings help us to conjure up the sight and sounds around
the Nazareth home: the streets and market-places where by night
'the outer darkness' reigned supreme and where by day the children
'made believe' at weddings or at funerals (Luke 7.32; Matt. 11.16f.
Q)—it was the boys, we are told,[2] who played at weddings, the girls
at funerals. Doubtless Jesus' parables cf the Apprenticed Son (John
5.19f.) and the Splinter and the Plank (Luke 6.41f.; Matt. 7.3–5 Q)
and his sayings about yokes (Matt. 11.29 M) go back to the days
when:

> The Carpenter of Nazareth
> Made common things for God,

as the sight of a ploughman at his job suggested the firm, quiet

[1] Aramaic for 'Dada' and 'Mama'.

[2] J. Jeremias, *The Parables of Jesus*[2], SCM Press 1962, p. 161.

'holding to it' which was the quality he later required in a true disciple (Luke 9.62 Q).

We know little about his education save by inference. Yet three books must ever have been open before him—the Bible (i.e. the Old Testament), nature and man. That he read well in all three, every page of the gospels attests.

His early education he must have received at home and in the synagogue-school. Its staple would be the Law, the prophets and 'the tradition'. The gospels show his knowledge of his people's scriptures to have been penetrating and profound. He read them of course with the eyes of faith, not of science, not as a manual of Hebrew history but as a means of grace. In them he discerned the long purpose and scope of God's salvation. What he found in them was not the prophets' thoughts about God but God's action in Israel by prophet, priest and king—God's invasion of his race by words and deeds of gracious power. Moreover, certain books seem to have spoken to him with peculiar force: Deuteronomy, the Psalms, Daniel and Isaiah in whose 'Servant Songs'[1] (as we call them) he saw as in a mirror, when the time came, his own face— and destiny. Whether his eyes ever lighted on extra-canonical books like *Enoch* we cannot certainly say.

Much has been written about his mother-tongue. It is certain that Aramaic, the language of his prayers, was the tongue in which he commonly preached and taught, and Mark has preserved a few of his actual words like *Talitha cum, Ephphatha* and *Abba*. It is very probable that he also knew Hebrew, for according to Luke 4.16f. he read from the Hebrew scroll of Isaiah in the Nazareth synagogue. (The evidence of the Dead Sea Scrolls suggests that Hebrew was more widely used than was once supposed.) Probably also he could make himself understood in the 'Common Greek' which was the international language of the time and must often have been heard in Galilee, where many were Greek-speaking Gentiles.

Of his deep reading in 'the open volume' of nature we have abundant evidence in the gospels:

> He spoke of grass, and wind, and rain,
> And fig-trees, and fair weather,
> And made it His delight to bring,
> Heaven and earth together.[2]

[1] Isa. 42.1–4; 49.1–6; 50.4–9; 52.13–53. 12.
[2] T. T. Lynch.

Study the sayings of Jesus, and you will find in them as good evidence that he was country-bred, as you will find in the poems of Burns or Cobbett's *Rural Rides* with their memories of boyhoods spent in Ayrshire and Surrey. Moreover, for Jesus 'nature' and 'super-nature' were one order. The sense of the divineness of the natural order is a major premiss of his parables, as he discerns the grace of God in the rising of his sun on good and bad alike and the falling of his rain on honest and dishonest (Matt. 5.45 Q).

'He knew men so well,' says St John of Jesus (2.24). Parable after parable attests his interest in people, his insight into human nature, showing that from his youth he must have walked with shrewd observant eyes amid the human scene. Doubtless it was during 'the hidden years' that he first watched or met those characters who people his parables: the resourceful rogue we call the Dishonest Steward, the jerry-builder who scamped his foundations, the callous, self-sufficient pagan we know as the Unjust Judge, that type of the crass materialist, the Rich Fool, the self-righteous Pharisee who thanked God he was not as other men—and many another drawn to the life in a few deft strokes—a testimony to Jesus' knowledge of common men and common things.

But all this is indirect evidence. With one exception the canonical gospels say nothing directly about the early years of Jesus. The exception is, of course, Luke's story of the boy Jesus in the temple courts (Luke 2.41–51 L)—a story which shows him from boyhood conscious of a unique sonship to God. 'Did you not know,' he said to his mother, 'that I was bound to be in my Father's house?' The apocryphal gospels, on the other hand, contain many tales of how the boy Jesus:

> made him small fowl out of clay
> And blessed them till they flew away,[1]

and the like; but they really add nothing to our sure knowledge of Jesus. It is enough to know that he 'increased in wisdom and stature, and in favour with God and man'; for 'he had to be made like his brethren in every respect'.

> He has been our fellow, the morning of our days,
> Us He chose for housemates, and this way went.[2]

[1] H. Belloc.
[2] G. Meredith.

4

THE FORERUNNER, THE BAPTISM
AND THE TEMPTATION

'As it is written in the prophet Isaiah,' Mark begins his gospel, 'John the Baptist appeared in the wilderness proclaiming a baptism in token of repentance, for the forgiveness of sins' (Mark 1.2f.).

Our knowledge of this lonely, austere man of God comes from the four gospels and Acts, plus a paragraph in the *Antiquities* of Josephus. This agrees in essentials with what the gospels tell, though it attributes Herod's arrest of John to his fear of an insurrection and not to John's condemnation of Herod's adultery with Herodias.[1]

John was an ascetic, 'eating no bread and drinking no wine', an apocalyptist expecting the imminent day of God's wrath, and a prophet calling his countrymen to repentance. Especially the last: in him the voice of prophecy silent for centuries rang out like a trumpet. 'In the fifteenth year of the emperor Tiberius,' says St Luke, with a fine feeling for God at work in history, 'the Word of God came to John the Baptist in the wilderness' (Luke 3.1f.). This was the call of John.

In his 'rough coat of camel's hair, with a leather belt round his waist' (Mark 1.6), he might have been Elijah come back to earth; in message and temper he recalled Amos: a strong, blunt, fearless man—'no reed-bed swept by the wind', no wearer 'of silks and satins', as Jesus said of him (Luke 7.24f. Q). The New Testament and Josephus alike testify to the tremendous impression he made on his countrymen. They also show that Herod saw in him a dangerous man who had better be quickly put under lock and key.

The bare facts of his career would seem to be these. Born of priestly stock in the hill-country of Judea (Luke 1.39f.), he stepped into public view as a preacher in 'the wilderness' near the Dead Sea.

[1] But John's condemnation of the unlawful marriage and Herod's political fears were merely different aspects of the same series of events. See C. Scobie, *John the Baptist*, SCM Press 1964, pp. 182ff.

Thither he drew large crowds from the Judean country-side and from Jerusalem. Many of these he baptized, among them a young man named Jesus from Nazareth; and around him there gathered disciples whom he taught to pray (Luke 11.1 L) and to fast like himself (Mark 2.18). John 3.22–30 (a passage based on reliable tradition) tells us that for a time John and the man from Nazareth worked in parallel, Jesus in Judea and John in Samaria. When these parallel ministries ceased, John evidently crossed the Jordan into Perea (which may have been the main centre of his work), only to be arrested and imprisoned by Herod Antipas in the fortress of Machaerus, where he was finally executed.

Jesus evidently took the news of John's arrest as the divine signal for him to begin his Galilean ministry (Mark 1.14).

John's ministry was a stern call to moral renewal with a clear reference to the messianic hope of Israel. His purpose was to prepare Israel to meet her God by gathering a people worthy of him. What was the burden of his preaching? First, the day of wrath is near— 'already the great Feller has laid his axe to the tree-roots'. Second, his agent will be the Coming One, i.e. the Messiah, who will sift the wheat from the chaff and 'baptize with the Holy Spirit and with fire' (Luke 3.16 Q; cf. Mark 1.8)—fire for impenitent sinners, the Spirit's power for the repentant. Third, in view of this men must 'repent'—turn back, in strong earnest, to God and prove the sincerity of their penitence by amended lives. For in the coming judgment there would be no preferential treatment for those who pinned their hopes on their descent from Abraham: 'God,' John said (and there would be word-play in his Aramaic), 'can make children (banim) for Abraham out of these stones (abhanim)' (Luke 3.8 Q).

For those who came to hear him, John had some blunt moral advice. To the crowds he said, 'Share with your needy brothers'. To the tax-collectors, 'Stop extorting more than your due'. To the serving soldiers, 'No bullying or blackmail' (Luke 3.10–14 L). In short, no epoch-making moral teaching, but essentially an 'interim ethic', telling them how best to amend their lives before the Dies Irae dawned.

But John did more than call for decision for God and his purpose. As a sign of their once-for-all break with their bad past lives he immersed his converts in the Jordan river. Some have thought John's baptism was patterned on proselyte baptism—that ritual immersion which Gentile converts to Judaism were required to undergo. But it is doubtful whether such baptism existed at the beginning of the first century AD. A closer analogy is to be found in the Essene baptisms practised at Qumran.[1] (These were confined to Jews, had a moral significance, conferred forgiveness on condition of repentance, granted admission to the new covenant and the new Israel, had an eschatological forward-look, and were probably performed in a river.) In any case, John's baptism was a piece of prophetic symbolism sealing the converts' repentance and initiating them into a new Israel fit to meet God and his Messiah.

Did John ever surmise that the man from Nazareth was the Messiah? According to the synoptics, John seriously entertained the possibility that Jesus was the Messiah while John lay in prison. According to John 1.29–36, John knew Jesus was the Messiah when he rose from his baptism in Jordan. Most scholars would hold that, for dramatic effect, St John has ante-dated this recognition of Jesus as the Messiah. Yet possibly, to begin with, John did glimpse in Jesus the Coming One, but later was vexed with doubts when Jesus' ministry did not measure up to his preconceived picture of the Messiah's role. Hence perhaps his troubled question from his Machaerus prison, 'Are you the Coming One, or are we to expect some other?' (Luke 7.18 Q).

For his part, Jesus saw in John the Messianic herald. His mission was 'from God' and no mere movement of man's contriving (Mark 11.27–33). Not simply another prophet, he was *the* prophet who, according to the Jewish hope, was to usher in the new age and make ready for the Messiah (Luke 7.26f. Q). For Jesus, John was the key figure at the turning-point of history, the greatest man in that old dispensation which ends with the advent of the kingdom of God (Luke 16.16 Q).

Through the mists of antiquity it is still possible to glimpse something of the grandeur of this 'grim old Puritan' who stands at the threshold of the gospel. What we glimpse is a man of vivid and trenchant speech, unbending resolution and splendid courage. His mission was the last attempt of Jewish legal religion to compel men to be good by threats of hell-fire. When it failed, the gospel took its place.

Call John's life a failure, if you like; yet it was a glorious one. It is the story of a great, simple man who played his part in a purpose of God which passed his understanding, and who paid for his integrity

[1] See C. Scobie, op. cit. pp. 107–10.

with his life's blood. His place is really with those who did not receive the promises, 'God having provided some better things for us, that they without us should not be made perfect' (Heb. 11.39f.). That 'better thing' was the reign of God, proclaimed by and embodied in the man whom John baptized and for whom he paved the way. John the Baptist is the bridge between the old covenant and the new—the clasp between the Testaments.

The Baptism of Jesus (Mark 1.9–11; Luke 3.21f., Matt. 3.16f. Q)

'In those days Jesus came from Nazareth of Galilee and was baptized by John in Jordan. And when he came up out of the water, immediately he saw the heavens opened and the Spirit descending upon him like a dove; and a voice came from heaven, "Thou art my beloved Son; with thee I am well pleased" ' (Mark 1.9–11).

Among the crowds who flocked to John's baptism came Jesus from Nazareth in Galilee. Why did one whom Christian tradition held to be sinless submit to 'a baptism in token of repentance, for the forgiveness of sins'? Was he conscious of sin? Did he come as a sinner among a crowd of sinners? (To this ancient difficulty Matt. 3.14f. attempts an answer. John sought to dissuade Jesus from being baptized. 'I need,' he said, 'rather to be baptized by you.' To which Jesus replied, 'Let it be so for the present; we do well to conform in this way with all that God requires.') But the issue is really an academic one, for we have no reason to suppose that the question of his own sinlessness occupied his mind at the time. From what he later said about him, it is clear that Jesus discerned the hand of God in John's mission, and sought to identify himself with it. If, even in Jordan (as the words of the heavenly voice suggest), Jesus found his own destiny prefigured in Isaiah's Servant of the Lord, he was, in accepting John's baptism, deliberately 'numbering himself with the transgressors' (Isa. 53.12), as he was to do all through his ministry.

At his baptism Jesus saw a vision and heard a voice. Mark is right in saying that the vision and voice came to him alone. (Matt. and Luke imply that others heard and saw). In vision Jesus saw God's Spirit gliding down upon him like a dove, and from the rent heavens heard a divine voice addressing him.

Here the first point to seize is that the story, which must have been told to the disciples by Jesus himself, is of symbol all compact. The dove-like descent of the Spirit and the voice from the opened heavens

are Jewish images to express what is imperceptible to outward eye
and ear. What happened as he came streaming from the waters of
Jordan was a climacteric experience in Jesus' life—even if (supposing
such facilities to have been available) it could not have been photographed or recorded on tape. Like the 'hour' of the great thanksgiving or of the transfiguration, it was a crucial event in that traffic
between two worlds which holds the last secret of Jesus' own spiritual
life.[1]

But what do the descending Spirit and the heavenly voice signify?

When later, in the synagogue at Nazareth (Luke 4.18 L), Jesus
applied to himself Isaiah's words about the Servant of the Lord
('The Spirit of the Lord is upon me, because he has anointed me to
preach good news to the poor,' Isa. 61.1), he was recalling his
experience in Jordan. The descent of the Spirit upon him meant that
from this time on he knew himself as 'the Lord's anointed', to be
equipped, like the Lord's Servant (Isa. 42.1; 'I have put my Spirit
upon him') with divine power; for the Spirit, whatever else it connotes, always carries with it the idea of power, and power in which
God is active (cf. Acts 10.38: 'God anointed Jesus of Nazareth with
the Holy Spirit and with power'—a reference to his baptism). Thus
only can we explain the sovereign note of authority which informed
his later words and works.

But how shall we interpret the words of the heavenly voice, 'Thou
art my beloved (or 'only'[2]) Son; with thee I am well pleased'? It is
commonly said that what Jesus received at his baptism was the
assurance that he was the Messiah. So stated, this view is unsatis-
factory. That Jesus knew himself to be the Messiah, albeit in his own
sense of the term, we shall argue later. But was 'Son of God' at the
beginning of the first century a commonly recognized title for the
Messiah? The evidence that it was, is not abundant. On the other
hand, we have to reckon with something even more fundamental to
Jesus' divine consciousness. Years before his baptism—how we can
only guess—he had become aware of a special filial relationship to
God (Luke 2.49) that was to deepen and mature as the years went by.

---

[1] In the synoptics, Jesus' 'divine consciousness' is present from the beginning of
the ministry, but it flames out at climacteric moments which illuminate the whole.
It is like the tall crests on a relief map, whereas in the Fourth Gospel the Sonship
of Jesus appears continuously like high points studded on a broad plateau. See
Vincent Taylor, *The Person of Christ*, Macmillan 1958, pp. 182f.

[2] The Greek word *agapētos* means literally 'beloved', but the word strongly
inclines towards the meaning of 'only beloved', as in Gen. 22. 2, 12, 16 LXX.

Remembering these things, we may reconsider the meaning of the heavenly voice. The Old Testament passages which it seems to echo are Gen. 22.2 ('your only son'); Ps. 2.7 ('The Lord said to me, You are my Son'); and Isa. 42.1 ('My servant . . . in whom my soul delights'). Sonship and service are the dominant motifs here. What Jesus experienced at his baptism was an inward authentication of his unique Sonship and the call of his Father to be a Messiah with a destiny like that of Isaiah's lowly Servant of the Lord.

The next 'historic occasion' in his life—the temptation—would seem to confirm this; for that ordeal in the desert was to test the quality of his Sonship ('If you are the Son of God . . .') and raise the implications of his vocation as the Servant of the Lord.

The Temptation (Mark 1.12f.; Luke 4.1–13, Matt. 4.1–11 Q)

After the baptism follows, with psychological fitness, the story of Jesus' temptation. Spirit-impelled, he retires into the rocky Judean wilderness, in order to decide

> How to begin, how to accomplish best,
> His end of being on earth, and mission high.[1]

Mark is content to record the fact of temptation, adding that in the wild scene of his conflict he was supernaturally sustained: 'Thereupon the Spirit sent him away into the wilderness, and there he remained for forty days tempted by Satan. He was among the wild beasts, and the angels waited on him.'

It is to Q that we owe the full account of his struggle. But how do we know anything at all about it? For 'forty days'—an oriental round number for a 'longish' time—he was quite alone. Obviously the Q account is a piece of spiritual autobiography told to the disciples by Jesus, perhaps in the days after Peter's confession at Caesarea Philippi. Such a dramatic dialogue between Jesus and Satan was never invented by the early church.

The first point is that to interpret the story in terms of an incarnate Devil engaging in some dialectical passage of arms with Jesus in some gloomy picture-book wilderness is to betray a crude occidental literalism. The story describes inward experiences, not external events. It is the record of a searching spiritual experience—a real, not a sham, fight—told in the figurative language of one who was steeped in the Old Testament.

[1] Milton.

Second: only against the background of the baptism does the story make sense. That high hour of revelation had brought to Jesus not only a divine authentication of his Sonship but also a call to be the Servant Messiah and an equipment with extraordinary powers. (The ensuing temptations are, strictly, not the temptations of Jesus but of the Christ: the temptations not of a private person but of one called to be God's vice-gerent in his kingdom.) How is he to fulfil his destiny as the bearer of God's rule to men? What course of action is open to one who, knowing himself to be God's only Son, is called to be the Lord's Servant? With such problems Jesus wrestles in the wilderness, and the Evil One is ever near to suggest all sorts of wrong roads to the kingdom.

The third point to note is that in each of his replies to the Tempter Jesus borrows the language of Deuteronomy. For an Old Testament key to Jesus' mind at this time consider the words of Moses to the people of Israel in the wilderness:

'You shall remember all the way which the Lord your God has led you these forty years in the wilderness, that he might humble you, testing you to know what was in your heart, whether you would keep his commandments, or not. And he humbled you and let you hunger and fed you with manna which you did not know, nor did your fathers know; that he might make you know that man does not live by bread alone, but that man lives by everything that proceeds out of the mouth of the Lord' (Deut. 8.2f).

The echoes of this passage from Deuteronomy in the gospel story are too numerous to be accidental. Just as old Israel, 'God's son' (Exod. 4.22; Hos. 11.1), had been tested in the wilderness, so now God's only Son who, as the Servant Messiah, is called to create the new Israel, is put to the proof.

We may now consider the three temptations, taking them in Matthew's order, which provides a more striking climax than Luke's.

'If you are the son of God, command these loaves to become bread.' Some find the clue to this temptation in Jesus' own physical hunger at the time. Around him lie the flat desert stones, and he hears the Tempter saying in his inner heart, 'You are hungry. If you really are God's Son and Messiah, use your powers to turn these stones into bread. So will you confirm your conviction of Sonship and preserve yourself for your mission.' Others have suggested that Jesus was being tempted, Moses-like, to repeat the miracle of the manna, to feed the starving multitudes. ('Show us manna falling from heaven, as Moses did', said the Galileans at a later date, John 6.30f.) They remind us that when contemporary apocalyptic writers pictured the good time coming, they often pictured it as an economic paradise, a miraculous abundance of material blessings, a 'feast of fat things' for Israel (Isa. 25.6). Between these two views we do not need to choose. Jesus was being invited by the devil to assume a role that would at once satisfy his own immediate need and fulfil popular expectations of the messianic age. The temptation touched Jesus at a point not of weakness but of strength—his compassion for the hungry and poor. But the good may so easily become the enemy of the best. To satisfy men's physical needs at the neglect of their spiritual ones would be to dehumanize man made in the image of God, and make him one with the beasts that perish. Jesus repudiates the suggestion, 'Man shall not live by bread alone but by every word that proceeds from the mouth of God' (Matt. 4.4; Deut. 8.3).

If the first temptation was to be an economic Messiah, the second was to be a wonder-working one. In imagination (cf. Ezek. 8.3, 'The Spirit . . . brought me in visions of God to Jerusalem') Jesus stands on the pinnacle of the royal porch of the temple. Below, the multitudes clamour for a 'sign'—some dazzling act that will blazon the truth of his claims across the sky. Why not fling himself from the pinnacle, assured that God will supply a flight of angels for his protection? The second temptation is to pander to the Jews' craving for a sign. ('The Jews demand signs,' said Paul, who knew them, in I Cor. 1.22.) But Jesus refuses the demand, as he was later to refuse it during his ministry. 'You shall not put the Lord your God to the test,' he replied (Matt. 4.7; Deut. 6.16). We may finish the quotation from Deuteronomy: 'as you tested him at Massah', comparing Exod. 17.7, 'Moses called the name of the place Massah, because they . . . put the Lord to the proof by saying, "Is the Lord among us or not?".' Now, as then, God was among his people. To doubt it by thus putting God to the proof would be to challenge God, not to trust him. Besides, Jesus well knew that no transient impression made on men's senses would establish God's sovereignty in the spirit. Later, he was to tell some sign-seekers, 'Neither will they be convinced if someone should rise from the dead' (Luke 16.31 L).

The third temptation likewise recalls Israel in the wilderness. On the far side of the Jordan valley rose Mount Nebo where of old the Lord had showed Moses the Promised Land (Deut. 34.1). Now it is not the land of Israel but 'all the kingdoms of the world' which are shown to the Servant Messiah. In imaginative vision—this is the meaning of Luke's 'in a moment of time' (Luke 4.5)—Jesus stands on a height commanding a prospect of all the kingdoms of the world and their glory. (As a youth, from the Nazareth hill-tops, looking down on the *Via Maris* running through the vale of Esdraelon, he must have had a fore-glimpse of such kingdoms.) This is evidence that Jesus was thinking of the whole world to whom Israel had a mission (Isa. 42.1ff.; 49.6). 'Here is dominion,' says the Tempter, 'such as even the great ones of the Gentiles might envy. All shall be yours on one condition—that you do homage to me.' It is the temptation to be a political Messiah—to heed the call of the Zealots and their like and lead them in a war of liberation against Caesar and all his works. 'Use the world's methods, force and domination,' says the Devil, 'and you cannot fail to rally men to you.' If only Jesus will stoop to the methods of 'the prince of this world' who now claims to have it in his power, 'the ends of the earth' (Ps. 2.8) will be his possession. But to employ the Devil's methods to win the world would be rank treachery to God. 'Homage,' Jesus replies, 'is due to God alone' (Matt. 4.10; Deut. 6.13). No man, let alone one who knows himself called to be the Messiah, can serve both God and the Devil.

Thus in all three temptations the Messiah is being invited to take the centre of the stage. In each of his replies Jesus puts God in the centre. Implicit obedience to the will of God ('living on every word God utters') is the first principle he lays down. The second is trust in God which asks no proof ('you shall not put God to the test'). And the third is a dedicated allegiance which excludes all lesser claims ('homage is due to God alone').

So, in travail of soul, Jesus fought his way through this tangle of specious alternatives to a clear vision of the Messiah God meant him to be. The first battle in the fight with the power of evil had been won—as Jesus himself put it in his little parable of the Duel (Mark 3.27; Luke 11.21f. Q): the Strong Man had been worsted by the Stronger. But there were to be further battles. We often speak as if the temptation were an isolated experience. But the pressure lasted right through his very ministry, to the very hour when he hung on the cross (Mark 15.32). Nevertheless, from the truth reached in the wilderness Jesus never swerved. The way he chose was one of utter self-dedication and obedience to the will of his Father: he would wait for the hour when the Father chose, and as the Father chose, to make him known as the Servant Messiah.

> The Kingdom that I seek
> Is thine; so let the way
> That leads to it be thine.[1]

Note

The narrative of the temptation presupposes belief in a personal devil, as indeed the whole New Testament does. But can a modern Christian continue to hold such a belief? In reply certain things must be said.

First: if there was to be a true incarnation, Jesus must have used the thought-forms and categories of his time. The gospels say he did so. He spoke of Satan, the Evil One, etc. And we could not expect him to do anything else, unless we are prepared to give up our conviction of his true manhood.

Second: if the ordinary man today apparently 'has no need of that hypothesis', viz. belief in a personal devil, not a few distinguished modern thinkers (Forsyth, Tillich, Sayers, C. S. Lewis) have, and they can point in evidence to the 'demonic' elements abroad in our world.

Third: the modern Christian may accommodate himself to the *Zeitgeist* (which denies the existence of *Geister*, whether good or evil) by saying that the New Testament's language about a personal devil is 'mythological'. But,

> Myth is the language which contains the clue
> To that which is at once both real and true,

and the 'myth' of a personal devil—if we choose to call it so—witnesses to the fact that moral evil is (*a*) real and (*b*) personal.

Fourth: though we very properly disavow all crude nonsense about a devil with two horns and a tail, it is quite another matter to conceive of God's antagonist as only human or only a principle. If we do this, we lower the whole tension of the conflict between the kingdom of God and the kingdom of evil, which is writ so large in the New Testament, as we blind our eyes to the fact that, as Jesus and his apostles held, the Lord has a controversy not only with his people but with a rival king and a rival strategy. While therefore we must always beware of thinking of Satan as a second God, there is evidence enough in our world of the existence of a giant power of evil to warrant us in holding that when Jesus spoke of it as God's great adversary, he was uttering profound and inescapable truth.

[1] Horatius Bonar.

Part Three

THE MINISTRY

5

SKETCH OF THE MINISTRY (i)

Excluding the last journey to Jerusalem and the ministry there, we trace three periods in Jesus' activity: an early Judean mission; the Galilean ministry; and the period of travel.

The early Judean mission

If we had only Mark's gospel, we might well conclude that Jesus' ministry was limited to Galilee, with one first and final visit to Jerusalem. This is unlikely, for three reasons:

(a) There is a gap between Mark 1.13 and 1.14 which leaves room for earlier activity outside Galilee.

(b) Even the synoptic gospels contain hints that Jesus was no stranger to the capital and its neighbourhood when he came up to it for the last time. Most impressive of all are those words of Jesus, uttered on the road to Jerusalem and 'wild with all regret': 'O Jerusalem, Jerusalem, killing the prophets and stoning those who are sent to you! How often would I have gathered your children together as a hen gathers her brood under her wings, and you would not!' (Luke 13.34 Q).

(c) We have the plain statement in John 3.22–30—a passage derived from reliable pre-Johannine tradition[1]—that Jesus and John the Baptist conducted parallel missions in the south before the Galilean ministry began. Of the nature and length of this early Judean mission of Jesus we can say little except that it must have been a time of preparation for his later ministry. That it was successful the Fourth Gospel tells us: 'Some of John's disciples had fallen into a dispute with Jews about purification; so they came to him and said, "Rabbi, there was a man with you on the other side of Jordan, to whom you bore your witness.

[1] C. H. Dodd, *Historical Tradition in the Fourth Gospel*, Cambridge University Press, 1963, pp. 270–87.

Here he is baptizing, and crowds are flocking to him." John's answer was: "A man can have only what God gives him. You yourselves can testify that I said, 'I am not the Messiah; I have been sent as his forerunner.' It is the bridegroom to whom the bride belongs. The bridegroom's friend, who stands by and listens to him, is overjoyed at hearing the bridegroom's voice. This joy, this perfect joy, is now mine. As he grows greater, I must grow less" (John 3.25–30 NEB).

St John adds that it was the Pharisees' jealousy of Jesus' success which made him move northwards, via Samaria, into Galilee (John 4.1ff.). For the sequel we have to turn from St John to St Mark. Mark 1.14 suggests that the interval was broken by Jesus' receipt of news that the Baptist had been cast into prison. The forerunner had run his course. It was time for the mightier one to appear in Galilee with 'news' which far transcended John's.

The Galilean ministry (Mark 1.14–6.56)

'Now after John was delivered up . . .' Jesus began his Galilean ministry after Herod Antipas had imprisoned the Baptist in the lonely fortress of Machaerus near the Dead Sea.

From now on we follow Mark's narrative which we may summarize. (The Galilean ministry, which seems to have lasted about a year, is to be fitted into John's framework between chs 5 and 7 of his gospel.)

After describing Jesus' appearance in Galilee and the call of four disciples, Mark relates a memorable sabbath in Capernaum. There follows a group of stories—often called 'the conflict stories'—narrating how Jesus came into ever sharper conflict with the Jewish authorities (2.1–3.6). Jesus now withdrew to the lakeside, and somewhere in the 'hill country' chose twelve disciples. His work of healing continued with such success that he was accused, by scribes from Jerusalem, of being in league with Satan (3.7–35). Mark now records some parables of the kingdom which Jesus told, followed by a series of 'mighty works' (4.1–5.43). Then come the mission and the return of the twelve disciples (the story of the Baptist's death being dovetailed between the two events). The Galilean ministry culminates in the feeding of the multitude, the voyage and the walking on the water (6.1–56). (Thereafter follow the period of travel and the last journey to Jerusalem.)

So Mark traces the march of events. Did they really happen in this order? The form critics have said that we cannot trust Mark's order. He likes (they say) to group his stories topically, and 'the generalizing summaries' with which he links them together are his own invention.

This view that Mark 'is a heap of unstrung pearls' is an exaggeration. If Mark groups some of his materials topically, he does give us a broad outline of how things developed—an outline we have reason to believe was derived from the tradition of the church's *kērygma* (compare Peter's speech in Acts 10.37–41).[1] It reveals three distinct stages:

(a) Synagogue preaching in Capernaum and elsewhere.
(b) Teaching and healing by the lakeside in the presence of crowds from all over Palestine.
(c) Retirement to the hill country with a disciple band who are sent out on a preaching and healing mission.

So the Galilean ministry developed, and we must now try to describe its main features.

'Jesus came into Galilee,' says Mark, 'proclaiming the Gospel of God: "The time has come; the kingdom of God is upon you; repent, and believe the Gospel" ' (Mark 1.14 NEB). Familiarity with these words has dulled our ears to their wonder. What they mean is something like this: 'The time of which the prophet Isaiah spoke (Isa. 52.7f.) has come. The reign of God is now a dawning reality. God has begun to invade history in his royal power. Therefore, turn back[2] to God and accept the good news I am bringing.'

Such, in summary, was Jesus' message. How did it differ from the Baptist's? John's was a 'burden' or 'doom' in the comminatory sense of the old prophets. Jesus' message was an *evangel*, the proclamation of good tidings (as in Second Isaiah). John declared 'the day of wrath is near'; Jesus said, 'The reign of God is here'.

A Q saying (Luke 7.33f.) tells how the two men appeared in the eyes of their contemporaries: 'John the Baptist came neither eating

[1] See C. H. Dodd, *New Testament Studies*, Manchester University Press 1952, ch. 1, and Vincent Taylor, *The Gospel according to Mark*, Macmillan 1957, 145–8.
[2] 'Repent' means 'turn back' in the prophetic sense. It denotes an act of the will, and in his parable of the Prodigal Son Jesus has given us a picture of it. 'It was not repentance when the prodigal son grew hungry,' Mrs. Booth is reported to have said, 'nor when he remembered his father's house, nor even when he said, "I will arise and go to my father". You see repentance when it is said, he arose and came to his father.'

bread nor drinking wine, and you say "He is possessed". The Son of Man came eating and drinking, and you say, "Look at him! a glutton and a drinker, a friend of tax-gatherers and sinners" ' (NEB). In other words, John was an ascetic, Jesus was not.

The same contrast marked their disciples: those of John fasted and apparently wore the grave looks of men in deadly earnest about their religion; but the disciples of Jesus were like members of a wedding party (Mark 2.18–20).

With this message of the inbreaking reign of God Jesus began his Galilean ministry. At first he proclaimed it in the synagogues and elsewhere in the towns. But before long he clashed with the religious authorities, and had to seek the freer atmosphere of the lakeside whither, as his fame spread, the crowds resorted. There followed the third stage when he retired to the hill country with a disciple band. These disciples, after training, he sent out to proclaim God's dawning kingdom by word and deed.

Before we fill in this rough outline, one important observation must be made. Under the influence of 'lives' of Jesus like Renan's, we have tended to think of the Galilean ministry as a time of quiet preaching and teaching in contrast with Jesus' later work in Judea when he is marching on the cross—the time of his passion—which we might equally well call his action. Such a picture we obtain only if we scale down the miracles, interpret the parables as charming stories about moral commonplaces, and evacuate Jesus' eschatological sayings of their mystery and depth. Something of Whittier's 'O Sabbath Rest of Galilee' there may have been in the ministry, but more of Bunyan's 'Holy War' in which there fights for us,

the Proper Man
Whom God himself hath bidden.

We ought to picture the Galilean ministry dynamically, not statically. 'Jesus,' observes Goguel,[1] 'never said, "I am come to teach", but "I am come to kindle a fire on the earth".' His words bear this out. He begins his ministry in Nazareth by announcing that he is sent to 'proclaim release to the captives' (Luke 4.18 L). He compares his mission to the binding of the strong man (the devil) by a stronger (Luke 11.21f. Q). His parables, as Jeremias has said, are 'weapons of war' and his 'mighty works' signs that the issue is being victoriously joined with the powers of evil. And all through that

ministry there rings a note of terrible urgency, as though a crisis
uniquely fraught with blessing or with judgment for 'this generation'
in Israel were upon them (see Luke 12.49–59; 13.1–5, and note
especially the little parable of the Defendant, which says that Israel,
like an insolvent debtor, is on the way to court—God's court—and
must decide which way she will go).

Only if we see the Galilean ministry thus, do we see it aright—
get the impression of 'tremendous power', as of 'a great wind sweep-
ing through Palestine',[1] which Jesus' ministry created. And the
emergent picture of the chief figure in that campaign of the kingdom,
so far from being that of a high-souled teacher patiently indoctrinat-
ing the multitudes with truths of timeless wisdom, is rather that of
the strong Son of God, spearheading the attack against the devil and
all his works, and calling on men to decide on whose side of the
battle they will be. 'Leave the dead to bury their own dead,' he
cries, 'but as for you, go and proclaim the kingdom of God' (Luke
9.60 Q). 'The kingdom of God exercises its force' (Matt. 11.12). 'If
I by the finger of God cast out demons, then the kingdom of God
has come upon you' (Luke 11.20 Q). 'Behold I cast out demons and
perform cures today and tomorrow, and the third day I finish my
course' (Luke 13.32 L). It was so, looking back on it many years
after, that St John saw the ministry: 'The Son of God appeared for
the very purpose of undoing the devil's work' (I John 3.8 NEB).

Now let us choose five salient features of the ministry. Of the call
of his disciples, which we shall discuss later, let us note that there
were three stages in the relationship between Jesus and his disciples.
First, he called certain men from their daily tasks—perhaps initially
five, as the Fourth Gospel and the Talmud suggest. Then, when the
number of his followers had grown, he selected twelve men to form
the nucleus of the new Israel, the new church which he was creating.
Finally, when these had been to school with him, he sent them forth
to preach and heal in his name and in the power of the dawning
kingdom.

Second, note the 'mighty works' (*dynameis*: acts of power) which
marked Jesus' ministry. (These we shall study in some detail later.)
For Jesus announced the dawning of God's reign not in words only
but by deeds, as 'as he went about doing good and healing all who
were oppressed by the devil' (Acts 10.38). His miracles were not
accidental or incidental—the spontaneous reactions of his compas-

[1] E. V. Rieu, *The Four Gospels*, Penguin Books 1952, p. XXX.

sion to dire cases of human need, though of course his heart was ever moved at the sight of human misery. So far from being an *addendum* to his gospel, they were an integral part of it; they were, in one phrase, the kingdom of God in action. Preaching and mighty acts were complementary parts in one great campaign against the dominion of evil.

Third, we notice Jesus' proclamation of the reign of God to the common people. To them he generally spoke in parables, not, as Mark 4.11f. might suggest,[1] because he wished to befog and blind his hearers, but because 'truth embodied in a tale' makes it memorable, and because the purpose of the parable is to tease into thought, to sift its hearers, and to challenge to decision. Mark records three of these parables: the Sower, the Seed growing Secretly, and the Mustard Seed. But there were others, e.g. the Dragnet and the Weeds among the Wheat. All imply, in one way or another, that the reign of God is now in some sense a present reality, a power of God already at work. If we study our other gospel sources, we can form a better idea of the various ways in which Jesus presented the claims and the challenge of the dawning kingdom. Thus, we can hear him in the Nazareth synagogue quoting the great prophecy of Isa. 61, 'The Spirit of the Lord is upon me', and summing it up with 'Today in your very hearing this text has come true' (Luke 4.16–22 L, NEB). Or we can imagine Jesus closing a sermon on the kingdom with the twin parables of the Precious Pearl and the Hidden Treasure (Matt. 13.44–46 M), as though to say 'The kingdom of God is wealth that demonetizes all other currencies. Is not such blessedness worth any sacrifice?' One day, certain candidates for the kingdom eagerly present themselves to him, only to be warned in the stories of the Tower Builder and the Warring King (Luke 14.27–33 L) to count well the cost. Another day, there are scribes and Pharisees within earshot who sneer at him as 'the sinner's friend', and he tells them the great parables of the Lost Sheep, the Lost Coin and the Waiting Father (Luke 15 L), as though to say, 'This is what the Almighty is like, and this is why I am acting as I am'.

Fourth, we observe the effect of Jesus' ministry on the people. Without doubt his mission deeply stirred the people of Galilee. After the wonderful sabbath in Capernaum the disciples could say to Jesus, 'They are all looking for you' (Mark 1.37). We read of a vast multitude following him to the Lake of Galilee—so great that he had

[1] See note at end of chapter.

SKETCH OF THE MINISTRY (i)

to have a small boat standing by lest he be mobbed (Mark 3.7–10).
And there were, on a very rough computation no doubt, five thousand men in the desert place where, at the height of the Galilean
ministry, he fed them with the bread of the kingdom (Mark 6.44).

For their part, the people found the teaching of Jesus altogether
'new' (Mark 1.22, 27), for he spoke and acted with conscious authority and not as their scribes did. When the rabbis taught, nothing
happened. All things happened when Jesus taught. He declared
men's sins were forgiven, and they were. A paralysed man rose to his
feet and walked. 'Never before have we seen the like,' said the on-
lookers (Mark 2.1–12). Layman as he was, there was a wonderful
'wisdom' about his words—a depth and insight unique in their
experience (Mark 6.2). Above all, as is shown by the rich variety of
verbs[1] used to describe the reactions of people to him, there was
about Jesus something other-worldly, 'numinous', or, as they say in
Scotland, 'uncanny', suggesting that in him the very power and
presence of God was at work. Small wonder that the man from
Nazareth attracted, thrilled and awed the crowds as his fame spread.
Jesus, however, was not deceived by this outburst of popular enthusiasm: not all, he knew, would receive the seed of the kingdom he
was sowing and, by a true repentance, align themselves with the
Great Sower's purpose; and in that simple story of a farmer's fortunes (though it was originally a ringing 'Have faith in God' to
despondent followers), we hear Jesus thinking aloud about his work
in Galilee, with its mixture of success and failure (Mark 4.3–9).

For—and this is the fifth feature—side by side with Jesus' fascina-
tion over the common people there was arising hostility against him
among the religious leaders of Jewry. At the causes of this it is not
hard to guess: Jesus' personal popularity with the crowds; his highly
irregular attitude to fasting (Mark 2.18ff.); his healing on the sabbath with which went a mysterious claim to be 'Lord of the sabbath'
(Mark 2.27; cf Luke 13.10–17 L, etc); his consorting with social
pariahs like prostitutes and tax-collectors (Mark 2.15–17; Matt.
11.19 Q, etc.); his trenchant criticism of the Pharisees and scribes
(Luke 11.37–52 Q); his attack on their 'tradition' (rabbinical

[1] Here are four of the 'numinous' verbs which Mark employs: *thaumazein*
'marvel'; *thambeisthai* 'be dumbfounded'; *ekplēssesthai* 'be astounded'; and *phobeis-*
thai 'be awe-struck'. On the whole subject see W. Lillie, *Jesus Then and Now*,
SPCK 1964, pp. 48ff.; R. Otto, *The Idea of the Holy*, Oxford University Press 1923,
pp. 162f., and *The Kingdom of God and the Son of Man*, Lutterworth Press 1938,
pp. 333ff.

interpretation of the Law) which, he said, made God's word null and void (Mark 7.1–13). All these things served to sharpen the antagonism of the religious leaders. Nor was this deep suspicion of Jesus confined to them. Herod the Tetrarch had decided that Jesus was 'John the Baptist all over again' (Mark 6.16). Clearly the success of the Galilean ministry had produced a situation ever becoming more difficult to control. Between the enthusiasm of his followers and the mounting hostility of his enemies a state of crisis was building up.

During this time Jesus made no public claim to be the Messiah, though in his reply to John the Baptist's question from prison he said, in effect: 'I am, but not the kind, you, John, were expecting' (Luke 7.18–23 Q). If he used a title for himself, it was the Son of man—a title which was at once mysterious and non-committal. To have made an overt claim to be the Messiah would have awakened wrong hopes in Jewish breasts (as the sequel to the feeding of the five thousand shows) and would have attracted to himself the attention of Rome, whose *Realpolitik* found swift ways of dealing with all such disturbers of the *Pax Romana*.

All this activity of Jesus may have lasted from one spring to another (if our chronology is right, from the spring of AD 28 to the spring of AD 29). The Twelve were sent out on their mission. On their return, in order to get them away from the excited crowd, Jesus took them off into a place of quiet retreat (Mark 6.32), only to find there was no escape from the multitudes. The crisis came to a head in a desert place at the north side of the Lake of Galilee.

When Jesus saw the crowd, 'his heart went out to them because they were like sheep without a shepherd, and he had much to teach them' (Mark 6.34). To Jesus they looked like a nation, or army, without a proper leader, and doubtless what he had to say to them concerned the dawning reign of God. Then, when evening wore on, he fed that crowd of five thousand men with five loaves and two fishes. Was it a miracle? *Prima facie*, yes. Yet Mark uses none of his 'numinous' verbs to describe the crowd's reactions, and he suggests that the disciples found it more a *mystery* than a miracle story (Mark 6.52). Perhaps, then, instead of arguing whether Jesus could, or could not, have performed a nature miracle like this, we would be better employed trying to discover the *meaning* of what Jesus did. What if it really were a great open-air sacrament, a kind of Galilean Lord's supper (as Schweitzer suggested)? The words Mark uses to describe Jesus' actions certainly recall what he said and did with bread and wine in the upper room (Mark 6.41); and in the Fourth Gospel, Jesus, on the day following, interprets the desert supper in terms of 'bread of life' (John 6.26ff.).

But if we are right in suggesting that it was primarily a sacrament, what place and purpose had it in Jesus' intention? We have three clues to guide us. First: St John calls it a 'sign' (John 6.14), that is, an action resembling the *'ōth*, or symbolic act of the Old Testament prophets, by which they believed they were entering into the divine purpose and helping it forward. Probably Jesus so conceived his act. Second: we recall that Jesus once told a story about God's kingdom using the figure of a great supper, in which the host summoned his guests with the invitation, 'Come, for everything is ready' (Luke 14.16–24 Q). We may then say that, when Jesus made the men sit down and gave them food by the hands of his disciples, he was acting out his own parable. Earlier in the day he had spoken to them about God's reign. The open-air supper at its close said in effect, 'The kingdom of God is upon you. Come, all is ready.' Third: Jesus had declared, 'I did not come to invite the righteous but sinners' (Mark 2.17). Now, as host at the supper, Jesus was doing just this—inviting sinners to the banquet of God's kingdom. The 'sign', or acted parable, was Jesus' last attempt to make the Galileans understand God's great call to them in his kingdom, of which he himself was God's agent and mouthpiece.

How did they respond to that call? John 6.14f. supplies the answer. Excited by the 'sign', the Galileans would fain have taken Jesus by force and made him a King Messiah after their own dreaming. What was being planned was nothing less than a Messianic 'revolt in the desert', with Jesus as its leader, against the occupying power of Rome. This role Jesus flatly refused to play. Long before, in the desert (Matt. 4.8–10 Q), he had rejected that Messianic role as of the Devil. And what he now did shows that our reading of the whole episode is right. First, he compelled his disciples (who may have shared the crowd's hopes) to put a lake's breadth between them and the crowd; then he himself induced the excited multitude to depart peacefully, before he retired alone into the hills for prayer (Mark 6.45f.; John 6.15).

More clearly than the first three evangelists St John saw that the Galilean Lord's supper had, in the result, political implications. Equally, in the discourse about the supper which Jesus made to the crowd the following day (John 6.26ff.), St John brings out the true spiritual implications of what Jesus had sought to say at the Galilean Lord's supper, 'In my person and mission God's saving rule has confronted you. I am the bread of life.'

Though it means anticipating our next chapter, a brief postscript on the sequel to the feeding of the five thousand seems necessary. It can be shown that John 6 (which begins with the feeding and ends with Peter's confession) preserves a more reliable account of events than Mark 6–8 (which records *two* cases of feeding and two journeys northwards) and makes more intelligible the situation which led to Peter's confession. According to John 6.66, after the abortive revolt in the desert, when Jesus dashed the hopes of the militants, 'many of his disciples withdrew and no longer went about with him'. Here is the background for Jesus' question, 'Do you also want to leave me?' Then Peter, speaking for the disciple band, said, 'Never! We know that you are the Holy One of God' (John 6.68ff.).

Note on Mark 4.11f.

Some take these two verses to be a piece of later church theology—an attempt to explain why the Jews as a whole rejected Jesus' 'good news'. Such scepticism is unnecessary if one accepts T. W. Manson's explanation of the passage (*The Teaching of Jesus*, pp. 177f.):

Mark 4.11f. is a genuine saying of Jesus, but v. 12 conceals a mistranslation from the Aramaic. We ought to translate:

11. 'To you is given the secret of the kingdom of God, but
    all things come in parables to those outside,
12. who see indeed but do not know,
    and hear indeed but do not understand,
    lest they should repent and be forgiven.'

Verse 12, which quotes Isa. 6.9f., reflects not the Hebrew (or the Septuagint) but the Targum, i.e. the Aramaic paraphrase of the passage used in the synagogues. (For example, the Targum ends, 'be forgiven', where the Hebrew has 'be healed'.)

For most people the difficulty is the *hina* ('so that') introducing v. 12. But here the Targum has the Aramaic word *de*, which, besides meaning 'so that', can also mean 'who'. Hence the right rendering is: 'Who see indeed, etc.'.

The parables (Jesus is saying) are a test of a man's insight, and determine whether he will enter the kingdom or stay out of it. The real cause of 'the outsiders'' blindness is their own fatal self-satisfaction—their refusal to repent and be forgiven. In other words, nobody can receive the secret of the kingdom without exercising his own responsibility towards it. Jesus does not regard 'the outsiders' as a fixed and immutable class, but merely those who, for lack of proper response, remain, for the time being, outside.

6

SKETCH OF THE MINISTRY (ii)

The travel period (Mark 7.24—8.26)

After the Galilean Lord's supper and its sequel, Jesus left Galilee, abandoning for a time his public ministry. Mark now narrates a time of travel outside Palestine in the direction of Tyre. This is followed by Peter's confession at Caesarea Philippi, the transfiguration, and the last journey south.

Mark's geographical data make it difficult to reconstruct the route Jesus took on this time of travel outside Palestine. (His phrase 'by way of Sidon' in 7.31 has suggested to one scholar a journey from Cornwall to London via Manchester.) Nor do the other evangelists help us here. St Matthew well-nigh eliminates the time of travel. Luke omits it. John is silent about it—unless John 7.35 ('Will he go to the Dispersion among the Greeks, and teach the Greeks?') betrays some knowledge that Jesus set foot on non-Jewish territory. Yet we need not doubt that Jesus did for a time travel north-west, outside Galilee. And if conjecture is permitted, we may surmise that he went first north-west in the direction of Tyre, before turning south-east to Bethsaida and the district of the Ten Towns (Decapolis).

Why did he thus withdraw from Galilee? Since he wished to remain incognito (Mark 7.24), he cannot have planned a mission to the heathen. The theory of a flight from the hostility of Herod Antipas has found little support. The cool defiance of Jesus' reply to some friendly Pharisees who advised him to flee because Herod meant to kill him, hardly suggests one who feared what men, even Herod, could do. 'Go and tell that fox,' he replied, ' "Listen: today and tomorrow I shall be casting out devils and working cures; on the third day I reach my goal." However, I must be on my way today and tomorrow and the next day, because it is unthinkable for a prophet to meet his death anywhere but in Jerusalem' (Luke 13.31–33 L, NEB).

If the time of travel was a flight, it was a flight from the dangerous enthusiasm of his friends. Jesus withdrew from Galilee because the people there had wrongly responded to the challenge of the Galilean Lord's supper. No Zealot-like revolt against Rome would serve the purposes of God's kingdom. Quite other was the destiny appointed by his Father for the Son of man. To think things out to their divine conclusions he must have time for privacy and prayer. What these were would be disclosed at Caesarea Philippi . . .

Appended Note on Mark 7.24–8.26

'Then he left that place and went away into the territory of Tyre' (Mark 7.24).

'On his return journey from Tyrian territory he went by way of Sidon to the Sea of Galilee through the territory of the Ten Towns' (Mark 7.31).

Between these two travel notes Mark places the story of the Syrophoenician Woman and, after the second one, the tale of the deaf-mute and the story of the feeding of the four thousand.

Now if you study Mark 6.30 – 7.23 and Mark 8.1–13, you cannot miss the striking parallelism between the two narratives. Each records a meal followed by a crossing of the lake and a controversy with the Pharisees, thus:

A	B
1. 6.30–44 Feeding of five thousand	1. 8.1–9 Feeding of four thousand
2. 6.45–53 Crossing to Gennesaret	2. 8. 10 Crossing to Dalmanutha
3. 7.1–23 Controversy with Pharisees	3. 8.11–13 Controversy with Pharisees

So close is the parallelism that most critics agree that the feeding of the four thousand and its sequel (B1 and B2) are a doublet (or variant account) of the feeding of the five thousand and the crossing to Gennesaret.[1] (Dalmanutha, on the west side of the lake, *may* be Magdala.) This means that the series—meal, crossing and controversy—is doubly attested and is therefore probably historical.

Moreover, since the sayings collected topically in Mark 7.1–23 might have been uttered at almost any time during the Galilean ministry, the original series of events looks like A 1, A 2, B 3, i.e. Mark 6.30–53 plus 8.11–13.

[1] A strong argument for this view is Mark 8.4. The disciples ask, 'How can one feed these men with bread here in the desert?' Yet in Mark 6.41 Jesus, with the disciples' help, had done just this.

If this is so, where in this historical series should we place Jesus' withdrawal to Tyrian territory? Between 6.30–53 and 8.11–13? Or after 8.11–13? The second suggestion seems likelier, for 8.14ff. relates a recrossing of the lake ending at Bethsaida.

Accept this, and you have an intelligible account of Jesus' movements. Quitting Gennesaret, after refusing the Pharisees' demand for a sign (8.11–13), Jesus crosses the lake to Bethsaida and withdraws in the direction of Tyre. From this retirement, after his encounter with the Syrophoenician woman, he returns to Bethsaida, near which he heals the deaf-mute (7.32–37) and the blind man (8.22–26), before moving north to 'the villages of Caesarea Philippi' (8.27–33).[1]

Caesarea Philippi (Mark 8.27–38 par.; Matt. 16.17ff. M; John 6.66–71)

Now, Mark tells us, as Jesus and his disciples set out for the region of Caesarea Philippi, almost in the shadow of snow-capped Hermon, he asked them, 'Who do men say I am?' He was putting, as we should say, the great Christological question. They replied, in effect, that popular speculation took different shapes: the Baptist risen from the dead, Elijah (who was expected to return as the Messiah's herald) or someone in the same spiritual line as the old prophets. Then Jesus pressed the question down on them squarely, 'But you— who do you say I am?' The answer was critical for both Jesus and his disciples. If the Twelve had penetrated no more deeply into his mind than the people with their dream of a 'king to slay their foes and lift them high' (John 6.15), he must still have stayed his advance. Peter, however, at once spoke out what was in all their minds, 'You are the Messiah!' He was more than the prophet of Nazareth; he was 'the Coming One', the bearer of God's rule to men.

According to Matthew (16.17f. M), Jesus replied by congratulating Peter, 'Blessed are you, Simon Bar-jona!' His confession was no mere human deduction but a revelation from on high. It is the kind of response almost demanded by the occasion. But, alas, Peter evidently regarded his confession as the last word on the secret of his master's person; for Jesus himself it was only the first one. At once, Mark says, Jesus forbade them to speak about him, i.e. as the Messiah. Messiah he was, but such a one as none was dreaming of. For, as he now told them frankly, 'The Son of man must suffer many

---

[1] For a full discussion see Vincent Taylor, *St Mark*, pp. 628ff.

things', be rejected by the rulers of Israel, and die before he came to his triumph. His words echo the general tenor of Isa. 53 (with, in the 'after three days', an echo of Hos. 6.2). So, hard on Peter's confession, which Jesus tacitly accepted, came the staggering truth that, in his vocation as the Son of man, Jesus must go the way of the suffering Servant of the Lord. 'Must', be it noted. It is 'a statement of divine destiny rather than of human inevitability'. Jesus sees himself as the chief actor in a drama of divine action rather than as the passive victim of human plotting.

But to Peter all this was a thing incredible. The paradox of a suffering Messiah swept him out of his spiritual depths; he reproved Jesus, only to be in turn rebuked with awful severity: 'Out of my sight, you Satan! Your outlook is not God's but man's.' As Jesus listened to Peter's protest, there came back to him his grim conflict in the wilderness. The devil was speaking to him through Peter's lips, urging him to follow a worldly course, tempting him to saviourhood without a cross.

It is commonly said that the central point in this narrative is the disciples' first realization of Jesus' Messiahship. Their first express avowal it may well have been. But some glimmering of it must have been in their minds before. They had heard him say, 'If I by the finger of God cast out devils, then the kingdom of God has come upon you.' He had claimed in their hearing to be 'Lord of the sabbath'. Demoniacs had blurted out his Messiahship, only to be silenced. The idea had even occurred to the Baptist in prison.

But the Twelve had not hitherto so confessed him; and evidently Jesus regarded that confession as the necessary first step before he led them on to a deeper disclosure. Now he could begin to tell them what kind of Messiah he was. The more we reflect on it, the likelier it appears that the sovereign truth revealed at Caesarea Philippi was that, as Messiah, Jesus must go to a cross.

But this truth carried with it a corollary for his disciples, as Mark 8.34ff. shows. So, with terrible clarity, Jesus now spelt out all that following a Servant Messiah would mean for them. Henceforward they must be like a band of criminals carrying their own crosses to the gallows, and 'whoever cared for his own safety would be lost' (Mark 8.35).

Caesarea Philippi was a real turning-point in Jesus' ministry. As we read on in the middle section of Mark's gospel, we note how general teaching about the dawning of God's reign is replaced by teaching about the Son of man and his mission and the suffering and danger attending it. Already Jesus is beginning to 'dwell in his passion', and in the narrative that follows we find three close-linked features: the inexorable claims of Jesus on his disciples (compare Luke 14.26f. Q, spoken 'on the road to Jerusalem'), the all too human ambitions of the disciples (Mark 9.34; 10.35ff.) and, like a solemn bell tolling through all, the re-iterated predictions of the Son of man's coming passion (Mark 8.31.; 9.31.; 10.32ff.).

The Transfiguration (Mark 9.2–8 par.)

'Six days' after Peter's confession there occurred, on a 'high mountain' (probably Hermon, a dozen miles north of Caesarea Philippi), an event which has been 'at once the paradise and the despair of commentators'. Some have regarded it as a misplaced resurrection narrative; others as a parousia story; and all sorts of typological meanings have been read into the details. We take the view that the story is based on an actual experience of the disciples in Jesus' lifetime. The precision of Mark's dating suggests that it must be linked with Peter's confession and its sequel, as the event is to be regarded as a heavenly ratification of the new teaching which Jesus had then given his disciples.

Our primary account is Mark's:

'Six days later Jesus took Peter, James, and John with him and led them up a high mountain where they were alone; and in their presence he was transfigured; his clothes became dazzling white, with a whiteness no bleacher on earth could equal. They saw Elijah appear, and Moses with him, and there they were, conversing with Jesus. Then Peter spoke: "Rabbi," he said, "how good it is that we are here! Shall we make three shelters, one for you, one for Moses, and one for Elijah?" (For he did not know what to say; they were so terrified.) Then a cloud appeared, casting its shadow over them, and out of the cloud came a voice: "This is my Son, my Beloved; listen to him." And now suddenly, when they looked around, there was nobody to be seen but Jesus alone with themselves' (NEB).

Specially interesting for its details is Luke's account (Luke 9.28–36). (Whether they are his own editorial comments or derived from a special tradition, who can say with certainty?) Jesus, he says, went up the mountain to pray. Before they saw Jesus' 'glory', Peter and his companions had been half asleep. Moses and Elijah who appeared in glory spoke of the *exodus*, or 'deliverance', which Jesus was about to accomplish at Jerusalem.

What is clear is that this was a critical stage in Jesus' ministry. This is why (as in Gethsemane) he takes companions with him. But what makes the whole narrative hard to interpret is the blending of what sounds like *remembered fact*—the precise date, the inner circle of disciples, the unearthly radiance of Jesus ('with a whiteness no bleacher on earth could equal'), the 'numinous' terror of the disciples—with what look like *symbolical elements*—the presence of Moses and Elijah and the heavenly voice out of the over-shadowing cloud (cf. Exod. 24.16).

What happened to Jesus on the mountain? As he prayed, he was transfigured with an extraordinary radiance. Somehow the rapture of his communion with his heavenly Father showed upon his face and person. We need not hesitate to accept this as historic fact if we recall the many records (collected by Evelyn Underhill and others) of the physical transfiguration of saints at prayer. (A friend of Sadhu Sundar Singh noted 'a faint luminosity' about his face as he prayed alone.) What we cannot do with any certainty is to enter the mind of Jesus as he prayed. Yet conjecture may be permissible. A week before, he had told his disciples about the Son of man who must suffer and die before he came to his glory, adding that they must be ready to share his suffering with him. In a day or two he would turn south for Jerusalem and, eventually, death. May we not say that on the mountain Jesus went through a momentous experience of self-dedication to his Father's will as he now saw it clearly in all its sombre significance? In Johannine phrase, he was consecrating himself afresh for his followers that they too might be consecrated in truth (John 17.19).

But, we are told, the three watching disciples saw more than Jesus in the rapture of his communion with God. In some way, at this high moment, they were so caught up in their Master's experience that they saw what Matthew calls a 'vision' (Matt. 17.9). In that vision two supreme representatives of the Old Covenant, Moses and Elijah, somehow materialized from the unseen world and conversed with their Master—conversed, Luke says, about the 'deliverance' he was about to fulfil in Jerusalem. Perhaps here we may invoke the psychology of mysticism to explain the vision. We may conjecture that, stimulated by the sight of Jesus in rapture of his prayer, they themselves experienced a vision accompanied by auditory and visual phenomena such as are elsewhere attested in the experiences of the mystics. But what are Moses and Elijah doing in this vision? It is not enough to say they represent the Law and the Prophets. For in the Old Testament Moses is a prophet (Deut. 18.15) as well as a lawgiver. And Elijah, besides being a prophet, is the final precursor of the Messiah (Mal. 4.5f.). Appearing together with Jesus they sum up the entire drama of the Old Covenant and point to Jesus as its consummator. Accordingly, as the vision fades, they 'vanish into thin air' and leave Jesus alone, with a heavenly voice from an over-shadowing cloud declaring Jesus to be the sole bearer of God's authority.

'This is my Son, my Beloved' are the first words of the voice. They are identical with the words spoken privately to Jesus as he rose from the waters of Jordan, except that here they are addressed to the disciples. The transfiguration is the counterpart in the disciples' experience of the baptism in Jesus' own experience. If the baptism was God's seal on the call of his Son to be the Servant Messiah, the transfiguration was, for the disciples, a like seal on the mission of Jesus as the suffering Messiah. No less significant are the second words of the voice: 'listen to him'. They recall the promise to Moses in Deut. 18.15: 'The Lord your God will raise up a prophet from among you like myself, and you shall listen to him.' Jesus, the disciples are to understand, bears an authority which is to replace that of Moses. And when the voice has ceased, Moses and Elijah have disappeared, and Jesus is seen alone.

On their way down the mountain Jesus bade his disciples be silent about the whole experience until the Son of man had risen from the dead. They were puzzled. They realized that this must mean a special resurrection of the Son of man before the general resurrection. 'Must not Elijah come first?' they asked. 'Yes,' replied Jesus, 'but in fact Elijah has already come and they have treated him as scripture said they would' (I Kings 19.2, 10). John the Baptist had found his Jezebel in Herodias.

There follows the story of how on their descent from the mountain Jesus cured an epileptic boy (Mark 9.14–29). Between the splendour of the scene on the mountain and the spectacle of human misery at its base—the theme of a famous picture by Raphael—there could be no sharper contrast.

7

THE ISRAEL-TO-BE

It is an indisputable fact that Jesus had disciples. But so had the rabbis. What distinguished his from theirs? First: they owed their discipleship to Jesus' sovereign call 'Follow me!', not to any free choice of their own to throw in their lot with him. Second: those so called were not invited to spend their days interpreting the Torah, but summoned to become 'apprentices' in the work of God's king-dom—labourers in God's harvest now ripe for reaping (Luke 10.2 Q; cf. John 4.35).

What had Jesus to say about discipleship to himself? (What he does say applies especially to the Twelve; but it does not appear from the gospels that the Twelve formed a close corporation to the exclu-sion of other disciples.) To begin with, he would have no disciples under false pretences. In modern terms, he would issue no lying prospectus. Candidates for discipleship were told to sit down and in cold blood count the cost (parables of the Tower-builder and the Warring King, Luke 14.28–32 L). This cost Jesus further elucidated in terms of sacrifice (Luke 9.57–62 Q; Luke 14.25f. Q), service (Luke 17.7–10 L) and—especially after Caesarea Philippi—suffer-ing (Mark 8.34f.; 10.39 etc.).

On the other hand, the kingdom was 'wealth that demonetizes all other currencies' (parables of the Hid Treasure and the Precious Pearl, Matt. 13.44–46 M); and for those who rose to the height of his challenge (as the 'rich young ruler' did not) he had both a special task and a special promise. Their task was, empowered with his authority, to 'catch' men for the kingdom (Mark 1.17; Luke 5.10). The promise was that faithfulness to him and his mission on earth would not go unrecognized in heaven (Luke 12.8f. Q). Yet the guerdon to be gained must never be the disciple's ruling motive. Reward hereafter there would be, but Jesus promises it to those who are obedient without thought of reward (Luke 17.7–10 L; Matt. 25.31–46 M). Their only ambition must be to serve. By so doing they would show themselves true followers (Mark 10.42–45; Luke 22.25–27 L) of the servant Son of man.

So Jesus conceived the calling, lot and destiny of those who would 'come after him'. Now we must look more closely at his dealings with the disciples—especially the chosen Twelve—and consider the great end he had in view.

The nucleus of the new Israel

According to Mark, there were three stages in Jesus' relations with his disciples—their call, their choice and their commissioning.

First comes the call, probably near Capernaum, of two pairs of brothers from their fishing nets—Peter and Andrew, James and John (Mark 1.16–20; cf. Luke 5.1–11; John 1.35ff.). A little later comes the call of Levi (probably the man later renamed by Jesus 'Matthew', i.e. 'gift of God') from the custom-house at Capernaum. No doubt these calls are meant to serve as typical of others not recorded.

The next stage—the choice—is recorded in Mark 3.13f. Somewhere in the hill-country round the lake Jesus 'chose twelve men' (cf. John 6.70) from a larger group of followers, that they might 'be with him' for training in the ways of the kingdom before he sent them out on mission.

Eleven of their names seem tolerably certain: Peter and Andrew, James and John, Matthew and Thomas, Philip and Bartholomew, James the son of Alphaeus and Thaddeus, Simon the Cananaean and Judas Iscariot. For Thaddeus Luke has 'Judas son of James'. Possibly this was the man's real name, Thaddeus being preferred to avoid any confusion with the betrayer (cf. John 14.22 'Judas, not Iscariot').

This Judas, James the son of Alphaeus and Bartholomew (i.e. *bar talmai*, possibly the patronymic of Nathanael, John 1.45ff.) are little more than names to us. To St John we owe a little more light on Peter's brother Andrew and on Thomas (his name means 'Twin'), the doubter. Matthew, or Levi, as a customs-officer, was probably a man of some education. Judas Iscariot (his second name probably meaning 'man of Kerioth'), who acted as purse-bearer to the Twelve (John 12.6), was possibly the only non-Galilean in the disciple-band. Simon the Cananaean (which Luke rightly Graecizes as 'Zealot') belonged to the extreme nationalists later known as 'Zealots'. The sons of Zebedee, James and John, formed, with Simon Peter, the inner circle of the Twelve (Mark 5.37; 9.2; 14.33). By the evidence of the gospels (Mark 9.38; Luke 9.54 L) they were men of ardent and fiery temper, their nickname 'Boanerges' (sons of thunder) suggesting their excitable and 'thundery' nature. Simon Peter we know best of all, not only because in the gospels he is the natural spokesman of the Twelve (as at Caesarea Philippi) but because after the resurrection he became the first leader in the Jerusalem church. A native of Bethsaida (John 1.44), in the gospels he is both brave and brash but hardly the incarnation of stability. Why did Jesus surname him Cephas, i.e. the Rock? Was the name given in order to steady him? Did Jesus (as Luke 22.31f. L might seem to suggest) foresee, beyond the *débâcle* of Calvary, his ultimate staunchness—the Peter of the day of Pentecost? There may be another explanation. A Jewish *midrash* (rabbinical comment on scripture) made God say of Abraham, 'Lo, I have discovered a rock on which to found the world'. When Jesus called Simon the Rock, was he in fact designating him as the basic or key figure in the new Israel?

Twelve men, then, belonging to what we might call the lower middle class—a tax-collector, four or more fishermen, a militant nationalist, and the rest we know not what—such were Jesus' chosen lieutenants for special training. Almost thirty years later Paul was to describe Christ's followers in Corinth as not many wise by wordly standards, not many powerful, not many of noble birth (I Cor. 1.26); but it had been true originally of the chosen Twelve. We are reminded of Chesterton's remark about the British jury. When (he said) our civilization wants to discover a solar system or to catalogue a library 'or any other trifle of that kind', it chooses specialists. But when it wants to do something really serious, it collects twelve ordinary men. 'The same thing,' he observes, 'was done by the Founder of Christianity.'

The third stage in Jesus' dealings with his chosen disciples was their mission (Mark 6.7–13, 30; Matt. 10.1–42; Luke 9.1–6; 10.1–20).[1] Since all our gospel sources—Mark, Q, M and L—have a version of Jesus' mission-charge, the mission is one of the best-attested facts in the life of Jesus. The Twelve now become the

[1] Luke has two missions and two charges. The first, Luke 9.1–6, comes from Mark 6.7–13. The second, Luke 10.1–20—a mixture of Q and L—is associated with the mission of the Seventy. Now Luke 22.35 ('no purse, no bag, no sandals') refers back to Luke 10.4 (where we find the same words), and in Luke 22.35 it is the Twelve who are addressed. This suggests that the mission of the Seventy (or Seventy-two) is a doublet of the mission of the Twelve.

accredited envoys of Jesus, their task to 'catch men'[1] for the kingdom. So Jesus sends them forth two by two, no doubt on the sound
scriptural basis that, in time of difficulty, 'two are better than one'
(Eccles. 4.8), as the testimony of two witnesses is likelier to be more
reliable than that of one (Deut. 19.15ff.). Before they go, he gives
them their marching orders.

First, they are to travel light. Dispensing with food, collecting bag
or money, they are to carry only a stick, a pair of sandals and one
tunic. (Matthew denies them even sandals and stick, and Luke, the
stick. Here Mark must be right.)

Second, they are to proclaim the advent of the kingdom, heal the
sick, and call for repentance (Luke 10.9; Matt. 10.7 Q; Mark 6.12),
as Jesus himself had done.

Third, they are to observe certain rules of hospitality. With well-
wishers they are to stay; but, if others reject their message, wasting
no time they are to quit them, solemnly shaking the dust off their
feet as a prophetic gesture of warning (Mark 6.11).

Fourth, they are never to forget whose emissaries they are. The
rabbis had a saying, 'A man's *shaliach* (accredited envoy) is as himself', that is, the agent's actions count as those of his principal. So
Jesus tells his special envoys: 'To receive you is to receive me, and to
receive me is to receive the One who sent me' (Matt. 10.40; Luke
10.16). They are messengers of Jesus who is himself the apostle of the
Almighty.

Then the curtain falls on their mission, except for one incident—
the case of the strange exorcist (Mark 9.38ff.), which clearly belongs
to a time when the Twelve were separated from Jesus—and we hear
no more of the missioners until they returned and reported to Jesus
who, noting the tell-tale signs of fatigue on them, sought, vainly, to
take them into quiet retreat (Mark 6.30ff.). How did Jesus estimate
the result of the mission? According to Luke 10.17f. L, when his
envoys reported to him jubilantly what had happened, he cried, 'I
saw Satan fall like lightning out of the sky'. The power of evil was
already toppling from his throne.

[1] The Greek verb is *halieuein* (fish for, with a view to catching) which gives us
our English term 'halieutics', art of fishing. This rough vernacular word was used
figuratively in much the same way as we talk about 'hooking' people. When the
prophets use the metaphor (Jer. 16.16f.; Ezek. 47.8ff.), God's fishermen are to
'hook' men for judgment. But in the gospels, Jesus' missioners are to be 'hookers of
men' for salvation, i.e. the kingdom of God.

Call, choice, mission—what was Jesus' intention in all these dealings with his disciples? He was creating the new Israel. When
modern scholars tell us that 'Jesus never intended a church'—one of
them[1] even saying that 'Jesus preached the kingdom of God and the
church came'—they show that they do not understand what the
kingdom of God means.

What is the basic idea of the church? It is that of the people of
God, a community living under the divine sovereignty, and its roots
go back into the Old Testament where Israel—or, as in the prophets,
the faithful remnant—is the *qahal* (LXX: *ecclēsia*) of God. Now this
idea of the *ecclēsia* is deep-rooted in the purpose of Jesus. His message
of the kingdom implies it. His doctrine of Messiahship involves it.
His ministry shows him creating it.

1. The burden of Jesus' good news was that the reign of God had
begun. But is God an *émigré* ruler? And what kind of king is he who
has no subjects? No more than any other rule can God's rule operate
in a void. It requires a sphere of sovereignty, a realm to work in.
This is the reason why sometimes the kingdom of God in the gospels
carries the secondary sense of 'realm' (as in the Beatitudes) and why
Jesus can speak of men 'entering' the kingdom or being 'cast out' of
it. The people of God is a necessary corollary of the kingdom of God.

Not surprisingly therefore, some of his parables—the Mustard
Seed, the Wheat and the Tares, the Dragnet, the Great Supper—
clearly envisage the gathering of a *community*. But this is only the
beginning of proof.

2. The correlate of the kingdom is the Messiah, and it is patent
from Jesus' conception of his Messiahship that he had a community
in view. For Jesus interpreted his Messiahship in terms of two Old
Testament figures—the Son of man in Daniel 7 and the Servant of
the Lord in II Isaiah. These are both *societary* figures. As the Son of
man in Daniel represents 'the saints of the Most High', so the Servant
in II Isaiah implies a community. If Jesus saw his destiny thus, he
saw his task as the creation of a new Israel.

Here we may note that Jesus spoke of himself and his disciples as a
shepherd and his flock (Matt. 10.16; Mark 6.34; Luke 12.32). This
is no mere picturesque pastoral phrase. Not only was 'shepherd' a
common name in the East for a divine deliverer, but in famous Old
Testament passages like Ezek. 34 and Micah 5 (cf. *The Psalms of
Solomon*, ch. 17) the Messiah's work is described as the gathering and

[1] Loisy, the French modernist biblical scholar (1857–1940).

tending of God's flock. If Jesus calls himself the shepherd (John
10.1–5), we expect him to seek out and shepherd his Father's flock.
And this is precisely what he does in the gospels.

3. Up till now we have been dealing with the theological theory
of the matter. Turn now to the ministry itself, and we see Jesus
translating it into reality.

First, he *called twelve men*. It is the number of the tribes of old
Israel. To a Jew of any penetration this acted parable must have
suggested, 'This is the Messiah and the new Israel'.

Second, he *taught* these men. Centuries before, Isaiah had formed
a circle of disciples and committed his teaching to them (Isa. 8.16–
18). 'This,' wrote Robertson Smith,[1] 'is the birth of the conception
of the Church.' So it is now in the ministry of Jesus. By appointing
twelve men and instructing them, Jesus signifies his intention of
creating a new people of God.

Third, he *sent* them on a mission to proclaim the advent of God's
reign. What was the mission's purpose? Let us recall that the
rule of God (a subject to be discussed more fully later) is essentially
dynamic. It creates a people ruled wherever its power is felt. So Jesus'
purpose in the disciples' mission is clear. It is to gather God's people.

Now (anticipating events) let us turn to the climax of Jesus' ministry. In a Jerusalem upper room, by means of broken bread and outpoured wine, Jesus gave his disciples a share in the new covenant to
be inaugurated by his sacrificial death for 'the many'. Centuries
before, at Sinai, God had constituted the Hebrews into a people of
God by making a covenant with them. The 'new' covenant now
prophetically inaugurated in the upper room implies the creation of
a new people of God. That night, round the supper table, the Twelve
sat as the nucleus of the New Israel, the church.

But Jesus also knew that only by the Son of man's obedience even
unto death could Israel in nucleus become the Israel God meant it
to be. The grain of wheat must die, he said in a parable about his
own death (John 12.24), if it were to yield a great harvest. Another
saying of his, probably best preserved by St John (cf. John 2.19 with
Mark 14.58), had prophesied a new sanctuary: 'Destroy this temple,
and in three days (i.e. a brief undefined time) I will raise it up.' The
'temple' represents a way of religion and a community based on it.
Jesus predicts a new way of religion and a new community embodying it. The saying is not merely a prophecy of personal triumph over

[1] W. Robertson Smith, *The Prophets of Israel*, A. and C. Black[2] 1928, pp. 274f.

death; it is the prophecy of a *new church*. Beyond his death he looks to a time when there will be a new shrine 'made without hands' for his 'little flock' now grown into a great one. On the day of Pentecost his prophecy began to come true.

The instruction of the new Israel

What teaching did Jesus give his disciples who had accepted the good news of God's dawning kingdom and become founder members in the Israel-to-be? He gave them a new revelation of God as *Abba*, Father; a new pattern of approach to him in prayer; and a new design for living as his children.

'To you (i.e. the disciples) the secret of the kingdom of God has been given' (Mark 4.11). (Note the 'reverential passive' voice of the verb. What it means is, 'God has given'.) The 'secret' was that the reign of God, so long an object of hope and prayer, was already present on earth, albeit in tiniest beginnings, like a mustard seed. But basic to this 'secret' was another one—that the king in the kingdom was a father: *Abba*, Father.

1. Once only in the gospels, in Mark's record of Jesus' prayer in Gethsemane (14.36), does the Aramaic word *Abba* occur; but beyond doubt it lies hidden behind those passages where Jesus says, 'Father', 'My Father', or 'the Father'. More particularly we may confidently affirm that in all his prayers to God Jesus used a word he had learnt more than thirty years before in the Nazareth home, *Abba*.

Here is a discovery of great importance for our understanding of Jesus' person and mission.

Modern scholars, particularly Joachim Jeremias,[1] have searched the prayer-literature of Judaism from end to end, to see if there is any parallel to Jesus' usage. Not a single real example of this use of *Abba* in prayer to God do the sources yield. Yet Jesus, when he prayed, regularly used it. How are we to account, on the one hand, for the astonishing refusal of the Jews so to address God and, on the other, for Jesus' equally astonishing preference for it?

Abba ('dear Father') is what the grammarians call a 'caritative'. It was the word little Jewish children used at home to their human father; indeed, we are told even grown-up sons and daughters went on so addressing him. It was a colloquial, everyday, family word. Yet precisely in this fact lay its 'offence' for the Jews *vis-à-vis* the

[1] *The Prayers of Jesus*, SCM Press 1967, ch. 1.

Almighty. 'God is in heaven, and thou on earth.' No pious Jew
would have dared to use this homely word in prayer to the high and
holy One who inhabits eternity. To do so would have savoured of
blasphemy (cf. John 5.17f.). The fact that Jesus did just this—
addressed God as *Abba*, spoke to him with the simplicity and inti-
macy a child uses with his earthly father—is remarkable testimony
to the kind of communion he had with God, the sense of unique
sonhood of which he was conscious. Jesus regarded this form of
address to God—*Abba*—as embodying the very soul of the revelation
granted him by the Father. *Abba* held the secret of his mission and
authority. He to whom the Father had granted full knowledge of
himself had, as the Messiah, the privilege of addressing him
familiarly as a son would.

But this privilege Jesus did not hug to himself. He shared it with
his disciples. They were of those to whom the Son 'chose' to reveal
God as *Abba* (cf. Matt. 11.27 Q). 'When you pray,' he said to them,
'say *Abba*' (Luke 11.2 L).

Here is a point worth pondering, for it runs counter to what is
commonly believed. By the evidence of the synoptic gospels, as
T. W. Manson[1] showed, Jesus did not speak of God as *Abba*, Father,
before all the people (though in a parable like that of the Prodigal
Son he came near it). Thus, of a dozen examples where Jesus speaks
of God as Father in our two primary sources, Mark and Q, eleven
occur in prayers or in conversations with his disciples; and the
twelfth example is no real exception to the rule. Why this reserve?
Manson answered, 'We are so made that we cannot speak lightly of
the things that most profoundly move us; and for every man the
Holy of Holies in his life is hedged about with silence . . . In this
matter the Jesus of our earlier records is one with us.'

The Fatherhood of God was not, therefore, a truth which Jesus
proclaimed to all and sundry but a secret he disclosed in private to
his disciples, because it was the uttermost reality in his own spiritual
life. We may surmise that he did it not by using 'much speaking' but
by so living out its truth in his own daily life that it became plain
where lay the deepest source of his person and authority. Only after
the resurrection, with the advent of the Spirit (witness Rom. 8.15
and Gal. 4.6), did Jesus' secret about the Father become an 'open
secret', and the chief word in his esoteric speech with his disciples the
precious possession of all the adopted sons of God. 'When we cry,

[1] *The Teaching of Jesus*, Cambridge University Press 1931, ch. 4.

Abba! Father!' Paul wrote, 'it is the Spirit himself bearing witness with our spirit that we are children of God.' To what was the apostle referring? Almost certainly to the corporate recitation of the Lord's Prayer by new converts as the first exercise of their Christian privilege. This brings us to the second thing that Jesus taught his disciples as the nucleus of the Israel-to-be.

2.   When the disciples besought Jesus, 'Lord, teach us to pray as John (the Baptist) taught his disciples' (Luke 11.1), they meant, 'Give us a distinctive prayer which will be the hall-mark of your followers.' Jesus' response was the *Abba*, Father prayer.

As is well-known, the gospels preserve two versions of the prayer —one in Luke 11.2-4 containing (in Greek) thirty-eight words, the other in Matt. 6.9-13 containing fifty-seven. There has been much debate about which is truer to the mind of Jesus. Some think it is Luke's briefer version, with its simple opening 'Father' (*Abba*) and its five petitions (as against six in Matthew). Others prefer the claims of Matthew's version, pointing to its finer poetic symmetry and what looks like the superior wording of the petitions about 'bread' and 'forgiveness' (where Luke has 'sins', Matthew has 'debts'; only in Aramaic is 'debt' a metaphor for 'sin').

Whatever be the truth, the general tenor of the prayer is plain. After the opening invocation of God as Father come, first, petitions for the hallowing of his name (his fatherly nature), the (fuller) coming of his reign, and (in Matthew only) the doing of his will on earth as it is done in heaven. Then, having 'asked for the big things', the disciples are bidden to ask for provision of 'daily bread', pardon for their sins, and protection in time of testing from evil (or the evil one). First world issues, then human needs; this is to be the order of things in the disciples' approach to their heavenly Father; for both are in the hands of him who at once shapes the course of history and provides for his children's individual needs.

That Jewish scholars can parallel this phrase or that of the *Paternoster* from Jewish sources should not surprise us. The work of a great artist is not to manufacture his paints but with them to paint a noble picture. So Jesus, using older materials, made his perfect prayer. Its originality lies in:

(*a*) Its brevity. Here is no *polylogia*—no holy loquacity, but six short petitions that go arrow-like to the unseen world.

(*b*) Its order. The prayer puts first things first, the heavenly things before the earthly.

(c) Its universality. It is wholly concerned with the needs common to all humanity, so that all men, whatever their class or colour, can make it their own. It is 'the prayer that spans the world' and (as Edwin Muir said) refers to human life 'seen realistically, not mystically', concerned as it is with 'the world and society and not with the everlasting destiny of the soul'.

3. Initiation into the secret of the dawning kingdom in which the king in the kingdom was a father, a pattern prayer to guide them in their approach to him—what further instruction did Jesus give his disciples? He gave them a design for living as God's children in the new order now beginning.

Pointers to it, in saying and parable, are scattered through the gospels; but it is best summarized in the great Sermon. Luke's version of it (Luke 6.20–49) is only one third as long as Matthew's (Matt. 5–7), and probably represents the Sermon as it stood in Q. Matthew's version, derived from the M and Q sources, is a masterly compendium of 'ripe teaching for ripe disciples', and gathers together the fruit of many teaching sessions at which Jesus instructed his men in the 'way' of the kingdom.

The Sermon handles six basic themes:

First, the people God delights in (Matt. 5.1–12). Here, turning the world's verdicts upside down, Jesus pronounces 'divinely happy' (*makarios*) those 'who know their need of God' and long for the triumph of his cause, the mourners and the lowly ones, the compassionate and the pure-hearted, the peace-makers and those who suffer for the sake of right. To such God promises the blessings of his heavenly kingdom.

Second, the goodness God demands (5.20–48). Here, in six great antitheses, Jesus calls for 'truth in the inward parts'. With his sovereign 'But I say to you' he contrasts the standards of the Kingdom with the precepts of the Law of Moses:

The Law said, 'No murder'. I say, 'No anger'.

The Law said, 'No adultery'. I say, 'No lustful look'.

The Law said, 'Divorce on condition'. I say, 'No divorce'.

The Law said, 'No false swearing'. I say, 'No swearing at all'.

The Law said, 'An eye for an eye'. I say, 'No retaliation at all'.

The Law said, 'Love your neighbour'. I say, 'Love your enemies'.

Third, the religion God approves (Matt. 6.1–18). Be it charity, prayer or fasting, the thing that matters with God is sincerity and secrecy. All piety done to win human approval wins none from God who sees and rewards what is done in secret.

Fourth, the service God requires (Matt. 6.19–24). Learn to delight in the things of heaven—of God, says Jesus, for they are the only treasures that last. What is needed is the single eye and the single service, i.e. undivided allegiance to God.

Fifth, the faith to which God calls (Matt. 6.25–34). Study the wild birds and the lilies, says Jesus, and from them learn that freedom from worry and that trust in God's providential care which accepts each day as it comes and leaves the future in his hands.

Sixth, the way God expects his children to treat others (Matt. 7.1–5, 12). Here the call is to 'gently scan your brother man', remembering that we too are liable to God's judgment, as the guiding rule should be to treat others as we would like them to treat ourselves.

Such is Jesus' design for living in that realm over which God rules as Father.

In all this Jesus was not laying down a new code of laws on the perfect keeping of which a man's salvation would depend. If he had been, then he who invited men to come and take his 'kindly' yoke upon themselves (Matt. 11.28ff.) would have been laying on his followers a far heavier burden than he accused the Pharisees of laying on theirs (Matt. 23.4 M). Jesus was no legalist. The ethic of the Sermon, as of all Jesus' moral teaching, is an *ethic of grace*. For (though it is not immediately clear in Matthew's setting) the *prius*, or presupposition, of all his teaching is the good news of God's dawning kingdom. Accordingly, if he says 'You must forgive', it is because his hearers have already had the assurance, 'Your sins are forgiven'. If he calls his men to be 'the light of the world', it is because they have already found in their master 'the world's light'. If he bids them live as 'sons of God', it is because, through his revelation, they already know themselves to be sons—and *noblesse oblige*! If he calls them to 'love their enemies', behind his command lies the dynamic of the boundless grace of God who makes his sun rise on evil and good and sends his rain on the just and the unjust. All the things that Jesus calls for—all the patterns of behaviour he desiderates—are therefore samples and illustrations of the kind of moral fruit to be produced in lives transformed by the grace of God. It is a case of 'Freely you have received; freely give'.

To sum up. What Jesus gives in his pattern for life in the new Israel is direction, not directions, a compass and not an ordnance map. Yet Jesus meant his teaching to be a design for actual living, not a blue-print for Utopia; and, in the parable of the Two Builders which closes the Sermon, he makes it pellucidly clear that the secret of security in any time of testing, as at the Last Judgment, will be a life based on his own teaching and person. 'It is,' he says, in effect, in that vivid story, '*my* way—or disaster'.

8

THE MIRACLES OF JESUS

'God,' wrote C. S. Lewis,[1] 'does not shake miracles into Nature at random as if from a pepper-caster. They come on great occasions: they are found at the great ganglions of history.' Such a one was the ministry of Jesus; indeed he himself saw it as the greatest of all ganglions, as a crisis inaugurating a new set of relations between God and men. If Lewis is right, the story of Jesus ought to contain miracles, as in fact it does. According to the gospels, Jesus proclaimed the dawning of God's reign not by words only but by acts which indicated, to the spiritually percipient, that God's power was at work in him for men's salvation.

Miracles we may define as extraordinary intervention of God in history; not necessarily breaches of what is called 'natural law', but exceptional occurrences bringing an undeniable sense of the presence and power of God. Let this serve as a working definition; for we are concerned not with the question whether Jesus worked miracles in the sense in which this or that philosopher (e.g. Hume) used the word, but with the question whether Jesus brought health to the sick in body and mind, cured demoniacs, restored people to life and on occasion exerted mastery over nature; and if he did, what place such acts had in his mission.

The synoptists call them *dynameis*, i.e. outgoings of divine 'power'; and if they talk of 'signs' (*sēmeia*), they usually mean spectacular wonders. By contrast, St John calls Jesus' miracles 'signs' in the sense of acts which suggest the superhuman personality of Jesus and are tokens of God's new order—not mere wonders but wonders with meanings in them which the evangelist is at pains to bring out. (In his sayings in the Fourth Gospel Jesus himself generally calls them 'works', *erga*. This term, which recalls 'the works of God' in the Old Testament, brings out the continuity between the Father's works

[1] *Miracles*, Fontana Books 1960, p. 171.

and those of Jesus. Cf. John 5.17: 'My Father is working still, and I am working.')

Miracles bulk large in the gospels. No gospel source lacks them, and almost one third of the earliest gospel, Mark, deals with miracle. Thus, so far as we can judge, the story of Jesus was told from the beginning as that of one who did miracles. They are not late importings into the story, but part of the primary stratum.[1] They are part of the total picture of Jesus in the gospels, and we can no more eliminate them from the record than we can eliminate the watermark from a piece of good note-paper.

How have men regarded the miracles? Orthodox divines of an older day (like Paley) took their purpose to be *evidential*, saw them as plain proofs of Jesus' divinity, seals which accredited him as the divine Son of God. Now, though Jesus did not wholly discount this aspect of them—witness his reply to the Baptist's question, 'Go and tell John what you have seen and heard, etc.'—this view is open to serious objections. For one thing, whether the request came from the devil, Herod or the Pharisees, Jesus refused to do miracles merely to show people that he was sent by God. No such legitimating proof of his authority would be given (Mark 8.12). The only sign they would get, he said, would be that of Jonah, i.e. that of a man preaching in God's name (Luke 11.29f.; cf. Matt. 12.39f.). Second: this picture of a heavenly bellman calling men to believe in him through his miracles is quite out of character in the Jesus of the gospels. Third, this evidential idea of miracle does violence, as we shall see in a moment, to the close connection between miracle and faith.

Very different was the view of the miracles taken by nineteenth-century liberal Protestants like Ernest Renan and Matthew Arnold. It was a time when science seemed to be explaining everything and disclosing a universe which was one vast closed system of cause and effect. In such a universe miracles appeared as violations of the uniform order of nature. Naturally they concluded that miracles were impossible and dismissed them as legendary accretions to the gospel story. The only trouble about this view was that they blandly assumed they knew the answer to the one question that really

[1] A serious weakness of form critics like Bultmann is their tendency to isolate the picture of Jesus as a mere wonder-worker and regard the miracle-stories as a later stratum in the gospel tradition, and so historically dubious. Yet they contend that the shape of the gospels was largely dictated by the needs of the early church. If the early proclamation of the gospel had no need of a saviour who worked miracles, how came the evangelists to include so many?

matters: Is nature really a closed system, quite impervious to inva-
sions from super-nature—from God? The mischief had really started
when the working hypotheses of natural science had been allowed
to become the dogmas of liberal Protestantism. Renan and Arnold
had really renounced the living God of the biblical revelation, the
God whose workshop is history, and who decisively invades it at its
'great ganglions'.

We cannot therefore accept either of these views of the gospel
miracles. Jesus' miracles are not seals appended to the document,
but part of the document itself. They are not a semi-legendary frame
which may be summarily discarded, but part of the picture itself.

Much more important is the question, How did Jesus himself
regard his miracles?

The burden of Jesus' preaching was the kingdom of God, i.e. the
sovereign activity of God in saving men and overcoming evil and the
new order of things thus established. It was the very heart of the
good news he came preaching that this new order was no longer
merely a shining hope on the far horizon but a dawning reality in his
own ministry. And for Jesus his miracles were tokens of that new era
in which the power of God was at work through himself and his
mission, meeting and defeating the devil and all his works, whether
it was the demonic distortion of man's personality, or the assault of
disease on his natural vigour, or the foretaste of death, 'the last
enemy'. In short, the mighty works of Jesus were the reign of God in
action, outgoings in power to sick and sinful people of that love
which was central to the kingdom of God.

Miracle he did not over-value: he steadfastly refused the role of
thaumaturge, as the gospels show. Nonetheless, he regarded his
'works' as an essential part of his message. If by word and parable he
proclaimed the coming of the kingdom and challenged men, by the
decision of faith, to accept the good news as true, his extraordinary
deeds were signs for those who had eyes to see that the Almighty was
now visiting his people in grace and judgment. Charged by his
opponents with using 'black magic', he replied, 'If I by the finger of
God cast out demons, then the kingdom of God has come upon you'
(Luke 11.20; Matt. 12.28 Q; Matt. has 'by the Spirit of God'). It
is but the other side of the same medal when we note that Jesus saw
his miracles as fulfilments of the prophets' predictions about the
Messianic age. Thus when the Baptist sent messengers from prison
to ask him, 'Are you the Coming One (the Messiah)?', Jesus replied

in effect, 'You remember what Isaiah prophesied about blind men receiving their sight, deaf men hearing, lame men walking and dead men being raised up? Well, these things are happening now in my ministry. Draw your own conclusions' (Luke 7.18–23; Matt. 11.2–6 Q). In the same vein he told his disciples, 'Blessed are the eyes which see what you see! For I tell you that many prophets and kings desired to see what you see, and did not see it, and to hear what you hear, and did not hear it' (Luke 10.23f.; Matt. 13.16f. Q). What they were privileged to see were the 'works' of the kingdom.

The characteristics of the miracles

If Jesus' miracles were tokens of the dawning reign of God, let us study their characteristics.

Regarding them from the human angle, we note first the stress Jesus lays on the need for *faith*. Faith in Jesus' God-given power to heal is the pre-condition of all his miracles—the sphere in which it comes to fruition—and this power is seriously hindered where such faith is wanting, as it was in his native Nazareth (Mark 6.5). 'Daughter, your faith has made you well', is his word to the woman with the haemorrhage (Mark 5.34). 'Fear not, only believe,' he says to Jairus while the professional mourners lament his daughter's death (Mark 5.36). 'All things are possible to him who believes,' he assures the father of the epileptic boy (Mark 9.23).

Of a piece with this is the demand which Jesus often makes for the patient's *active co-operation* in a cure. 'Have you the will to health?' he asks the cripple at the pool of Bethesda (John 5.6). Elsewhere his commands to the sick are invitations to co-operate in the divine work he is doing. 'Rise, pick up your bed and walk' (Mark 2.11). 'Go and wash in the Pool of Siloam' (John 9.11). Or, again, observe the sheer pertinacity of the people who seek a cure either for themselves or for those they represent: the paralytic's friends who took down a bit of the roof to get him into Jesus' presence, the woman with the haemorrhage resolved at any cost to touch the hem of his garment, blind Bartimaeus who refused to be silenced by the bystanders. In all these cases faith is no mere pale and passive belief; it is 'the energetic and importunate grasping after God's help present in Jesus'.[1]

---

[1] This demand for faith, the stress laid on the human emotions of Jesus and his frequent injunctions to silence after a cure contrast sharply with the form critics' portrait of Jesus as a mere wonder-worker.

Along with this we may note the emphasis Jesus lays on *prayer* which is really faith in action. Cf. Mark 9.29: 'The kind cannot be driven out by anything but prayer.' We moderns, half hypnotized by the apparently 'steel-and-concrete' order of nature, ask timidly, 'What may we pray for?' Jesus has no such inhibitions. 'Whatever you ask in prayer,' he says (Mark 11.24), 'believe that you receive it, and you will.' We wonder whether we may pray for material blessings in any shape or form. In his pattern prayer for his disciples, Jesus includes a petition for 'daily bread'. Clearly he believed in the power of prayer to influence the circumstances of life, and he saw his miracles as divine answers to his prayers.

But faith and prayer are only one half—the human half—of the secret of his miracles. What of the divine side? 'By the finger (or Spirit) of God' is Jesus' answer. His miracles he regards as tokens of God's Spirit working in all its fullness through himself.

At his baptism Jesus knew himself to be 'the anointed with the Spirit'. Whatever else this meant, it meant equipment with divine power. Except on this assumption, his 'temptations' in the wilderness are unreal. His words in the Nazareth synagogue carry the same implication. 'The Spirit of the Lord is upon me,' he says, quoting Isa. 61.1, 'because he has anointed me to preach good news to the poor. He has sent me to proclaim release to the captives and recovering of sight to the blind' (Luke 4.18 L). Not only his preaching of the 'good news to the poor', he implies, but also his conquests of disease and the devil are inspired by God's Spirit. His 'acts of power' reveal the energizing of God's Spirit through himself for the saving of sick and sinful men and women. 'The Father who dwells in me,' he says in John's gospel, 'does his works' (John 14.10).

'I think,' wrote David S. Cairns, author of one of the best modern books on the miracles, 'I think the Gospel view of the miracles is quite plainly that they are the work of Jesus' own faith in God, and of the Divine Spirit in answer to the appeal of his faith.'[1]

The credibility of the miracles

We come last to the question of credibility. What is a modern Christian who values his intellectual integrity to make of Jesus' miracles?

Before we essay an answer, two things fall to be said. First, and

[1] *David S. Cairns, An Autobiography*, SCM Press 1950, p. 193.

granting the possibility of miracle, we must always be satisfied that there is strong evidence for any particular miracle. After all, on any definition of it, a miracle is a highly unusual event and needs to be well attested.[1] (Thus we should require only slight evidence if a man told us that he had once seen King George the Sixth riding in Windsor Great Park. But we should need quite overwhelming evidence if somebody assured us that he had seen Charles the First riding in the Park with his head underneath his arm!) On this view, some of Jesus' miracles are much more soundly based historically than others. The healing of the officer's son, for example, which occurs not only in Matthew and Luke (who presumably found it in Q) but also in the independent Gospel of John, is better attested than the miracle at Cana found only in the Fourth Gospel. Let it also be said that doubt about any particular miracle (e.g. the cursing of the fig tree) does not of course discredit the lot.

Second: The miracles of Jesus were done among a people who had no doctrine of 'secondary causes' and sought a supernatural explanation for any event which baffled popular understanding. They were not unlike Defoe's pious lady who on seeing a bottle of over-ripe beer explode and fly in froth to the ceiling exclaimed, 'O the wonders of Omnipotent Power!' The point is that, with our understanding of 'secondary causes', we are entitled to that extent, to 'rationalize' this or that miracle, provided we do not, in so doing, travesty the historical evidence. Such a caricature would be, in our judgment, the suggestion that what Jesus stilled was not the storm on the lake but the storm of fear in the disciples' hearts.

With these two provisos, we may now face the question of credibility.

First: we need not hesitate to accept the historicity of Jesus' *healing* miracles. Even the arch-sceptic among New Testament scholars, Bultmann,[2] has no doubt that 'Jesus healed the sick and cast out demons'. To be sure, here and there the miraculous element may well have been heightened in the course of oral transmission; but in face of the abundant evidence that Jesus restored sight to the blind, helped the deaf to hear, made the lame walk, cleansed lepers and

---

[1] When that agreeable atheist, David Hume, declared that 'no testimony is sufficient to establish a miracle', all he was really saying was that the more surprisingly an event runs counter to our experience, the stronger will have to be the testimony before we accept it. Alan Richardson, *History Sacred and Profane*, SCM Press 1964, pp. 188f.

[1] *Jesus and the Word*, Fontana Books 1958, p. 124.

cured demoniacs, scepticism is wholly unwarranted. (The question of the reality of demon-possession is still disputed. Modern psychiatrists would probably include it under the category of 'morbid psychology'. But whether we accept the hypothesis of demon-possession or not—and many who have worked among primitive peoples have no doubt about its reality—Jesus undoubtedly healed those believed to be possessed by evil spirits. Jesus' recorded raisings from the dead also tax modern man's credence; but it is worth noting that they appear in four of our five gospel sources: Mark 5.35–43; Luke 7.22 Q; Luke 7.11–17 L; and John 11.)

Moreover, in favour of the healing miracles of Jesus we may justifiably point to the advances made by modern psychological medicine. The potent part played by the mind in the cause and cure of disease is now freely acknowledged. (If paralysis has sometimes a psychogenic origin and worry can produce stomach ulcers, certain types of skin disease yield to psychiatric treatment, and even warts have been cured by suggestion.) To these advances we may also add the evidence of spiritual healing to be found in such books as Cameron Peddie's *The Forgotten Talent*. All these things conspire to bring the healing miracles of Jesus within the range, if not of our powers, at least of our credence. True, we cannot match the speed of Jesus' cures, and his ability to heal at a distance presents problems. But if, to put it at its lowest, we remember the extraordinary personality of Jesus—the charismatic man *par excellence*, as Otto[1] called him—we shall wisely refuse to say we will accept only those healing miracles which we, with our present knowledge, can effect. And the secret of his 'telepathic' healings—the officer's son and the Syro-Phoenician woman's daughter—is surely to be sought in the person of Jesus and the divine answers to his prayers.

It is the half dozen or so *nature* miracles in[2] the gospels which perplex modern man. His perplexity is twofold: (*a*) a suspicion that science has shown them to be quite impossible; and (*b*) a sense that some of them are out of character in Jesus. (Multiplying loaves to feed a crowd might be construed as yielding to the temptation to be 'a bread Messiah'; walking on the water a 'prodigy' of the kind he elsewhere abjured; and cursing a fig-tree which had leaves but no fruit in early April, the peevish act of a wonder-worker.)

---

[1] See *The Idea of the Holy*, p. 182; *The Kingdom of God and the Son of Man*, pp. 333ff.
[2] Neither Jesus nor the evangelists made the distinction between healing and nature miracles.

On the first point of perplexity it must be said that reputable modern science has long since departed from the notion of the universe as a cast-iron system of natural law. Matter as a 'hard fact' has been replaced by entities so intangible that it no longer seems outrageous for a scientist like Sir James Jeans to speak of the universe as more like a great thought than a great machine. Whatever the science of the popular press may say, responsible physicists would agree that the natural laws which appeared so rigid to our grandfathers are simply the hitherto observable ways in which nature seems to work. They would also agree that with the fresh flood of discoveries about the behaviour of matter we hardly know what is, or what is not, possible.

On the second point of perplexity, it may be said that historical criticism relieves some of the difficulties. Thus apart from the statement that 'all ate and were satisfied' (Mark 6.42, which is hard to reconcile with Mark 8.16), the feeding of the multitude suggests, as we have seen, a sacrament rather than a miracle. In John's gospel, which is independent of the synoptics, Jesus' walking on the water does *not* necessarily involve a miracle, its chief point being the recognition of Jesus unexpectedly present to the disciples in the hour of their fear and need. The cursing of the fig-tree was probably in origin an acted parable of the divine judgment overhanging Israel (like the '*ōth* of Jeremiah—Jer. 19.1–13). The stilling of the storm may be regarded as a miracle of divine providence: 'Jesus trusted in God, and his trust was not deceived.'[1]

What, then, should be the attitude of the modern Christian to the nature miracles?

While respecting the confessed ignorance of the responsible scientist in face of encompassing mystery, he can hardly rest content in his agnosticism. His faith is in the God of biblical revelation, the living God who acts in history and is known by what he does. For this God the divine art of miracle is not that of breaching 'the laws of nature' (which are merely summaries of existing knowledge in constant need of revision), but that of feeding new and extraordinary events into the pattern of history of which he is Lord, and intervening sovereignly in that order of nature which is his creation.

But for the Christian there is another consideration even more important. If Jesus was, as he claimed to be, the only Son of God, in whom the divine Spirit was uniquely incarnate and active, and if his

[1] Vincent Taylor, *St Mark*, p. 273.

ministry was nothing less than the living God decisively invading history to defeat the powers of evil that had lodged not only in human beings but in the created world, who will dare to limit the power Jesus may have had over not only the bodies and spirits of men but over nature itself?

One last word on the whole subject of miracle. Earlier we quoted the testimony of E. V. Rieu on completing his translation of the gospels: 'Superimposed on all my previous impressions is one of power, tremendous power, utterly controlled.' Now it cannot be denied that many modern attempts to retell the story of Jesus signally fail to leave this impression on the reader; and if we ask why, is not the explanation that, in deference to modern man's doubts about miracles, they tend to play them down and concentrate on Jesus' teaching? Yet should not any true portrait of the 'strong Son of God' leave us with the impression not only of dynamic word but also of dynamic deed, and suggest one whose acts were as surely stamped as his sayings with the unique authority of the Almighty?

9

JESUS' TEACHING ABOUT THE KINGDOM OF GOD

What is the dominant theme of the synoptic gospels? This question, scholars agree, has only one right answer—the kingdom of God.[1] With this theme Jesus began his Galilean ministry; it is the central theme of his parables; it is the theme on his lips at the last supper. In the thought of the kingdom of God he lives, and works, and dies.

But what does it signify? For the phrase is one thing, its interpretation quite another; and into it, down the centuries, men have read very diverse meanings. Consider only four. As early as St Augustine men began to equate the kingdom of God with the church, and some still do.[2] The error here is to confound the divine rule with those who live under it, the people of God. Liberal Protestants like Harnack in the ninteenth century took the phrase to mean the rule of God in the hearts of men—and so men's obedience to God's will. This is to confuse human response with divine activity; for according to the Bible God's rule exists whether men respond to it or not. To be sure, it claims the obedience of man, but it is there before the claims are made, and it is still there if men reject them. Towards the end of the nineteenth century, when the science and religion debate was in full swing, Christian apologists[3] took it to be a kind of biblical equivalent for the evolutionary process, on the principle of

'Some call it Evolution, and others call it God'.

They forgot that, for the fulfilment of history, the men of the Bible look not to *e-volutio* but to *in-gressio*, not to an evolution from within

---

[1] Mark has 'the kingdom of God' 14 times and Luke 32. In Matthew 'the kingdom of God' occurs 4 times and 'the kingdom of heaven' 33.

[2] Cf. R. A. Knox, *New Testament Commentary*, Vol. I, p. 58: 'The kingdom of heaven means, as usual, the Church.'

[3] 'First the blade, then the ear, after that the full corn in the ear—what is that,' said Henry Drummond of Christ's parable of the kingdom (Mark 4.26–29), 'but Evolution?'

but to a divine invasion from without. A more popular view was to regard the kingdom of God as some kind of earthly Utopia to be built by men on the moral teaching of Jesus. It found its rallying-cry in Merrill's hymn:

> Rise up, O men of God,
> His Kingdom tarries long,
> Bring in the day of brotherhood,
> And end the night of wrong.

But in the gospels, as we shall see, the kingdom of God is not man's deed but God's seed. It is not men creating a new and nobler Christian society on the basis of the Sermon on the Mount; it is the holy God breaking into history from outside it to deliver and redeem sinful men. But this is to anticipate later findings. Meanwhile, amid all these conflicting views, obviously the wise course is to hark back to first-century Judaism and the gospels and discover what this key phrase means there.

The Jewish background

The Greek word in the gospels for 'kingdom' is *basileia*. But 'kingdom' is not a very happy translation, for *basileia* represents the Aramaic *malkuth*, whose primary meaning is 'kingly rule', not 'kingdom' in the sense of territory. 'Reign' or 'rule' is therefore the better rendering. Yet since a 'rule' does not operate in the void but implies a sphere of rule—since moreover in the gospels the *basileia* of God is something which a man can 'enter' and from which he can be 'shut out', 'realm' rather than 'rule' sometimes conveys the proper sense. But the dominant meaning of 'the kingdom of God' is dynamic, not static: it signifies God acting in his royal power.

The other point commanding general assent is that 'the kingdom of heaven', the phrase preferred by Matthew for 'the kingdom of God' in the other gospels, does not differ in meaning. 'Heaven' means 'God' (as it still means today in the phrase 'Please heaven'). Matthew's phrase simply illustrates the pious Jew's avoidance of the ineffable name.

What did 'the reign of God' mean for a Jew in the first century AD? It might mean three things:

(*a*) God is now and always king: his reign is eternal, and therefore beyond time. This thought finds expression in the Psalms:

'Thy kingdom is an everlasting kingdom
And thy reign endures through all generations' (Ps. 145.13).

(b) God's reign, however, is only partly recognized. Israel is his special people, and among them his rule is realized in so far as Israel obeys his will revealed in the Law. Thus, according to the rabbis, if a man daily recited the *Shema* (Deut. 6.4f.) he was said to 'take on himself the yoke of the kingdom of heaven'.

(c) But there was a third and important sense in which the Jews spoke of the reign of God. God might be sovereign of the world in the *faith* of the pious Jew; in *fact* he was not acknowledged as such. Amidst the evil and misery of the present the pious Jews dreamed of a blessed coming time when the living God would finally manifest his rule, overthrow the powers of evil, and show his grace and mercy to his people. So, in the first century, Jews prayed (as they still pray) the words of the *Kaddish*:

'May He establish His Kingdom during your life and your days, and during the life of all the house of Israel.'[1]

Likewise, early in the first century AD a Pharisaic quietist[2] wrote of the future kingdom:

And then His Kingdom shall appear throughout all his creation,
And then Satan shall be no more,
And sorrow shall depart with him.

These three senses we may call respectively the eternal sovereignty, the covenant relationship and the divine intervention. We may sum them up in one sentence: 'The eternal sovereignty, now acknowledged in Israel, will one day be effectively manifested in the world.'

It is this third meaning that matters now. In this sense the reign of God is an 'eschatological' concept. When we use the word 'eschatology' here, we use it not so much in the popular sense of the doctrine of post-mortem rewards in heaven and hell, as in the Jewish sense. Eschatology means the doctrine of the end—the *eschaton*—the end conceived as God's age-long and final purpose to be realized in the future and to give meaning to the long travail of history. Now, in Jewish thought, the reign of God (in this third sense) is the one great hope of the future—the *eschaton* with which all eschatology is

---

[1] See the Jewish *Authorized Daily Prayer-Book*, p. 86.
[2] *The Assumption of Moses*, x.1.

concerned. It is another name for the good time coming, the Messianic age, and it connotes the whole salvation of God.

Before we turn to the gospels, one more thing falls to be said. 'The New Testament lies hidden in the Old,' declared Augustine, 'and the Old is made plain in the New.' And one feature of twentieth-century study has been the scholars' rediscovery of the truth of this ancient dictum. More particularly, they have realized anew how important are the prophecies of Second Isaiah (Isa. 40–66) in providing the clues to Jesus' mission and message. Thus, it is in words from Isa. 42 that God speaks to Jesus at his baptism. His sermon in the Nazareth synagogue takes up some great words from Isa. 61 and declares them to be fulfilled. With words from Isa. 49 about the strong man and his spoils Jesus replies to the charge of being in league with Satan. Above all, there is good evidence that Jesus consciously identified himself with the Servant of the Lord by whose sacrifice 'the many' were to be redeemed (Isa. 53). Now we must add that it was from the same source that his whole gospel of the reign of God took its origin.

More than half a millennium before 'the fullness of the times' the great unknown whom we call 'Isaiah of Babylon' had prophesied the return of the exiles. He foresaw them returning triumphantly to Jerusalem with God in their midst and a herald going before them with a *euangelion*—a proclamation of 'good news'. Thrice in Isa. 40–55 there is the promise of 'one who brings good tidings'; but it is in the last of the three passages, Isa. 52.7, that we see most clearly the nexus of Old and New Testaments. All Jerusalem is pictured on the walls when suddenly, on the hill-top, the herald is descried:

> Look, 'tis the feet of a herald
> Hastening over the hills
> With glad, good news,
> With tidings and relief,
> Calling aloud to Zion,
> 'Your God has become king!'

So Isaiah foresaw the coming of the reign of God. No doubt he expected the glorious day to dawn soon. However, in the providence of God, the stream of that great hope was to run underground for more than five centuries till the decisive time came. It came in the reign of the Roman emperor Tiberius when a young man from Nazareth appeared in Galilee saying in effect, 'The time which

Isaiah predicted is here. The good news of the reign of God is ringing out. Turn again to God and accept this message as true.' The *eschaton* was becoming fact. The reign of God was invading history. The final purpose of God was being realized.

Inaugurated eschatology

Nowadays scholars are generally agreed that the most accurate description of this is 'inaugurated eschatology'. There is ample evidence to justify the phrase, inelegant though it be. Thus, out of twenty-seven references to the kingdom of God in our two primary sources, Mark and Q, no fewer than eighteen imply that the reign of God has begun.

The phrase means two things. First, the kingdom of God is not some moral disposition in the heart of man, neither is it some Christian Utopia to be reared on earth by human endeavour; it is power breaking in on men from without through the direct and personal action of God. It is God himself intervening on the stage of history to 'visit and redeem his people'.

Second: the heart of Jesus' gospel was that this was no longer a distant hope but a dawning reality. The 'one far-off Divine Event', so long the object of pious prayers, had projected itself into history. The eternal God was now laying bare his arm and manifesting his saving sovereignty in the person and work of Jesus, and men must consider how to get into this realm of redemption.

Now let us deploy the evidence:

(*a*) First there are direct statements like:

Blessed are you poor, for yours is the kingdom of God (Luke 6.20).

If I by the finger of God cast out demons, then the kingdom of God has come upon you (Luke 11.20; Matt. 12.28 Q).

To you God has given the secret of the kingdom of God, i.e. as a present reality (Mark 4.11, addressed to the disciples).

From the days of John the Baptist until now the kingdom of God exercises its force (*biazetai*)[1] (Matt. 11.12; cf Luke 16.16).

The kingdom of God is in the midst of you (Luke 17.21 L: this to the 'kingdom-curious' Pharisees).

---

[1] *Biazetai* is probably a middle voice ('shows its power'), not a passive (is 'violenced'). On the question of how to translate *ēngiken* in Mark 1.15 see my *Introducing New Testament Theology*, SCM Press 1957, p. 27.

Truly I say to you (the religious leaders of Israel) the tax-collectors and harlots are entering the kingdom of God ahead of you (Matt. 21.31 M).

(b) Now take the evidence of the parables, especially those of growth. (NB The Old Testament prophets, when telling of the new age, had depicted God as the Great Sower: Isa. 55.10f.; Jer. 31.27; Ezek. 36.9; Hos. 2.23; Zech. 10.9. Jesus was therefore using a metaphor about God's action in the new age which would be familiar to his hearers.)

In the parable of the Seed growing secretly (Mark 4.26-29) Jesus is thinking of his ministry in Galilee. Having, as God's agent, sown the seed, he can say (like Mark Antony in the play) 'Now let it work!' A new divine force has been released in the world and grow it will, as surely as the sown seed, by the gracious ministry of God's sun and rain, ripens to harvest.

In the parable of the Sower (Mark 4.3-8) Jesus says in effect, 'In spite of all hazards and failures, God's reign advances as the harvest exceeds all expectations.' It is a ringing 'Have faith in God' to despondent followers.

In the parable of the Leaven (Luke 13.20f.; Matt. 13.33 Q) he says, 'When the reign of God invades history, nothing can be unaffected by it. Like yeast in a batch of flour, it creates a disturbance from which nothing is secure. The ferment has begun—God's great ferment—which no time or society can escape.'

In the parable of the Seine Net (Matt. 13.47f. M) he is saying, 'Like a drag-net shot in the lake, the rule of God is gathering into its meshes all sorts and conditions of men.'

The point of the Mustard Seed (Mark 4.30-32; Luke 13.18f.; Matt. 13.31f.) is like that of the Leaven: 'Small beginnings, great endings': 'The reign of God, now present like a tiny seed in your midst,' says Jesus, 'will one day become an empire embracing in its sweep the Gentiles from afar.'

All these parables, it should be noted, compare the kingdom not to some dead, static thing but to something in movement, to somebody doing something; and each of them says to those who have ears to hear: 'God is among you in his royal power: now is the day of salvation. Come, for all things are now ready.'

(c) Consider, finally, those passages which, though they do not mention the kingdom, sound the note of *fulfilment*; which, Luke tells us, Jesus had struck in the Nazareth synagogue (Luke 4.16-21 L).

'Blessed are the eyes,' says Jesus to his disciples, 'which see what you see! For I tell you that many prophets and kings desired to see what you see, and did not see it, and to hear what you hear, and did not hear it' (Luke 10.23f.=Matt. 13.16f. Q).

Or, 'The queen of the South will arise at the judgment with the men of this generation and condemn them; for she came from the ends of the earth to hear the wisdom of Solomon, and behold, something greater than Solomon is here. The men of Nineveh will arise at the judgment with this generation and condemn it; for they repented at the preaching of Jonah, and behold, something greater than Jonah is here' (Luke 11.31f.=Matt. 12.41f. Q).

In the first of these sayings Jesus declares that what for all former generations lay still in the womb of the future is now a blessed reality —for those who have eyes to see. In the second, the 'something greater' which is now here is beyond doubt the kingdom of God.

The same note rings through Jesus' reply to the Baptist's question from prison (Luke 7.22f.=Matt. 11.4ff. Q). He answers John with a list of tokens of the actual presence of the kingdom: the blind are receiving their sight, the lame are walking, lepers are being cleansed, deaf men are hearing, dead men are being raised up, and the poor are hearing the good news (cf. Isa. 29.18f.; 35.5f.; 61.1).

The conclusion is inescapable. Jesus declared that in his ministry the reign of God had begun. And here, as we have already seen, his 'mighty works' fall into their true place, appear in their proper light. They are not mere acts of wonder-working. They are tokens of the inbreaking reign of God. They are the kingdom of God in action.

The kingdom of God and the future

The reign of God had been initiated. Did Jesus ever say it would come in the future, and, if he did, in what sense?

The relevant passages[1] here are as follows:

> Mark: 9.1 and 14.25.
> Q: Matt. 8.11=Luke 13.28f.
> L: Luke 11.2; 22.16; and 22.29f.
> M: Matt. 6.10.

[1] We have excluded three M passages as 'secondary': Matt. 5.19f. (see T. W. Manson, *Sayings*, p. 154); 13.43 (see Jeremias, *Parables*[2], p. 84); and Matt. 7.21 (Luke 6.46, which is more original, contains no reference to the kingdom).

Mark 9.1 reads: 'I tell you this: there are some standing here who will not taste death before they have seen the kingdom of God already come in power' (NEB). The saying contrasts a kingdom in some sense already begun with one to come 'with power', or 'with a miracle' (*en dunamei*). The phrase occurs also in Rom. 1.3, where the reference is to the resurrection. When therefore Jesus says that the reign of God will, at some not far distant date, 'come with power', he is probably referring to the triumph of his cause (the kingdom) in the resurrection and all that followed.[1]

Mark 14.25 is Jesus' saying at the last supper: 'Never again shall I drink of the fruit of the vine until that day when I drink it new (*kainon*) in the kingdom of God.' Here the mention of wine of a 'new' kind—compare the use of 'new' in Rev. 21.1, 'I saw a new heaven and a new earth'—points to the transcendent order beyond time and space—to 'a better world than this'. Of the same tenor are the two L sayings: Luke 22.16 (the L version of Mark 14.25?) and 22.29f.: 'As my Father appointed a kingdom for me, so do I appoint for you, that you may eat and drink at my table in my kingdom.'

The solitary Q saying, in Matthew's version, reads: 'Many will come from east and west and sit at table with Abraham, Isaac and Jacob in the kingdom of heaven' (Matt. 8.11). Here is no reference to a 'coming' of the kingdom. Moreover, Abraham, Isaac and Jacob, so far as their mortal bodies were concerned, were long dust. Jesus is not thinking of any kingdom to come on this earth, or on this side of eternity, but of the *supernal* kingdom where God's reign does not come or go but eternally *is*[2] (cf. Luke 16.22, where the patriarchs are conceived of as being already in the heavenly realm).

But did not Jesus bid his disciples pray, 'Thy kingdom come'? And what did he mean by it? In interpreting this petition in the Lord's Prayer we must lay account with the many sayings, already quoted, which imply that the kingdom has already been inaugurated. The petition must therefore be for a *fuller* coming of the reign of God. If so, we must say that it was in part fulfilled in the resurrection, the coming of the Spirit and the rise of the church. The other thing to be said is that in the twin parables of the mustard seed which grows

---

[1] If the ministry of Jesus was the *initiation* of the kingdom, we may say that the resurrection and Pentecost were the *effectuation* of the kingdom. For the *consummation* of the kingdom see Chapter 13.

[1] In Jewish thought the Age to Come (or Messianic Age) is conceived both as a future event and as an *eternally existent reality*—a realm that always *is*. See W. D. Davies, *Paul and Rabbinic Judaism*, SPCK 1955, pp. 315–20.

into a tree and the bit of leaven which permeates the whole lump, we have Jesus' own pictorial exegesis of the petition. He bids his disciples pray for a time when the rule of God, now present in tiny nucleus, will extend its sphere over the whole earth.

The kingdom of God

To sum up. The kingdom of God is not a product of human effort or of natural evolution, neither can it be identified with the church, though the rule of God implies (as we have seen) a people of God living under his rule, a church. It is the *eschaton*—God's final purpose —invading history. It is God breaking dynamically into human affairs, God in conflict with the powers of evil, through Jesus and his ministry, for men's deliverance, and the new order of things thus established. It is a divine crisis—nay, *the* divine crisis, the crisis which gives meaning to all history before and after it. And, for Jesus, this new order has been decisively initiated in his ministry.[1]

But, to complete our summary, three further things must be added:

First, as shown in an earlier chapter, the king in the kingdom is a father. At the end of his masterly study of the sayings of Jesus, T. W. Manson[2] asked the question, What single phrase best sums up the teaching and ministry of Jesus? His answer was: 'the kingdom of my Father'.

The second point may be made in Jesus' words: 'It is your Father's good pleasure to give you the kingdom' (Luke 12.32 L). The kingdom is not man's achievement but God's gift. Men receive it like little children, i.e. as a child takes a present from his father's hands; it is a gift of God's pure grace (Mark 10.15). Yet it calls for decision. Confronting its challenge a man must count well the cost before he decides (Luke 14.28–32 L); and no man who, having set his hand to the plough, later looks back, is fit for it (Luke 9.62 Q). On the other hand, no sacrifice is too great to win its wealth (Matt. 13.44–46 M).

Third, as we have already seen, the moral teaching of Jesus is a design for living as God's children in the Father's kingdom. Essentially an ethic of grace, it has, as its major premiss, 'The kingdom of

---

[1] In the Fourth Gospel this 'inaugurated eschatology' is expressed in the formula 'The hour cometh and now is'.

[2] *The Sayings of Jesus*, p. 345.

my Father has come upon you', and men who accept it are called to respond by living in a 'kingdom way'. It is not a new code of rules and regulations which a man must keep perfectly if he is to be saved. It provides direction rather than directions. It is the moral ideal—the new pattern for life—for those who live in that new order in which *Abba*, Father, is king.

The kingdom and the cross

One 'crucial' question remains: What is the connection between the kingdom and the cross?

Jesus opened his ministry with the proclamation that the reign of God had 'come upon' men. Near its ending he said, 'The Son of man came not to be served but to serve and to give his life a ransom for many' (Mark 10.45). Since Jesus is both the messenger of the kingdom and the Son of man who must die, he poses in his own person the problem of the kingdom and the cross.

Now, if the kingdom has been initiated in the ministry of Jesus, we may not say that he died to bring in the kingdom. The cross must fall *within* the kingdom—must be its burning focus and centre—the climactic act in the warfare of God's kingdom against the kingdom of the Devil.[1]

Here we may ask, Where in scripture is it laid down that the reign of God involves a cross? Once again we find the answer in Isaiah's prophecies. If the word 'gospel' as he used it and his proclamation of the reign of God have their roots in Isa. 40 and 52, where else shall we look for 'the word of the cross' but in Isa. 53, that prophetic song about the Lord's Servant destined to bring sinners weal by his woe and life by his death?

If then the cross falls within the kingdom, is the end which crowns Jesus' work, we may say that for him it was the condition not of its initial coming but of its coming 'with power'.

Nor is this merely unsupported speculation. There is another remarkable saying of Jesus which chimes in with Mark 9.1:

'I have come to cast fire on the earth, and how I wish it were already kindled! But I have a baptism to undergo, and how

[1] 'The parables were instruments forged for warfare and the means by which Jesus' strategy was vindicated—until no further words could serve but only an act. The parables are the precipitate of a campaign, the final step of which was surrender to the Cross' (C. W. F. Smith, *The Jesus of Parables*, Westminster Press, Philadelphia 1948, p. 78).

hampered I am till the ordeal is over!' (Luke 12.49f. Q, NEB).

The 'fire' must be the fire of his gospel (cf. Jer. 20.9 and 23.9 for 'the word of God' as 'fire'), as his 'baptism' is undoubtedly his baptism in blood. And the thought behind the saying appears to be this: 'My mission is to kindle the divine fire in the world. But only by my death can it be kindled, and the reign of God come with power.' Jesus is the new Prometheus, and he must pay the same price. The grain of wheat must die if it is to yield a rich harvest (John 12.24). The planted seed of the kingdom must be watered by the bloody sweat of his passion.

What in fact happened? By the cross and the resurrection the reign of God was effectuated, 'came with power', and on the day of Pentecost (as Bengel said) 'the fire was lit'.

All we have been saying has implied a close connection between the Son of man and the kingdom of God. Thus to become a disciple of Jesus is equivalent to being in the kingdom. If Jesus exorcizes evil spirits, through him the reign of God comes upon men. Where he is, there is the rule of God. The kingdom of God is bound up with the person of Jesus, the message with the messenger. Long ago Marcion perceived this. 'In the gospel,' he said, 'the kingdom of God is Christ himself.' Who then is Jesus, and what does he teach about himself? This is the next question to be faced.

Note

In the synoptic gospels 'the kingdom of God' is the central theme of Jesus' preaching. When we turn to Paul's letters, we read mostly about preaching 'Christ'. In the Acts the apostles sometimes 'preach the kingdom' and sometimes 'preach Christ'. Why this apparent change of theme? Why does 'the kingdom' tend to be replaced by 'Christ'?

Let a great theologian answer: 'The Gospel of Christ replaced the Gospel of the Kingdom because by his death he became the Kingdom, because he became all that the Kingdom contained . . . The Gospel of the Kingdom was Christ in essence; Christ was the Gospel of the Kingdom in power. The Kingdom was Christ in a mystery, Christ was the publication, the establishment of the Kingdom . . . He was the truth of his own greatest Gospel. It is wherever he is. To have him is to ensure it.'[1]

[1] P. T. Forsyth, *The Person and Place of Jesus Christ*, Independent Press 1909, pp. 122f.

10

JESUS' TEACHING ABOUT HIMSELF

Near the end of his life Karl Barth, being asked by an interviewer, 'Has your view of the person of Christ changed over the years?', replied, 'Yes, at first I thought he was the prophet of the kingdom of God. Now I have come to see he *is* the kingdom.' Our studies have been moving in the same direction. We have seen how Jesus opened his Galilean ministry with the message, 'The kingdom of God is upon you'; but, as we have proceeded, it has become evident that the kingdom is bound up with the person of Jesus himself, that message and messenger are not to be separated, that somehow he is the reign of God incarnate.

This appears perhaps even more impressively in sayings of Jesus where no titles of majesty are involved. But, before we come to these, we must say something about the titles: Messiah, Son (of God), and Son of man.

The Messiah

Messiah (*Mashiach*) is a Hebrew word meaning 'anointed'. In Greek it becomes *Christos* and in English Christ. Originally it was not a personal name but the index to a historical role. For its beginnings we have to go back to the Old Testament's use of the word 'anointed' to denote offices of divine appointment, whether Israel as the elect people of God,

> Thou wentest forth for the salvation of thy people,
> For the salvation of thy anointed (Hab. 3.13),

or the king as pre-eminently the Lord's anointed, as in II Sam. 1.14: 'How is it you were not afraid,' said David to the Amalekite who had slain King Saul, 'to put forth your hand to destroy the Lord's anointed?'; or even to be a heathen ruler like the Persian Cyrus raised up to do God's will in history:

Thus says the Lord to his anointed, to Cyrus (Isa. 45.1).

The word, however, soon acquired a special meaning. According to II Sam. 7.16, God, by his prophet Nathan, had promised King David that his throne would last for ever. So was born the hope of an ideal king, sprung of David's line, who would deliver Israel and reign in righteousness. To this hope, through centuries of adversity, Israel clung: it finds expression in their great prophets (e.g. Isa. 11; Jer. 23; Ezek. 34); it survives through the period between the Testaments; and in the first century BC it is still alive. Not in Judea and Galilee only were they dreaming of Messiah's coming, but in heretical Samaria (John 4.25) and down at Qumran where dwelt the Essene sectarians who wrote the Dead Sea Scrolls.[1]

If in Judea the 'doctors of the law' were dreaming of a 'great David's greater son' (Mark 12.35f.), the man who wrote *The Similitudes of Enoch* (I Enoch 37–71) thought of the coming deliverer as a super-human personage who would be manifested as judge at the close of history. But the popular view was probably that to be found in *The Psalms of Solomon* (a Pharisaic document written about 50 BC). Here the Messiah is portrayed as a kind of second and greater Judas Maccabaeus who will 'purge Jerusalem of the Gentiles' and 'gather a holy people whom he will lead in righteousness'.

Yet if there was no uniform picture of the Coming One, one basic idea underlay the variant hopes—that the Messiah, when he came, would be the divinely-appointed head of the people of God and the bearer of his rule of men.

Did Jesus believe himself to be the Messiah? According to the gospels once, and not in public, he made the claim (John 4.26). Once he tacitly accepted the title when Peter gave it to him (Mark 8.29f.). And once (Mark 14.62), when the high priest asked him if he was the Messiah, he assented openly, 'I am'. (According to Matt. 26.63f. and Luke 22.67f. his answer was more equivocal: 'You have said so', i.e. 'Have it so if you choose'.)[2]

This reticence about Messiahship has led some to say that Jesus never thought of himself in this historical role. Thus the German Wrede, in his book *The Messianic Secret in the Gospels* (1901), argued that Jesus never claimed to be the Messiah and that it was only after the resurrection his followers so acclaimed him. Note, he said, those

---

[1] See, e.g., F. M. Cross, *The Interpreter's Bible*, Abingdon Press, Nashville, 1957, Vol. XII, pp. 663f.

[2] That is, 'Yes but—'.

frequent injunctions to secrecy about Messiahship found on Jesus' lips in Mark's gospel. They are not historical, but have been read back by the early church into his earthly life. They are the church's attempt to explain why Jesus was not recognized as the Messiah till after his resurrection.

Though Bultmann and his followers still accept Wrede's view— well illustrating the dictum that 'no ghost in German theology is ever truly laid'—the evidence is firmly against it.

1. The rise of such a belief in the early church is quite inexplicable if Jesus had not in his lifetime suggested to his disciples that he was the Messiah. It would never have *originated* after the catastrophe of the cross.

2. Wrede's denial involves casting wholesale doubt on the gospels as historical records. Messianic are the stories of Peter's confession, of the transfiguration and of the entry into Jerusalem; and it is beyond doubt that Jesus was crucified as a Messianic claimant.

3. There was indeed a 'Messianic secret'. But Jesus, not the early church, was its source. Most of the injunctions to secrecy in Mark are to be explained (*a*) by Jesus' desire to avoid futile Messianic demonstrations (cf. John 6.14f.) and (*b*) above all, by the sharp Messianic cross-purpose between Jesus and his contemporaries. He was not the Messiah whom either the Baptist, or Peter, or the Galilean crowds expected.

Jesus knew himself to be the Messiah, albeit in his own terms, during his ministry. What does this mean? That he was the person through whom God's rule was being realized and the ancient prophecies fulfilled. Yet when Peter or Caiaphas sought to apply the title to him, Jesus seemed to shy away from it and talk instead of the Son of man. Why? The only convincing answer is that Jesus conceived his Messiahship in spiritual and eschatological terms, not in nationalist and political ones. One indication of what it meant to him comes in his reply to John the Baptist's question. 'I am,' he replies in effect, 'the fulfiller of the great Isaianic prophecies (Isa. 29.18f.; 35.5f.; and 61.1) come to bring healing, life and good news to God's needy children.' Another clue he gives in his mode of entry into the holy city, and it recalls Zechariah's prince of peace (Zech. 9.9f.). Not the Psalms of Solomon but the Servant Songs of Isaiah and the Psalms of the Righteous Sufferer (22, 69 etc.) shaped his thought of the Messiah, and when,

'They all were looking for a King

To slay their foes and lift them high,'

he was thinking of one called to serve and destined to go to his triumph by way of a cross.

There was, however, another title much more congenial to one for whom the king in the kingdom was a father.

The Son of God[1]

In the Old Testament the phrase 'the son of God' is variously applied to Israel (Exod. 4.22; Hos. 11.1), to kings (as to Solomon in II Sam. 7.14) and to angels (as in Gen. 6.2; Job 1.6). There is also evidence—though not so abundant as we could wish—that in the first century AD it was a synonym for the Messiah. Thus (a) they related the 'royal psalms' to the Messiah (e.g. Ps. 110 in Mark 12.35ff.); (b) in a Dead Sea scroll, II Sam. 7.14, 'I will be his father, and he shall be my son', is applied to the Branch of David; and (c) in the gospels we find 'Messiah' and 'Son of God' in a cheek-by-jowl equation (Matt. 16.16; Mark 14.61).

When we turn to the gospels, we must distinguish others' use of the title and Jesus' employment of it. Thus demoniacs (Mark 3.11; 5.7), Caiaphas (Mark 14.61) and the centurion at the cross (Mark 15.39) designate Jesus as 'the son of God'. Here it is probably a synonym for the Messiah, though in the last passage it may mean no more than 'a righteous man' (cf. Luke 23.47 and Wisd. 2.18).

But what are we to say of the phrase in the stories of the baptism and the temptation? Does 'son of God' in these contexts mean merely Messiah? When we recall the boy Jesus' question, 'Did you not know that I must be in my Father's house?' (or 'about my Father's business'), and (more important) his later and unparalleled mode of addressing God as *Abba*, must we not say that the phrase on Jesus' lips implies something more than simply a consciousness of Messiahship?

Happily we can shed light on that 'something more'. Five passages in the synoptics—two from Mark, one from Q, one from M and one from L—hint at something uniquely filial in Jesus' self-consciousness, testify to a sense of divine sonship.

We take the M and L passages first. In Matt. 16.17 Jesus

[1] To argue, as some do, that 'the Son' and 'the Son of God' are distinct titles to be treated separately is to be wiser than the New Testament writers (Mark, John, Paul), who are unaware of the difference.

congratulates Peter, 'Blessed are you, Simon, Bar-Jona! For flesh and
blood has not revealed this to you, but my Father who is in heaven.'
The Semitic style of this saying (even if, as some hold, it was not
uttered at Caesarea Philippi) argues its authenticity. The point to
note is Jesus' description of God as 'my Father'.

Luke 22.29 L: 'As my Father appointed a kingdom for me, so do
I appoint a kingdom for you, that you may eat and drink at my
table in my kingdom, and sit on thrones judging the twelve tribes of
Israel' (cf. Matt. 19.28 M). Again, in a saying which is probably
authentic, Jesus speaks of God as 'my Father'.

When we turn to the Marcan passages, we have to reckon first
with the sentence in the allegorical parable of the Wicked Tenants,[1]
'He had still one other, a beloved (or 'only') son; finally he sent him
to them, saying, "They will respect my son" ' (Mark 12.6). Could
Jesus have so spoken of himself before the Jews in Jerusalem? There
is no compelling reason why he should not. We have to distinguish
between what Jesus himself meant and the way his audience understood him. In the sending of the son in the story he had his own
sending by God in mind, but the mass of his hearers would not
necessarily take it so. Jesus was using language inspired by his own
filial consciousness, which would be meaningful to his disciples but
which would not flaunt his secret before the rulers of Israel. The
point of importance here is that all God's previous messengers to
Israel are 'slaves': Jesus is not a slave but a son: nay, he is the only
son of the Father; he is the heir—all that is the Father's is his.

Next, we note Mark 13.32, a saying, as even Schmiedel admitted,
beyond the power of the early church's invention: 'But of that day
or that hour no one knows, not even the angels in heaven, nor the
Son, but only the Father.' Here the Son occupies a place of lonely
splendour, above both men and angels, subordinate only to God
himself.

But among all these passages concerning Jesus' divine sonship
pride of place must go to the Q passage Matt. 11.27; Luke 10.22. It
forms the second stanza of 'the Great Thanksgiving' and is more
faithfully preserved by Matthew:

> All things have been delivered to me by my Father
> And no one knows the Son except the Father,
> And no one knows the Father except the Son

[1] On the authenticity of the parable as a whole see my *Interpreting the Parables*,
SCM Press, pp. 116f.

And anyone to whom the Son chooses to reveal him.

No saying of Jesus has been put oftener under the critical micro-scope. It has been called 'a bolt from the Johannine blue' and radical critics have questioned its genuineness on various grounds: its 'Johannine ring', its alleged Hellenistic use of the verb to 'know', its absolute use of the phrase 'the Son', its description of God as 'my Father'. None of these objections is convincing.

First, the days are long past when men could dismiss a synoptic saying as inauthentic because it had parallels in the Fourth Gospel as this one has (John 5.19f.; 10.15; 14.6; 16.15). A 'point' in the synoptic tradition has become 'a star' in St John.[1] Second, when we remember the Hebraic conception of 'the knowledge of God', as we find it for example in Hosea or the Dead Sea Scrolls, it is quite arbitrary and perverse to call this saying (as Bultmann does) 'a Hellenistic revelation word'. Finally, as we have seen, the absolute use of 'the Son' and the description of God as 'my Father' occur elsewhere on Jesus' lips.

The Jewish scholar Montefiore once expressed the hope that scholars would demonstrate the inauthenticity of this saying if only because, if proved genuine, it would give notable encouragement to orthodox Christianity! Besides admiring his honesty, we can take his point. For it reveals in Jesus a unique, intuitive and personal appre-hension of God. It suggests an 'I-thou' relationship initiated and sustained by the Father and fulfilled by the Son's own response of obedience and love. In the saying Jesus claims that he alone truly knows God as Father and for that supreme spiritual experience all men must become debtors to him. Here is 'unshared sonship', and it forms the deepest thing in Jesus' self-understanding. This was the mainspring of his messianic ministry as the Son of man and the Servant of the Lord. A filial relationship, expressed in the phrases 'My Father' and 'the Son', to which there is no parallel, this is the last secret of the works and words of Jesus.

The Son of man

If 'Son of God' holds the key to Jesus' self-consciousness, the name

---

[1] In the Fourth Gospel 'the Son' occurs no fewer than sixteen times in the Johannine sayings of Jesus, while the phrase 'my Father' is found twenty-four times on Jesus' lips. Interpretation by St. John? Maybe, but it is founded on good pre-Johannine tradition. The 'interpretation' has 'the mind of Christ' behind it.

which he preferred during his ministry was 'the Son of man'. (About its meaning there has been long debate,[1] of which the end is not yet. Here we content ourselves with setting down what seem to us the likeliest conclusions.)

In Jewish literature 'the son of man' occurs in a variety of senses. In the prophet Ezekiel it means simply 'a human being', man in his weakness *vis-à-vis* the Almighty. In Ps. 8.4 it signifies 'man' frail and insignificant, yet destined for authority second only to that of God. In Ps. 80.17 it stands for Israel made strong out of weakness. In the vision of Dan. 7, after four beasts symbolizing successive despotic empires and their rulers, there comes 'one like a son of man' who represents 'the saints of the Most High' to whom God is about to entrust judgment and sovereignty. In the Similitudes of Enoch (I Enoch 37–71)[2] this representative figure becomes less of a symbol and more of an individual—in fact, a supernatural heavenly being destined to be revealed as judge at the end.

When, with this background, we turn to the gospels, we find (discounting parallels) about fifty separate Son of man sayings (Mark 14; Q 11; M 6; L 7 and John 12). It is customary to classify them, according to their contents, in three groups: A. Sayings which speak of the Son of man as an earthly figure, possessing authority, eating and drinking, having no place to lay his head, etc.; B. Sayings which refer to the sufferings and triumph of the Son of man; C. Sayings which predict the Son of man's future coming in glory as judge. Radical critics think, with no good reason, that only the C sayings are authentic. It is altogether probable that the three groups are complementary and reveal different aspects of the Son of man's destiny.

Beyond reasonable doubt the title goes back to Jesus, and if we ask whence he derives it, the probable answer is Dan. 7, a chapter echoed elsewhere in his sayings (Mark 14.62; Luke 12.32; cf. Mark 4.32). Those who hold the title to be a creation of the early church quite fail to explain the fact that in all four gospels the title is used many times by Jesus of himself, but never by anyone else in address to him. On the other hand, save for a single use of it by the dying Stephen in Acts 7.56, it is not applied to Jesus by the earliest

[1] See the summaries of it by A. J. B. Higgins in *New Testament Essays* (memorial volume for T. W. Manson), Manchester University Press 1959, pp. 119ff., and by I. H. Marshall in *The Evangelical Quarterly* for April–June 1970.

[2] The date of the *Similitudes* is still disputed. Some think they belong to the first century BC, others assign them to the first century AD.

Christians.

But if the title was of Jesus' own choosing, it was deliberately mysterious and ambiguous. Cf. John 12.34: 'Who is this Son of man?' ask the crowds. The ambiguity lay in Jesus' original Aramaic. *Barnasha* could mean 'man' (with a small 'm') or 'one' (with reference to the speaker himself). It could also mean 'the Man' as a darkly mysterious messianic figure. In fact, no title was better calculated both to conceal and, at the same time, to reveal to those with ears to hear, the real identity of the Son of man.

Why did Jesus prefer this title? First, it enabled him, without making overtly messianic claims, to declare his essential unity with mankind, especially the humble, the unfriended, the despised. Second, it indicated (as Dan. 7 suggests) his special function as the predestined representative of the new Israel he was creating and the bearer of God's sovereignty and judgment. It was thus at once a title of majesty and of humility.

Yet when Jesus used it, its strongly corporate overtones[1] (as in Dan. 7) made it not simply a title but an *invitation* to join him in the high destiny he had accepted. And when he spoke of the future glory of the Son of man, he was predicting not so much his own personal victory as the triumph of God's cause which he served.

But—and this is the new thing in the usage of the gospels—with the concept of sovereignty and judgment he conjoined that of service and suffering. Not once but several times he told his disciples that the Son of man must suffer many things before he came to his triumph: and in Mark 10.45, where the Son of man's mission is described in words strongly recalling Isa. 53, we see what the new thing was: 'The Son of man came not to be served but to serve and to give his life a ransom for many.' In Judaism the two figures of the Son of man (Daniel) and the Servant of the Lord (II Isaiah) had existed more or less separately. The clear synthesis in Mark 10.45 must go back to Jesus. He knew himself called of God to fuse in his own person the two roles of the Son of man and the Servant of the Lord. He was born to suffer, born a king.[2]

---

[1] See T. W. Manson, *The Teaching of Jesus*, ch. 7, where the Son of man is collectively interpreted of Jesus and his disciples.

[2] In Iranian, Chaldean and Egyptian religious circles men spoke of a heavenly (or primal) man. It is improbable that this doctrine influenced Jesus' usage, though it may have influenced Paul's (see Rom. 5.15f. and I Cor. 15.45–47). In the gospels it is the final man rather than the primal man who is in view.

The Self-revelation of Jesus

From titles let us now turn to what may be called testimonies—to the claims, the demands, the declarations which Jesus made where no titles are on his lips.

The story of the paralytic (Mark 2.1–12) may introduce the subject. When Jesus told him, 'Your sins are forgiven', his words were ambiguous. They could mean simply, 'God has forgiven you'. Or they could imply that Jesus himself was forgiving the man. So, apparently, his critics took them: 'Only God can forgive sins,' they said. Jesus was exercising the divine prerogative. Now such covert claims are found also in his parables. The early church fathers, we know, had a way of finding Christ everywhere in them. If nowadays we do not indulge in such exegetical ingenuities, this does not mean that the parables do not contain veiled claims. They do. 'When a parable describes God's goodness,' writes E. Fuchs, 'it is that goodness made effective in Jesus. When a parable speaks about the kingdom, Jesus is hidden behind it as its secret content.'[1]

Christological overtones are to be detected in many parables—in small ones like the Stronger Man (Mark 3.27; Luke 11.21ff. Q) and the Apprenticed Son (John 5.19f.), in John's parable of the True Shepherd (John 10.1–5) and Luke's of the Great Supper and the Prodigal Son (Luke 14.15–24; 15.11–32) as well as in the Two Builders (Matt. 7.24–27 Q) and the Last Judgment (Matt. 25.31–46 M). Especially is this true of the parables Jesus uttered during his final challenge to Jerusalem. In them he revealed himself as the sole bearer of Israel's destiny, as he said things which none but the Messiah had a right to say. And in his last parable, that of the Wicked Tenants (Mark 12.1–9), those who had ears to hear could not have missed the tremendous claim he was making.[2]

Not less remarkable, christologically speaking, are the direct demands Jesus makes. These are not simply for ethical obedience; they are for utter self-committal to himself. They express the totalitarian claim of Jesus and are full of authority.

'Everyone who acknowledges me before men, I will also acknowledge before my Father who is in heaven; but whoever denies me before men, I will also deny before my Father who is in heaven'

---

[1] 'Bemerkungen zur Gleichnisauslegung', *ThLZ* 79, 1954, cols. 345–8: reprinted in *Zur Frage nach den historischen Jesus*, Tübingen 1960, pp. 136–42.

[2] See C. W. F. Smith, *The Jesus of the Parables*, ch. 8; J. Jeremias, *The Parables of Jesus*[2], pp. 132, 230.

(Matt. 10.32; Luke 12.8f. Q; cf. Mark 8.38).

Could words say more clearly than this that fidelity to Jesus is that on which a man's destiny finally depends?

'He who receives you receives me, and he who receives me receives him who sent me' (Matt. 10.40; Luke 10.16 Q; cf. Mark 9.37; John 13.20).

Here is one who knows his cause to be the cause of God.

'He who loves father or mother more than me is not worthy of me; and he who does not take up his cross and follow me is not worthy of me' (Matt. 10.37f.; Luke 14.26f. Q; cf. Mark 8.34).

In such demands speaks one who knows himself uniquely authorized by God. He acts for God; his doings are God's doings. It has been said that Jesus never asked men to believe in him (but cf. John 14.1). But even if, as a mere matter of words, this were true, how utterly untrue in fact it is! For through such phrases as 'Follow me!', 'Learn of me' and 'Forsake all and follow me' sounds a demand for faith in himself as insistent as in Paul's words to the Philippian jailer, 'Believe in the Lord Jesus, and you will be saved'.

No less astounding are the 'I-sayings' of Jesus. We are all familiar with the great 'I am's' of John's gospel, but 'I-sayings' are not absent from the synoptics. Take first those sayings where the emphatic pronoun *ego* is found on the lips of Jesus. Those who do not read the gospels in the original Greek are apt to miss this remarkable feature, for it is not easily translatable into English—an italicized 'I' is our best equivalent. In Greek, which does not insert such pronouns except for special emphasis, this sovereign 'I' is infinitely suggestive of his self-consciousness. Every New Testament student has noted the authoritative 'I' which sounds through the six antitheses of the Sermon on the Mount: 'You have heard that it was said to the men of old . . . but *I* say to you.' But we find the same emphatic pronoun in other places:

> I (*egō*) command you (Mark 9.25).
>
> Look, it is I (*egō*) who send you out (Matt. 10.16 M).
>
> If it is by the finger of God that I (*egō*) cast out demons etc. (Luke 11.20; Matt. 12.28 Q).
>
> As my Father appointed a kingdom for me, so do I (*egō*) appoint for you, etc. (Luke 22.29 L?).

To these fall to be added the 'Amen I say to you' sayings. 'Amen' is a Hebrew word meaning 'truly' which the early Christians, like

the Jews before them, used as a response at the end of prayer, doxology and scripture-reading, to endorse the words of their spokesman.
Not so did Jesus employ it. When he had something specially solemn
or significant to say, he *prefaced* it with 'Amen I say to you'. There is
no parallel to this in Jewish literature. About sixty examples are
found in our gospel sources (Mark 13; Q 9; M 9; John 25), and all
on the lips of Jesus. For a parallel we naturally think of the Old
Testament prophet's 'Thus saith the Lord'; but what prophet ever
dared to say, 'Amen I tell you'? The formula hints at the authority
of which Jesus was conscious. It implies that his utterance is not his
own but God's, that he is but passing on what he has received from
on high.

Many of his 'Amen I tell you's' have to do with the kingdom of
God (e.g. Mark 9.1; 10.15; 14.25; Matt. 11.11 Q; Matt. 13.17 Q).
But, as we might expect, remembering the close connection between
Jesus and the kingdom, many concern his own person and destiny.
A doubled Amen compares his own relation to God with that between an apprenticed son and his father (John 5.19f.). An Amen
saying promises blessing and reward to all who have sacrificed home
ties for his sake (Mark 10.29). With a 'Truly I tell you' he declares
that it will be more tolerable for Sodom and Gomorrah on judgment
day than for those who reject his messengers (Matt. 10.15 Q). 'Amen
amen I tell you' prefaces his parable about the grain of wheat which
must die in order to yield a rich harvest (John 12.24). An 'Amen I
tell you' introduces, in the vignette of the Last Judgment, the great
'Inasmuch as you did to one of the least of these my brethren, you
did it unto me' (Matt. 25.40, 45 M).

Here, then, we have a unique feature of Jesus' speech. It expresses
the certainty of one who knows and promulgates what he has learned
from his Father. And if we ask what in fact it implies, the answer is,
'He is the one who speaks as the Father has bidden him' (John
12.49), and therefore speaks with divine authority.

Very similar are the 'I came' sayings which, when we recall how
the Baptist named Messiah 'the Coming One', testify to Jesus' extraordinary sense of divine mission:

I came not to call the righteous but sinners (Mark 2.17).

I came not to destroy but to fulfil (the law and the prophets)
(Matt. 5.17 M).

I came not to bring peace but a sword (Matt. 10.34 M).

I came to cast fire on the earth (Luke 12.49 Q?).

Only familiarity has dulled our ears to the wonder of these statements: some of them remind us of detonating bombs. Yet one and all attest a mission to men which moves the thoughtful reader to ask, 'Who then is this who knows himself so sent, so authorized by God?'

Finally, we must lay account with those declarations in which Jesus implies that with his own coming the messianic age has dawned: his sermon in Nazareth with the words from Isa. 61 to which Jesus adds, 'Today has this scripture been fulfilled in your hearing' (Luke 4.16–22 L); his reply to the Baptist's question which says in effect, 'I am the Messiah, but not the kind you expected' (Luke 7.22ff. Q); and his words of congratulation to the disciples, 'Blessed are the eyes that see what you see' (Matt. 13.16f. Q), so radiant with the sense that they are living in the blessedness of God's new order.

Yet perhaps the most remarkable self-revelation of all Jesus kept to the last night of his earthly life. 'This is my body' is extraordinary enough, but his word over the cup (whether we accept Mark's or Paul's phrasing of it: Mark 14.24; I Cor. 11.25) is even more so. Centuries before, at the very nadir of his people's fortunes, Jeremiah had seen their only salvation in the hope that God would make a 'new covenant'—a 'new deal' with his people—a new order of things established not in stone but in the heart of man: in that day all would know God, he would forgive their sins, and they would be truly his people (Jer. 31.31ff.). Then what manner of man is this who knows that by his dying he will inaugurate this new and blessed order of relations between God and man? No mere mortal makes such a claim, or we know him to be mad. We are driven back on the words of wise old 'Rabbi' Duncan: 'Christ either deceived mankind by conscious fraud, or he was himself deluded, or he was divine. There is no getting out of this trilemma.'[1]

Down nineteen centuries Christians have not been slow to declare which of these propositions is the true one.

[1] John Duncan *Colloquia Peripatetica*, 1870, p. 109.

11

JESUS' TEACHING ABOUT HIS DEATH

Why did Jesus 'steadfastly set his face to go to Jerusalem'? Men have found out various answers to this question. To die for the sins of the world, replied the older dogmaticians. But this was altogether too dogmatic and *a priori* an answer for the Liberal Protestants. They tended to answer: to tell his countrymen, in the very home and heart of Jewry, that God was their Father and all men brothers, but, when they would not hear, Jesus went to the cross to move men's hearts by his heroic self-sacrifice for the truth as he saw it. Very different was Albert Schweitzer's answer. History, he held, is moulded by theological beliefs. Jesus went up to Jerusalem in order by his own death to force God to bring in his kingdom cataclysmically. But it was 'an unsuccessful gamble, something like what happens when a chessplayer sacrifices his queen in the hope of forcing a mate, and it does not come off'.[1] None of these answers is satisfactory. What we may say, before we look at the passion sayings of Jesus, is that Jesus saw the cross neither as a glorious after-thought nor as a means of compelling God to act but as the very soul of his vocation as the Servant Messiah.

Our first question suggests a second one. How early in his ministry did Jesus foresee the possibility of the cross? Some have argued that he began that ministry with brilliant hopes of success, and that only later, when these faded and he realized that his enemies, being what they were, must surely compass his death, he accepted the cross and explained it, believing that by it he would move men to penitence for their sin. Yet it is hard to believe that even in the spring-time of the Galilean ministry the skies held no dark clouds for Jesus.

1. The common destiny of prophets he knew, and before him, as matter of recent history, lay the fate of the Baptist.

2. The heavenly voice at the baptism suggests that Jesus saw his own destiny in terms of the Servant of the Lord, and he was

[1] T. W. Manson, *The Servant Messiah*, p. 76.

surely not unaware of the tragic progress of the Servant as Isaiah had delineated it in prophecies he knew well—labour in vain, bitter persecution, ignominious death.

3. Even during the Galilean ministry, when his disciples were as light-hearted as men at a wedding-party, he was hinting at a time when 'the bridegroom would be taken away from them' (Mark 2.19f.). While therefore we may not say that Jesus clearly foresaw Calvary from the hour when he emerged streaming from the waters of Jordan, he must always have reckoned with the possibility of rejection and death in fulfilment of his mission.

The Messiah who must suffer

'When Jesus unfolds Messiahship, it contains death.'[1] Caesarea Philippi was a turning-point in Jesus' ministry. Now it had become clear to him that what had always been a possibility was a grim certainty. He had proclaimed the good news of God's dawning reign to the people at large and challenged them to lay hold on salvation by the decision of faith. But the masses had responded in the wrong way, as at the Galilean Lord's supper; or the religious in Israel had turned a deaf ear to God's call, as Jesus declared in the parable of the Contemptuous Guests (alias the Great Supper, Luke 14.15–24 Q). Now God was calling the Son of man to action—action which would end in a passion. 'He began to teach them that the Son of man must suffer many things . . .' (Mark 8.31).

'Must suffer.' The Greek for 'must' is dei: 'it is necessary'. What lies behind the verb? Is it the 'must' of outward constraint? Did Jesus realize that his foes, being what they were, must finally kill him if he remained true to God and himself? Is it not far more likely that the 'must' is one of inward constraint, that the dei is 'the dei of divine necessity'? It was a destiny appointed for him by God and, as John 10.18 says, freely accepted by Jesus. In the historical necessity Jesus discerned a divine necessity, saw that his passion must become a great action, if the reign of God was to 'come with power' (Mark 9.1). As he put it later, in the very penumbra of that passion, the grain of wheat must die if it was to yield a rich harvest (John 12.24). This was why he could not

return home,
Comfort his mother, live as other men,

[1] J. Denney, The Death of Christ, Hodder & Stoughton 1911, p. 32.

And taste the happiness of men on earth,
With wife and children, friends, and fair old age.[1]

Did he first learn this from his own study of Isa. 53? Or was this terrible truth, so unwelcome to flesh and blood, first revealed to him in personal communion with his Father and confirmed to him by his study of scripture? Whichever it was, most of his sayings about his passion—and there are about twenty in the synoptic gospels plus those in the Fourth Gospel[2]—either echo Isa. 53 or have its sombre music somewhere in the background.

To be sure, once only, in Luke 22.37 L, do we find an express quotation on Jesus' lips: 'For I tell you that this scripture must be fulfilled in me, "And he was reckoned with transgressors".' But this is cause for confidence in the gospel record, not the reverse. Had there been more such explicit quotations, we might have suspected the early Christians of reading back their own 'Servant Christology' into the mouth of Jesus. What are impressive, because so unforced and so unobtrusive, are the numerous echoes of Isa. 53 in Jesus' sayings. It is their very veiled allusiveness that argues their authenticity.

Does Jesus declare that the Son of man must be 'rejected' (Mark 8.31; Luke 17.25) and 'set at nought' (Mark 9.12)? He is echoing Isa. 53.3 ('He was despised and rejected . . . we esteemed him not'). Does he speak of 'laying down his life' like a good shepherd for his sheep (John 10.11, 15, 17)? The verbal phrase goes back to Isa. 53.10. Does he foresee himself buried like a common criminal, without anointing (Mark 14.8)? The Servant was to make his grave with malefactors (Isa. 53.9). Does he say, in the hour of his arrest, that 'the Son of man goes as it is written of him' (Mark 14.21)? Who can doubt which scripture he means? Does he speak in the upper room of his 'blood' as about to be 'poured out for many' (Mark 14.24)? The reference to the 'many' recalls Isa. 53.11f. and one who would vindicate 'many' by bearing their sins. Above all, does he describe his whole mission to men as one of service—a service that must issue in death for the common salvation (Mark 10.45)? Then it can only be one Servant, the Servant of the Lord who 'poured out his soul

[1] Masefield.
[2] See Vincent Taylor, *Jesus and His Sacrifice*, Macmillan 1937, pp. 82–249. He lists 12 from Mark and 7 from the L source. Among the chief Johannine sayings of Jesus are: 1. three about the need for the Son of man to be 'lifted up' (John 3.14; 8.28; 12.32); 2. three about the good shepherd 'laying down' his life for the sheep (John 10.11, 15, 17) which echo Isa. 53.10; and 3. the parable of the grain of wheat (12.24).

unto death' for sinners, whom he has in mind.

The conclusion is not in doubt. If we are to understand how Jesus conceived of his passion, we must begin with Isa. 53. And the doctrine of that chapter is one of representative and redemptive suffering for others, with the idea of substitution well in the foreground (see Isa. 53.4–6).[1]

The passion sayings

According to Mark Jesus thrice predicted his passion and resurrection (Mark 8.31; 9.31; 10.33f.; with which take also Mark 9.12). These predictions radical critics have summarily dismissed as 'prophecies after the event', i.e. they betray knowledge of what actually happened. This is quite gratuitous scepticism. Only the last one (10.33f.) is really open to this charge. The others are couched in such general terms that we need not doubt their authenticity. 1. None speaks of a 'cross', as we might have expected, were the charge true. 2. Mark 8.31 and 9.31 make Jesus predict his resurrection 'after three days', i.e. a short indefinite time, not 'on the third day' as it should read if it were a prophecy after the event. 3. If you eliminate from the predictions what may be credited to the early church, what remains is significant. Put the 'expurgated' predictions into one sentence and you get—a description of the suffering and triumphant Servant of the Lord, altogether credible on the lips of Jesus: 'The Son of man must suffer many things and be rejected and set at nought, and delivered up into the hands of men, and they shall kill him, and after three days he will rise again.'[2]

From these predictions we may now turn to Jesus' chief sayings about his passion.

---

[1] The classical study of this subject is that of Jeremias in *The Servant of God* by W. Zimmerli and J. Jeremias, SCM Press 1957. There Jeremias shows, with a wealth of evidence, (a) that the Christological interpretation of Isaiah's Servant goes back to the Aramaic-speaking church; and (b) that Jesus knew himself called to be the Servant. He argues the authenticity of Jesus' sayings on three main grounds: 1. their Semitic style; 2. their firm anchorage in the context; and 3. their quite general tenor showing that they could not well have been shaped 'after the event'. In *Jesus and the Servant*, SPCK 1959, Morna Hooker denies Jesus' whole debt to the Servant passages. Her argument fails to convince, (a) because she makes no detailed reply to Jeremias's massive linguistic case; and (b) because, in general, she deliberately 'plays down' the significance of the Servant concept in the time of Jesus.

[2] R. H. Fuller, *The Mission and Achievement of Jesus*, SCM Press 1954, pp. 55f.

First, Jesus saw his passion as a 'baptism'. 'Can you be baptized,' he said to James and John, 'with the baptism I am baptized with?' (Mark 10.38). On another occasion he declared, 'I have a baptism to undergo, and how hampered I am until the ordeal is over!' (Luke 12.49, Q? NEB). Baptism, a metaphor for suffering (cf. Ps. 42.7; Isa. 43.2), here refers to his death. Before the fire of the gospel can blaze in the world, Jesus says, there must come for the kindler his own baptism of blood. And yet that tense verb 'hampered' (*synechomai*, 'constricted') suggests that the 'ordeal' of death will be also the gateway to a fuller and freer activity. Confirmatory of this is his parable of the grain of wheat (John 12.24) in which Jesus declares that his death is the ineluctable condition of his ministry becoming greatly fruitful.

Second, Jesus spoke of his passion as a 'cup' that God had given him to drink. 'Can you drink of the cup that I am drinking?' he asked James and John (Mark 10.38). And in Gethsemane he cried in agony, 'Abba, Father, all things are possible to thee; remove this cup from me; yet not what I will, but what thou wilt' (Mark 14.36). Now, in the Old Testament, of twenty metaphorical uses of the word 'cup', in seventeen it is a figure for divinely-appointed suffering, even punishment.[1] (See especially Isa. 51.22 'the cup of stupor, the chalice of my wrath'). Some have been content to describe Jesus' 'cup' as simply one of suffering. But, were this so, it is hard to understand why he should pray so earnestly for the cup's removal or explain why, in Gethsemane, 'horror and dismay came over him' and he cried 'My heart is ready to break with grief'. Rather was it the cup of God's wrath against human sin. What wrung from Jesus the prayer that, 'if it were possible the hour might pass from him', was not the anticipation of pain but the anticipation of that experience when the Father would put into his hands the cup men's sins had mingled. So closely had he identified himself with those he came to save—so irrevocably had he 'betrothed himself to the human race, for better, for worse'—that he had to experience, in all its horror, the reaction of God's holy love against the sin of man. Only such an explanation does justice to the agony in the garden and the later cry of dereliction on the cross (Mark 15.34) which describes his feeling of descent into the hell of utter separation from his Father.

Third, Jesus spoke of his passion as a road to be travelled. 'The Son of man,' he said, 'is going the way appointed for him in the

[1] See C. E. B. Cranfield's article in *The Expository Times*, Feb. 1948.

scriptures' (Mark 14.21 NEB). What that road was he had already suggested on the descent from the Mount of Transfiguration: 'How is it written of the Son of man, that he should suffer many things, and be treated with contempt?' (Mark 9.12 with its echo of Isa. 53.3). The road is that *via dolorosa*, that path of rejection and death, mapped out five centuries before for the Servant of the Lord.

Thus, in his vivid picture-phrases—a baptism to be undergone, a cup to be drained, a road to be travelled—Jesus declares the necessity of his passion, with a strong hint in the 'cup' saying that he was for the sake of sinners exposing himself to God's judgment on men's sin, and another in the 'baptism' saying that beyond the 'ordeal' of death he hoped for a fuller and richer ministry in the world.

There remain the two most important sayings of all: the ransom saying and the word over the cup at the Last Supper.

Somewhere on the road to Jerusalem Jesus gave his disciples a luminous hint at the whole purpose of his mission and ministry: 'The Son of man came not to be served but to serve and to give his life as a ransom for many' (Mark 10.45). The staggering claim here made has caused some modern critics to deny its authenticity. They have called it a secondary variant of Luke 22.27, 'I am among you as one who serves', which, because it says nothing about a redemptive death, they have declared more original. A curiously *a priori* and perverse comment on one who said that he came to 'seek and save that which was lost' (Luke 19.10)! Others have dismissed it as a 'Paulinism' from the pen of Mark. They assume that Paul's was the one creative mind in the early church and that he infected the earliest evangelist with his own peculiar brand of redemptive theology. In fact, Paul himself tells us that 'Christ died for our sins' was part of the 'tradition' he had received from his Christian predecessors (I Cor. 15.3ff.). More recently one or two scholars have sought to weaken the saying's connection with the Old Testament passage, Isa. 53, which affords the clearest clue to its meaning.

Thus there are no good reasons for doubting the genuineness of Mark 10.45. Cast in the form of Semitic parallelism, it uses the language of Isa. 53. 'To serve' means to fulfil the mission of the Servant; 'to give his life as a ransom' reflects the Hebrew of Isa. 53.10; 'for many' echoes Isa. 53.11f.

What light does the saying shed on Jesus' mind about the meaning of his death? If we are to do justice to the metaphor of the 'ransom', we must say that by reason of their sins the lives of 'the many' had become forfeit and that Jesus saw it as the very soul of his vocation to release them, by his expiatory death, from the doom which overhung them. 'Truly,' the Psalmist had said, 'no man can ransom himself or give to God the price of his life; for the ransom of his life is costly' (Ps. 49.7f.). What 'the many' cannot do for themselves Jesus, by his representative suffering, will do for them. The sacrifice of the innocent one, according to God's will, will exempt the guilty.

We turn last to the word about the covenant at the last supper.

According to Mark 14.24 it was, 'This is my blood of the covenant which is poured out for many.'

In I Cor. 11.25 (where Paul is quoting what he had 'received from the Lord', i.e. through oral tradition going back to Jesus himself) it reads: 'This cup is the new covenant in my blood.'

Both texts speak of a covenant to be established by the blood of Jesus, of which the cup with its red wine is the symbol. Our English 'covenant' suggests a compact made between equals; but the Hebrew *berith* underlying the Greek *diathēkē* lays the stress on the divine 'prevenience'. It denotes a reciprocal relationship in which the initiative is on God's side; and its central idea is of God entering history with a gracious purpose to create a new order of relations between God and men. So 'blood' in this context means Jesus' life sacrificially released by death.

What passage underlay Jesus' use of the word 'covenant'? Mark's 'blood of the covenant' recalls Exod. 24.8; Paul's version, Jeremiah's 'new covenant' of grace (Jer. 31.31). But remembering how Jesus' thought was influenced by the Servant Songs of Isaiah, we cannot rule out Isa. 42.6 where God says to his Servant, 'I have given you as a covenant to the people, a light to the nations (cf. Isa. 49.8).

The essential meaning of both versions is the same. As the old covenant at Sinai had been established by the sprinkling of sacrificial blood, so God's new covenant is about to be sealed by Jesus' death, and the 'cup', i.e. the wine it contains, enables those who drink it to share in the benefits of God's new dispensation.

Which version is nearer to the actual words of Jesus? If a choice has to be made, it must be Mark's, if only because it gives 'the harder reading'—the very idea of drinking blood, even symbolically, would have been abhorrent to the average Jew.

Now in Mark's version the meaning of 'my blood of the covenant' is elucidated in the words, 'which is poured out for many'. With its allusion to Isa. 53.12 ('he poured out his soul to death . . . he bore the sin of many') this is evidence that Jesus saw his death as a vicarious sacrifice for the common salvation ('many' being the Hebrew way of saying 'all').

In the word over the cup Jesus is therefore saying, 'In virtue of my sacrificial death as the Servant-mediator men will be able to enter into a new order of relations between God and men and to find, through the forgiveness of their sins, a new fellowship with God.

The atonement

What do the passion sayings of Jesus tell us? Are they simply a collection of scattered *obiter dicta*? Or, taken together, do they give us what might be called Jesus' rationale of his suffering and death?

They do not yield a systematic doctrine of atonement, nor should we expect one. In his passion Jesus was *viator*—a traveller by faith, not *apprehensor*—one who saw the goal clearly from the beginning. Besides, any true doctrine of the atonement must be based not on a few sayings but on the whole set of facts provided by the life and teaching of Jesus and on the experience of countless Christians since he died and rose. Nonetheless, as we have seen, Jesus had clear convictions about the necessity and value of his suffering and the ends they would achieve.

Men's theories of the atonement can be roughly divided into three classes. According to 'the moral theory', associated with the great name of Abelard, Christ on his cross reveals the love of God in conflict with human sin, and by that revelation of suffering love moves the hearts of sinful men to repentance and new life. The truth in it is an essential element in any true doctrine of the atonement. All begins in the loving purpose of God (Rom. 5.8; John 3.16). Yet it must be said that in Jesus' passion sayings there is none which says he dies to reveal the love of God.

According to the 'patristic' theory (so-called because favoured by the early church fathers), in his ministry and supremely on the cross Jesus raided the dark empire of evil, vanquished the Devil, and 'led captivity captive'. The cross is his death-grapple with Satan, a conflict through which he comes victorious by the resurrection. Now it is true that Christ's whole ministry was a campaign against the kingdom of evil and its king, and among the passion sayings we find such utterances of Jesus as: 'This is your hour and the power of darkness' (Luke 22.53 L) and 'Now is the judgment of this world, now shall the ruler of this world be cast out' (John 12.31). But this view is but one element, not the master-idea, in Jesus' thinking about the cross.

The third type of theory is built on what has been called 'the sacrificial principle', and is expounded by modern theologians like P. T. Forsyth and Vincent Taylor. Under this heading we may include theories which hold that Christ's sufferings were, in some sense, 'penal'—penal not in the sense that God punished Jesus but in the sense that Jesus entered into the blight and judgment which men's sins must incur at the hands of a God who is holy love. According to this third theory, Jesus on the cross offers an expiatory sacrifice for the sin of men against holy God. It is with this doctrine of the atonement that Jesus' sayings seem best to agree. His death he saw as a representative sacrifice for 'the many'. Not only is his thought steeped in Isa. 53 (which speaks of representative and vicarious suffering unto death), but his words over the cup—indeed the whole narrative of the last supper—almost demand to be interpreted in terms of a sacrifice offered in obedience to his Father's will—a sacrifice into whose virtue his followers could enter. The idea of substitution, prominent in Isa. 53.4–6, appears in the ransom saying with its preposition *anti*, 'instead of'. And it requires only a little reading between the lines to find in the 'cup' sayings, the record of the agony and the cry of derelection, evidence that Christ's sufferings were what, for lack of a better word, we may call 'penal'.

No theory of course—not all of the theories put together—may claim to preserve the whole truth of that act in which God in Christ took the responsibility of evil on himself and subsumed evil under good. Yet enough survives in the gospel records to show why the first article in the earliest Christian creed declared that 'Christ died for our sins according to the scriptures' (I Cor. 15.3), and why it has been the testimony of Christians down the centuries that 'he has given us rest by his sorrow and life by his death'.

12

JESUS' TEACHING ABOUT THE FUTURE

What did Jesus foresee as he looked into the future? If he predicted doom for the Jewish temple and people, what did he see lying beyond this time of disaster? What did he teach about the day of judgment? If he spoke of the coming of the Son of man, what did he mean by it?

It is Jesus' predictions, some of a historical kind, others of a supra-historical nature, that we must now study.

This is the most difficult part of our enquiry. Two observations may be made at the outset. One is that Matthew has demonstrably heightened the apocalyptic element in Jesus' teaching. Not only does he alone use the word 'Parousia' (4 times) and the phrase 'the end of the world' (5 times); but in passages where he depends on Mark, he gives the Marcan saying an apocalyptic turn. Cf. Mark 9.1 ('the kingdom of God having come with power') with Matt. 16.28 ('the Son of man coming in his kingdom'). The other problem is the use to be made of Mark 13. Here the signs preceding the end are carefully marked out, stage by stage,[1] till the end comes. Yet elsewhere Jesus refused to give 'signs', and in Luke 17.22–37 (Q) and Luke 21.34–36 (L) the end supervenes with complete suddenness. That Mark 13 contains many genuine sayings of Jesus is certain; but the way in which they are now arranged gives a wrong impression of Jesus' teaching about the future. We must use Mark 13 with care.

The historical predictions

What historical predictions did Jesus make?

To begin with, he forecast *suffering, for himself and his followers*. All four gospel sources contain such predictions:

> Mark 8.31–34; 10.39f.; 13.11–13.
> Q: Luke 12.4–12; Luke 14.26ff.

[1] Wars (7ff.), tribulations (14ff.), the end (24ff.).

L: Luke 22.35–38 (the two swords).

M: Matt. 5.10 and 10.24f.

Sometimes Jesus speaks of 'bearing a cross'; at other times he warns his disciples not to fear those who 'kill the body'; at others, he foresees his disciples brought before the authorities. Though the original setting of these sayings is not always certain, Mark does record that on the last journey to Jerusalem, Jesus warned his disciples to be ready for suffering and that he once particularized it as 'a cross' (Mark 8.34).

The second sure conclusion is that Jesus predicted *disaster for the Jewish temple and people*. We find explicit sayings like Mark 13.2, 'Not one stone shall be left on another'; Luke 13.35 Q: 'Your house (i.e. the temple) is forsaken'; and his pathetic lament over Jerusalem 'If thou hadst known . . .' (Luke 19.41ff. L) To these we must add allusive warnings in several parables.

The disaster which Jesus foresaw was the fatal clash with Rome,[1] and he prophesied it would happen *within the existing generation*. Speaking of Israel's persecution and killing of the prophets, he declared that 'the blood of all prophets, shed from the foundation of the world, would be required of this generation' (Luke 11.49f. Q). We recall Mark 13.30, 'This generation will not pass away before all these things take place'.

We have thus two well-attested predictions: one of suffering for himself and his followers, the other of disaster for the Jewish temple and people. How did Jesus connect the two coming events in his own mind?

We find the clue in Luke 12.49f. (Q?): 'I came to cast fire on the earth, and how I wish it were already kindled! But I have a baptism to undergo, and how hampered I am till the ordeal is over! Do you think I have come to give peace on earth? No, I tell you, but rather division.' And he goes on to predict the family and social chaos which will ensue.

Clearly then Jesus expected his mission to culminate in a great crisis in human affairs, and connected it with his own death which he called his 'baptism'. We trace a similar train of thought in the parable of the Wicked Tenants (Mark 12.1–9). There the killing of the 'heir' is followed by the destruction of the tenants of the vineyard. All this, Jesus said, would happen in 'this generation'. If in

[1] Cf. John 11.48ff. Even Caiaphas and the Jewish rulers foresaw this peril for the Jewish nation and temple.

fact the crisis broke almost forty years later, this is a very mild example of prophetic foreshortening of the historical perspective. Jesus' predictions did come true.

All these predictions deal in doom and disaster. Was there another and brighter side to the picture in Jesus' mind? Did he foresee a time of restoration beyond the coming tragedy?

We have already seen that he expected a coming of the reign of God 'with power' (Mark 9.1), with some mighty divine act like the resurrection, and that he expected the sphere of God's rule to grow from small beginnings to great endings, as the mustard seed grows into a tree affording shelter to 'the birds of the air' (the Gentiles). Did he expect some kind of paradise on earth to follow the calamities he foretold? And ought we, on the authority of Jesus, to cherish the hope that one day wars and tyrannies and exploitations will give way to a perfect society on earth?

Our gospel sources hardly encourage such a view. Jesus' promise in Mark 10.29f. does not authorize such a hope; for the blessings promised in this 'time' are to be mixed 'with persecutions' and 'eternal life' is reserved for 'the age to come'. Nor does the obscure saying about 'twelve thrones' (Matt. 19.28; Luke 22.29f.) justify it: what clues there are point to a better world than this. Our verdict must be that Jesus never taught his disciples to expect a time of un-alloyed bliss on this earth when the divine judgments were overpast. Christians must work for the improvement of human society, as they must pray that God's 'will may be done on earth as it is in heaven'; but they are not committed by their Lord's recorded teaching to any dream of Utopia in this vale of time and tears. For them, the ultimate meaning of history—and the fulfilment of their highest and holiest hopes—lies beyond history, in the supernal world.

The supra-historical predictions

We turn now to the supra-historical predictions of Jesus, i.e., those which describe not coming events in history but events of a super-natural kind: in particular, the day of judgment and the day of the Son of man.

(a) *The day of judgment*

The chief passages are seven:

Mark: 12.40.

Q: Luke 6.37; Luke 10.12–15; Luke 11.31f.

M: Matt. 5.22; 12.36; 25.31–46.

There are fewer references than we might have imagined. Moreover, in three of them Jesus, while teaching men's liability to divine judgment, does not actually refer to the day:

Mark 12.40: 'They will receive the greater condemnation.'
Luke 6.37: 'Judge not, and you will not be judged.'
Matt. 5.22: 'Everyone who is angry with his brother shall be liable to judgment.'

There remain four passages for study. According to the first Q passage (Luke 10.12–15), Jesus, in sending out his missionaries, declared that 'on that day' it would be more 'tolerable' for Sodom than for the Galilean city which rejected them:

'I tell you, it shall be more tolerable on that day for Sodom than for that town. Alas for you, Chorazin! alas for you, Bethsaida! for if the mighty works done in you had been done in Tyre and Sidon, they would have repented long ago, sitting in sackcloth and ashes. But it shall be more tolerable in the judgment for Tyre and Sidon than for you. And you, Capernaum, will you be exalted to heaven? You shall be brought down to Hades.'

The judgment in which Sodom figures must lie *beyond history*; for irretrievable judgment, in a historical sense, had overtaken the cities of the plain centuries before. Likewise, when Jesus contrasts the lot of Tyre and Sidon with that of the Galilean cities 'in the judgment', he cannot be thinking of a historical judgment in terms of war due to a clash with Rome; for no Roman threat overhung Tyre and Sidon.

The same must be said of the second Q saying (Luke 11.31f.):

'The queen of the South will arise at the judgment with the men of this generation and condemn them; for she came from the ends of the earth to hear the wisdom of Solomon, and, behold, something greater than Solomon is here. The men of Nineveh will arise at the judgment with this generation and condemn it; for they repented at the preaching of Jonah, and, behold, something greater than Jonah is here.'

So far as their mortal bodies were concerned, Sheba and the Ninevites were long dust. A judgment in which they figure must lie beyond history.

There remain two passages from the M source. In one (Matt. 12.36) Jesus declares that 'on the day of judgment men will render account for every careless word they utter'. The other is the parable of the Last Judgment (Matt. 25.31–46 M), whose substantial authenticity must be affirmed,[1] and to which we will come back later when speaking of the coming of the Son of man.

What shall we conclude from this survey? Jesus indeed spoke of a divine judgment, but for him it lay beyond history. There is a Q saying (Matt. 10.32f.; Luke 12.8f.) which implies that the scene of the judgment will be in heaven, that God will be the judge, and that Jesus will be the advocate, or witness, for men:

'So everyone who acknowledges me before men, I will also acknowledge before my Father who is in heaven; but whoever denies me before men, I will also deny before my Father who is in heaven' (for the last phrase Luke has 'the angels of God', i.e. in the divine presence).

In all these matters of judgment to come Jesus spoke with some reserve, not elaborating the picture but emphasizing men's final accountability to God and using the idea of doomsday to persuade men that eternal issues hung upon their response to the reign of God decisively being manifested in his person and mission. Cf. John 9.39: 'For judgment I came into this world.'

(b) *The triumph of the Son of man*

Jesus foresaw his death; but beyond death he foresaw also triumph for the cause of God embodied in his own representative person. The question is, How did he conceive of his coming triumph?

In the gospels we find two sets of predictions: 1. predictions in which Jesus says that as the Son of man he will rise 'after three days'; and 2. predictions in which he speaks of the coming (or day), of the Son of man. We must study both.

1. According to Mark 8.31; 9.31; 10.33f., Jesus thrice predicted that as the Son of man he would rise from the dead 'after three days'. In the Bible 'after three days' commonly means 'after a short (indefinite) interval' (the 'short time' of John 14.19 and 16.16). So it is in Hos. 6.2 and it is probable that Jesus' prediction echoes that prophecy: 'After two days he will revive us; on the third day he will raise us up.' This not only comes from a chapter familiar to Jesus (see Matt. 9.13 and 12.7) but refers both to 'the third day' and to 'resurrection'. Moreover, in Jesus' sayings about 'the new sanctuary' (John 2.19f. and Mark 14.58) we find him similarly referring to a three days' interval and a 'raising'. Not surprisingly scholars[2] trace

---

[1] See Theo Preiss, *Life in Christ*, SCM Press 1954, pp. 44f., and H. E. W. Turner's article in *The Expository Times*, May 1966.

[2] F. C. Burkitt, *JTS* ii, pp. 112f.; G. Delling in *TDNT* II, p. 949.

the origin of Jesus' phrase to Hos. 6.2f. We conclude that Jesus foretold his triumph over death and that he phrased his prediction in
Hosea's words.

2.   In the other set of predictions Jesus foretells the coming (or
the day) of the Son of man. There are nine[1] relevant passages:

> Mark: 8.38; 13.26; 14.62.
> Q: Luke 12.40; 17.22, 26, 30.
> M: Matt. 10.23; 25.31.

Note first that in Luke 12.8f., the Q parallel (to Mark 8.38), which is
commonly regarded as more original, the scene is laid in heaven—
there is no allusion to a 'coming'. Matthew 10.23, peculiar to Matthew, most probably reflects the expectations of the primitive
Palestinian church.[2]

We start then from sayings above serious suspicion. Luke 12.40
describes the unexpectedness of the Son of man's coming: 'The Son
of man,' we read at the end of the parable about Waiting Servants,
'is coming at an hour you do not expect.' On Jesus' lips this parable
and its warning probably referred not to what the early church
called the Parousia, but to the crisis of the kingdom created by his
ministry.[3]

We come next to Luke 17.22–37, commonly called the Q apocalypse. Verses 22–30 refer to the 'days' (22, 26) or 'the day' (30) of
the Son of man. On the other hand, most of 31–37, beginning with a
Sauve qui peut! and ending with the picture of 'eagles' and a 'corpse',
suggests a Roman attack on Jerusalem. We learn that the Son of
man, after his suffering, will be like lightning (24) and then that the
day of the Son of man's 'revelation' will take men unawares as did
Noah's flood and the ruin that befell Sodom (26–29). But we are not
told what role the Son of man will play in all this.

Much more illuminating is Mark 14.62. To the high priest's question 'Are you the Messiah?' Jesus replies, 'I am', and proceeds, 'And
you will see the Son of man sitting at the right hand of power and
coming with the clouds of heaven.' The words are from Dan. 7.13,
with an echo of Ps. 110.1. Now in Daniel the verse which begins
'Behold, with the clouds of heaven there came one like a son of man,'
ends, 'and he came to the Ancient of Days and was presented before

---

[1] Luke 18.8b sounds like an early church saying. Not only does it bear traces of
Luke's own style, but it consists ill with the confident mood of the parable.
[2] See T. W. Manson, *The Sayings of Jesus*, p. 182.
[3] See my *Interpreting the Parables*, p. 85.

him.' That is to say, the Son of man's destination is *the immediate presence of God*, his 'coming' to the right hand of God. Jesus must have taken the plain meaning of the passage. Thus his reply to the high priest is an impassioned assertion that, despite the apparent ruin of his cause, he will yet be exalted on high. Mark 14.62 therefore stands for a directly impending historical event—the death and resurrection of Jesus conceived as his vindication.

Is this what is meant by the 'coming' of the Son of man? Is it possible that, for Jesus, resurrection 'after three days' and the 'coming' of the Son of man are two different ways of saying the same thing?

Some have found this solution tempting. They have pointed out that in the synoptic gospels Jesus never speaks of 'coming again'. They have deemed it significant that, though Jesus predicted his resurrection and his coming as the Son of man, no recorded saying of his predicts both. Yet, tempting as it is, this view is open to two objections: 1. It fails to do justice to all the gospel evidence; and 2. it does not account for the early Christians' hope of Christ's coming in glory.

The best solution of our problem is therefore that Jesus predicted not only a 'coming' in history—of which the resurrection and the advent of the Spirit were the reality—but also a coming in glory at the consummation of the kingdom.

As evidence that Jesus expected a coming in history we can point to three passages: Mark 8.31 (resurrection 'after three days'); Mark 9.1 (the coming of God's reign 'with power') and Mark 14.62 (his reply to the high priest). All three express Jesus' certainty of speedy triumph and, with his own, the triumph of God's cause which he embodied. What they assert is swift vindication after apparent defeat. Of this Jesus was quite sure.

What actually happened we know: the Easter victory over death, the advent of the Holy Spirit, the rise of the apostolic church. This was Jesus' coming in history; and St John, who tends to interpret the Parousia in terms of the coming of the Spirit, was not wrong.

But there are other sayings of Jesus which refer to another coming —a coming with cosmic implications.

Luke 17.26–30 refers to a 'revelation' of the Son of man against the background of the end of the existing order.

Again, the great parable of the Last Judgment (Matt. 25.31–46 M) sets the Son of man's coming in another world; for surely it is not in this world of space and time that the dead as well as the living will be gathered before the Son of man. The reference is (in Addison's phrase) to 'that great Day when we shall all of us be contemporaries, and make our appearance together'.

To these sayings we may add another: 'But of that day or that hour no one knows, not even the angels in heaven, nor the Son but only the Father' (Mark 13.32). This undoubtedly genuine saying must refer to Christ's 'glorious coming' and judgment day.

Possibly these passages, notably the second, may have taken some colouring from the theology of the early church. Nor need we take their tremendous imagery with prosaic literalness, since they are attempts to express the almost unimaginable in human symbols. Yet, taken together, they provide dominical warrant for a belief in Christ's coming in glory:

> Heaven and earth shall flee away
> When he comes to reign.

This coming is the consummation of the kingdom of God. If we ask what it means, we may say three things. First: it must mean the final triumph of God over all evil. Second: it must be the point at which time—and all in it well pleasing to God—is taken up into eternity. (Locate the coming *in* the time series, says Reinhold Niebuhr;[1] and you make the ultimate vindication of God *over* time— which is what the consummation of God's kingdom means—into a mere point *in* history.) Third: it must mean the confrontation of all men by God in Christ. Here our clue is the first coming; the second must be *homoousios*—of the same kind—with it. God has already revealed himself in a man from whom we may learn what sort of person it is with whom we shall finally have to do. We shall encounter the same person whose holiness, goodness and truth are writ large for us in the gospels. Studdert Kennedy took the point well:

> Then will he come with meekness for his glory,
>   God in a workman's jacket as before,
> Living again the eternal gospel story,
>   Sweeping the shavings from his workshop floor.

That it will involve judgment is the teaching of Jesus as well as his apostles. It is Jesus' teaching also that the criterion of judgment will be men's response to such manifestation of God's truth as was

[1] *The Nature and Destiny of Man*, II, Nisbet 1943, pp. 299f.

given to them in their own day (Luke 11.31ff. Q), and the compassion they have shown to all the poor and needy folk in whom the hidden Christ meets them in divine disguise (Matt. 25.31–46 M). And, with St Paul, we may well believe that the Christ who died for us and now in heaven intercedes for us, will be men's advocate at the great day.

13

THE JERUSALEM MINISTRY
AND THE WITHDRAWAL

(Here we pick up again the thread of narrative where we laid it down. For the journey south to Jerusalem Mark must be our main guide. Luke's long narrative, 9.51–19.28, sheds little light on the path Jesus took, but Luke 9.51 at least shows how deep a mark this journey had left on the gospel tradition: 'When the days drew near for him to be received up, he set his face to go to Jerusalem.' Once Jerusalem is reached, we shall find cause to be grateful for the special tradition preserved by St John.)

On the road south

After the transfiguration Jesus and his disciples struck south from the neighbourhood of Caesarea Philippi. Though Mark does not have detailed information about this journey, he indicates its chief stages: south to Galilee with a halt at Capernaum, then 'into the regions of Judea and beyond Jordan', and finally via Jericho up to Jerusalem (Mark 9.30, 33; 10.1, 46; 11.1).

'It is unthinkable,' Jesus had said, 'for a prophet to meet his death anywhere but in Jerusalem' (Luke 13.33 L, NEB). Did he go south deliberately to court death, or did he contemplate a ministry in Jerusalem and its neighbourhood? The evidence suggests that, though he knew death awaited him at the end of the road, he knew also that he had a mission to fulfil in Jerusalem.

Mark says that Jesus wished his journey through Galilee to be secret (9.30f.). Why? He was seeking to initiate his men more deeply into the secret of Messianic suffering and glory. This part of Mark's gospel contains three predictions of passion and resurrection. Are they merely variants of the same tradition? If they are, we have a triply-attested tradition, even if in the third version (Mark 10.32f.) the phrasing reflects what actually happened. But is it not as likely that the doctrine of a suffering Messiah, so abhorrent to Jewish ears, had to be repeated? (Men are ever reluctant to believe what they do not wish to hear. Let us recall how few people in Britain were prepared to hear Churchill's warnings in the 'thirties' about the menace of Hitlerism.)

At any rate, in Capernaum the disciples were still much more interested in status than in suffering, so that Jesus, taking a child, had to read them a lesson in humility (Mark 9.33–37). Then the little band continued southwards—perhaps traversing for a time Samaritan soil (cf. Luke 9.51–56 L, the story of the inhospitable Samaritans)—till they reached 'the regions of Judea and beyond Jordan'. This strange phrase probably means (as some MSS in fact read) to Judea by way of Perea on the east side of Jordan.[1] So, fording the Jordan, they came to Jericho, fifteen miles from Jerusalem. Here Jesus restored his sight to blind Bartimaeus and gave new life and hope to a despised superintendent of taxes called Zaccheus (Mark 10.46–52; Luke 19.1–10 L).

Of that southward journey Mark preserves two vivid glimpses. One is the picture of the little band 'on the road to Jerusalem', with Jesus, a great lonely figure striding ahead of his men, wholly absorbed in his purpose and destiny, while his followers straggled behind in awe and amazement—fit symbol of the spiritual gulf which separated them (Mark 10.32). The other is the story of the request of James and John for the chief places in his coming 'glory'. 'Can you drink of the cup that I am drinking?' he answered, 'or be baptized with the baptism I am baptized with?' His reply shows clearly what his thoughts were at the time, and evokes from him a saying which not only expresses his concept of true greatness but hints, in one tremendous metaphor, at the aim and end of his whole Messianic mission (Mark 10.45).

In Jerusalem

If we had only Mark to guide us from this point on, so quickly do events seem to follow each other that we might easily suppose that everything from the healing of Bartimaeus in Jericho to the finding of the empty tomb on the first Easter morning was over in about a week. This is incredible.

[1] Others have thought Jesus went south through Samaria to Judea and hen to Perea.

Even Mark 14.49 suggests otherwise: 'Day after day,' says Jesus to the arresting posse in Gethsemane, 'I was teaching in the temple.'

Second: scholars have long felt that the controversies between Jesus and the Jewish authorities in Mark 11–12 cannot all have taken place on what is traditionally known as 'the day of questions'.

Third: a critical study of Mark 11–13 confirms this suspicion. In Mark 11.1–25 the narrative is set in a framework of three days (11.1, 12, 19), and apparently all recorded in Mark 11.27–13.37 took place on the third one. This passes belief: (a) The third day is absurdly over-crowded; (b) Mark 13, the apocalyptic discourse, is a composite document; and (c) most of the 'conflict' stories in Mark 11–12 probably form a pre-Marcan complex which the evangelist inserted here because the first of them ('By what authority are you doing these things?') had its right historical context here.

Fourth: at Mark 14.1 the real passion story begins with a fresh note of time: 'It was now two days before the Passover and the feast of Unleavened Bread.' This has no connection chronologically with what went before; it is manifestly a new start.

We conclude that in Mark 11–13 the course of events has been telescoped. Not a week but something like six months must have intervened between the healing of Bartimaeus and the finding of the empty tomb.[1]

It is here that, if we are to recover the true course of events, we must turn to the Gospel of John, chapters 7–12. At the beginning of this century William Sanday[2] drew attention to the 'extraordinary vividness' and 'peculiar verisimilitude' of the details of these chapters. In the last two or three decades C. H. Dodd and others have taught us to set a new value on the historical tradition embedded in the Fourth Gospel. But it was M. Goguel,[3] no conservative critic, who in 1933 showed what valuable historical tradition underlay John 7–12 and how, with its help, we could reconstruct Jesus' movements during the last phases of his mission. The chief 'traditional' passages are: John 7.10, 14, 32, 37; 8.20; 10.22, 40–42; 11.54; 12.1, and they reveal the following sequence of events:

(a) Jesus left Galilee with his disciples just before Tabernacles and went up to Jerusalem for the Feast (September—October), John 7.10. Cf. Mark 9.30.

[1] See T. W. Manson, *BJRL* 33, 2, March 1951, pp. 271–82.
[2] *Outlines of the Life of Christ*, T. and T. Clark 1905, p. 131.
[3] *The Life of Jesus*, pp. 238–50, 401–28.

(*b*) There he taught for three months till the Feast of Dedication (about the winter solstice), John 10.22.

(*c*) Soon after, because of mounting hostility, he withdrew across Jordan, i.e. into Perea (John 10.40), eventually moving to Ephraim on the edge of the wilderness (John 11.54).

This chronological scheme implies (roughly) three months of ministry in Jerusalem followed by a three months' withdrawal before he returned to the capital. What was Jesus doing in Jerusalem from Tabernacles to Dedication? The answer is that for him it was (*a*) a time of controversy about his authority coupled with, on his part, criticism of Israel's rulers and teachers and (*b*) a time when he urgently sought to awaken the people to the supreme historical crisis which overhung the nation.

Mark records some of the controversies Jesus had with the religious authorities and others (Mark 11.27–12.44). They asked him by what authority he was acting as he did, and whether it was lawful or not to pay taxes to Caesar. The Sadducees tried to catch him out with a trick question about the resurrection—only to be decisively discomfited—and Jesus for his part (in a passage where some suppose he was playing with his secret) asked his critics, 'How can the scribes say that the Messiah is the Son of David?'

Always in the background was the question of his authority. If now, making due allowance for John's strong sense of the dramatic, we turn to John 7–11, we find a clear and life-like impression of the excitement and controversy which Jesus' presence in the capital evoked, as we note how again and again the words he uttered and the things he did raised the question of his authority. Consider, for example, passages like John 7.25–27, 41–42; 8.19f.; 10.1–5, 22f. Always at the centre of the Jews' concern is the question of questions, 'Can this Galilean possibly be the Messiah?' On his part, Jesus does not give them the unequivocal answer which they desire, but in a simple parable 'drawn from ancient Palestinian tradition',[1] John 10.1–5, he does make a veiled Messianic claim. 'I am no interloper,' he says in effect, 'but the rightful shepherd of God's flock. I need no signs to prove my authority which is self-authenticating: it lies in the fact that my sheep follow my leadership because they recognize in me the accents and actions of Israel's true shepherd' (see Ezek. 34).

During this Jerusalem ministry Jesus did not, however, remain

[1] J. Jeremias, *TDNT* VI, p. 494.

wholly on the defensive. To this time must belong his outspoken condemnation of the scribes for their many-sided forms of religious play-acting. Mark preserves briefly the criticisms he made of their love of long robes, respectful greetings in the street, the best places 'in church' or at banquets, their victimization of widows and their hypocritically long prayers (Mark 12.38–40). Of this indictment Matthew gives us a fuller account, mainly drawn from his special source (Matt. 23), and possibly sharpened in the course of transmission. Just as the Sermon on the Mount (Matt. 5–7) represents not a single long sermon but *didache* ('teaching') given to his disciples on many occasions, so the 'woes' against the Pharisees and 'the doctors of the law' must represent criticisms made over many days.

But this record of controversy and criticism does not exhaust the tale of Jesus' ministry during these three months in Jerusalem. All through this time he was also challenging his countrymen at large to awaken to the fateful crisis which was now upon the nation, and, as earlier in his Galilean ministry, the medium in which he presented his challenge was parable.

Among the parables in the gospels there are about a dozen 'parables of crisis', i.e. stories heavy with a sense of impending doom and the urgent need for decision for or against God and his purpose. What is their historical setting in the life of Jesus? It can hardly be the Galilean ministry when Jesus was announcing the dawning of God's reign and calling on men to lay hold on salvation. Neither can it be the time of retirement when he was on the fringe of Tyre. Nor again can it be the time when he was secretly making his way south to Jerusalem. The only possible historical locus for these parables charged with this sense of supreme crisis is the Jerusalem ministry we have been describing.

Israel, Jesus said, like an insolvent debtor on his way to court, was walking to disaster (a collision course with Rome, Luke 12.57–59 Q); but his contemporaries, so wise at reading weather signs, could not see that God was visiting his people in blessing and judgment and that they should change their course accordingly (Luke 12.54–56 Q?). If they did not, like the barren fig-tree (Luke 13.6–9 L) they were doomed to be cut down, or, like the contemptuous guests in the story of the Great Supper (Luke 14.15–24 Q), shut out of the kingdom of God. God had entrusted Israel's leaders with a unique revelation of his will and purpose, but, like the barren rascal in the tale about Money in Trust (Matt. 25.14–26 M), they had fallen down on their trust and were in danger of being rejected like salt that had lost its savour (Luke 14.34f.; Matt. 5.13). What was needed was resolute action in face of the great emergency—action like that of the rascally steward who 'got his books' from his employer (Luke 16.1–8 L). Like servants waiting for their master's return, readiness must be the order of the day (Luke 12.35–38 Q?). Otherwise they might be caught unprepared like the foolish bridesmaids (Matt. 25.1–13 M) or the man whose house was burgled (Luke 12.39f. Q). Like a traveller, when the shades of evening are falling fast, they must act before the darkness overtook them (John 11.9f.; 12.35f.).

Thus Jesus saw his ministry moving inexorably to its climax, and in a final parable (whether spoken during the Jerusalem ministry or on his final return to the city) he forecast the doom that awaited them if they rejected God's last appeal to his people in his own person and mission (Mark 12.1–9).

We have previously discussed Jesus' teaching about the future. Suffice it now to repeat that, as Mark 13.1f. shows, he foresaw the historical disaster impending on temple and city. In what has been called 'the Q apocalypse' (Luke 17.23–37), he not only declared that the Son of man must suffer much and be rejected by this generation before his 'day' came, but in *Sauve qui peut!* language (suggesting the quick-marching Roman armies) foretold the coming clash with Rome. So he sought to alert his hearers to the gravity of the shape of things to come. Yet we should get things out of perspective if we supposed that Jesus during these three months spent all his time making prophecies of doom and disaster. 'I have a baptism to undergo', he had said. Facing him all through this time was the prospect of suffering, rejection and death. And this he met as he had done earlier in Galilee, by withdrawing from public teaching and controversy. The clamour of Jerusalem he now exchanged for the peace of Perea.

Withdrawal across Jordan (John 10.40; 11.54)

Jesus now retired across the river Jordan to the place where earlier John had baptized (John 1.28). For a brief time, in a place still echoing with the Baptist's witness, he sojourned and the crowds came to him. Later, with his disciples he moved to the country bordering on the desert and a town called Ephraim.

Why did he thus withdraw? Goguel believed it was Jesus' claim that he would destroy the temple and rebuild it in three days which brought the final rupture with the Sadducees and Pharisees and drove him from the city. Yet there is no evidence that Jesus had lost favour with the masses. On the contrary, the gospels agree that only his favour with the people (Mark 12.12; Luke 19.47f.; John 7.44; 8.20) prevented the Jerusalem authorities from arresting him. When, earlier in his Galilean ministry, he had withdrawn, his had been a flight not from his foes but from the dangerous enthusiasm of his friends. So it was now. He had been defeated not by failure but by success. What had happened after 'the Galilean Lord's supper' had happened again. The people of Jerusalem, like their Galilean counterparts, wanted a Messiah after their own hearts' dreaming. Jesus' preaching and teaching in Jerusalem—his insistence that God was now visiting his people in a supreme crisis of blessing or judgment—had either fallen on uncomprehending ears or been misconstrued. In their own cynical way, as John 11.47–53 shows, the Jewish ecclesiastics saw the issue more realistically—saw that it was a case of either the destruction of this man or the ruin of their nation. The other significant point is that, when Jesus did return to Jerusalem, he gave no more teaching. The time for this was past. A stage had been reached when 'the highest could not be spoken, but only acted', when only by giving his life as a ransom for many, could the Son of man consummate his ministry by his sacrificial death, in obedience to his Father's will.

Jesus withdrew from Jerusalem, not because he was driven out by the implacable hatred of his enemies, but because in quietness he wished to ponder the secret of his messianic suffering and death. If this is to 'theologize', is not history (as Schweitzer reminded us) moulded by theological beliefs? Though Jesus went to the cross as *viator*, not as *apprehensor*—as a traveller by faith, not as one who sees clearly the end from the beginning—we have seen how false is the idea that Jesus went to the cross with no idea of the ends his death would serve. Moreover, we cannot read the record of his last few days, after he came back to Jerusalem, without realizing that, despite the brief wavering in Gethsemane, he saw his destiny moving to its ineluctable climax, knowing that it was of his Father's ordaining. Historical reminiscence undoubtedly lies behind John 11.54. The fact that we do not know for certain where the town of Ephraim was, so far from telling against the historical value of the reference, rather favours it. (The author writing years later in Ephesus could hardly be expected to be interested in an obscure Palestinian town.) This unknown town on the fringe of the desert was probably 'the crucible of his thinking'. There his purpose finally crystallized in the decision to return to Jerusalem and (in Johannine phrase) finish the work God had given him to do.

14

THE PASSION

The events now to be related are those which began on what we call Palm Sunday and culminated in the finding of the empty tomb—that is, the prelude to the passion and the passion proper. We have three independent accounts of the passion—one in Mark, one in Luke and one in John. If they vary in details, they agree on the basic course of events. We shall follow Mark's, but reserve the right, at this point or that, to use the evidence of Luke or John to supplement, or correct, the testimony of Mark.

The entry (Mark 11.1–10; Matt. 21.1–9; Luke 19.28–44; John 12. 12–19)

At least three of the events in passion week may be called acts of prophetic symbolism or, since Jesus knew himself to be far more than a prophet, acts of Messianic symbolism. They resemble the *'ōth* of the Old Testament prophet. This was more than just an acted parable. By his action the prophet conceived of himself as entering into the divine purpose and helping it forward. His act was an 'earnest' of what would come to pass in its fullness.

Mark 11.1–6 makes it clear that Jesus' first *'ōth*, or act of Messianic symbolism, was deliberately planned. Borrowing an ass from some friend near Jerusalem, he rode the last two miles from Bethany and Bethphage, via the Mount of Olives, into the holy city, while his followers carpeted the road with their cloaks or spread brushwood[1] on the way, and they chanted 'Hosanna! (Hebrew for 'save now'.) Blessings on him who comes in the name of the Lord! Blessings on

[1] John says they carried palm branches, the emblems of victory—hence the traditional title 'the triumphal entry'. Palms do not grow in Jerusalem, but the carrying of palm-fronds was prescribed for the feast of Tabernacles, so that obviously they were obtainable, perhaps in 'the city of palms', Jericho, which was not far away.

the coming kingdom of our father David! Hosanna in the heavens!'
(Mark 11.9f. NEB. Cf. Ps. 118.2f.).

Why did Jesus ride on an ass into Jerusalem? His action was a
deliberate attempt to foil any kind of 'militantly Messianic' acclama-
tion. He was dramatizing his spiritual conception of Messiahship,
and there was nothing in what he did which the authorities could use
in evidence against him. In their accounts Matthew and John cite
Zech. 9.9, which was probably in Jesus' mind, even if (as John
says) his followers at the time did not fully take the scriptural point.
Centuries before, a seer had pictured Messiah as 'lowly and riding
on an ass' (the beast of peace as the horse was of war), adding that
'he would speak peace to the nations' and 'his dominion would be
from sea to sea and from the River to the ends of the earth'. This
prophecy Jesus now fulfilled, showing, to all the spiritually percipient at least, that he was the Messiah, but a Messiah without arms
or an army who was riding in lowly pomp that road of the spirit
marked out for the Servant of the Lord.

Since the words 'Blessed is he who comes in the name of the Lord'
were the normal welcome by priests to pilgrims arriving for the
feast, some have held that their was nothing Messianic in the accla-
mation. But the words about 'the coming kingdom of our father
David' (Mark 11.10; cf. John 12.13; 'even the king of Israel') imply
that the crowd were determined to find in Jesus a Messiah after their
own hearts' desire. A wave of enthusiasm seized them. So great was
the huzzaing as they began the descent from the Mount of Olives
that the Pharisees, fearing trouble from Rome, bade Jesus silence his
disciples. 'I tell you,' he replied, 'if these were silent the very stones
would cry out.' Were men voiceless, the very stones would cry out
that the kingdom and the Messiah were nigh (Luke 19.39f. L).

As they proceeded, the city broke full on his view. With tears
Jesus declared its coming ruin and his grief that it should be so, in
words which, though found only in Luke, ring with authenticity:
'Would that even today you knew the things that make for peace!
But now they are hid from your eyes.' And he went on to predict the
fatal coming clash with Rome and the ruin of the city because 'it
knew not God's moment when it came' (Luke 19.41–44 L, NEB).
In Jesus God's kingdom had drawn near in grace and mercy. But
Israel was rejecting the proffered mercy and walking headlong to
disaster. Such was the tragedy over which Jesus wept. 'It was the
agony of an old nation not only dying but damned; and all its vast

tragedy transpiring within the soul of one Man but (chief horror!) by the solemn choice and act of that one Man himself, and he its lover. Think of a whole nation proud, stubborn and passionate, with an ingrained belief in a world prerogative and mission, expiring in one Man, in whom also by a dreadful collision was rising the Kingdom of God they had forsworn.'[1]

When it was all over, Jesus went into the temple, noted what was happening there and retired to Bethany (or perhaps, as Luke 21.37 suggests, found a bivouac on the Mount of Olives).

The cleansing of the temple (Mark 11.15–19 par.; John 2.13–22)

What Jesus saw in the temple on the first Palm Sunday inspired his second symbolic act the following day. (If St John sets the cleansing early in Jesus' ministry, he probably does so for a doctrinal reason. His purpose is to show that the judgment, or purgation, effected by the Messiah's presence among men operated right from the beginning of his work. 'The Lord had come suddenly to his temple' and his coming was 'like a refiner's fire' (Mal. 3.1ff.). Even so, by his allusion to Ps. 69.9[2] and the reference to 'three days', St John shows himself aware that this event was linked with the passion, and his independent account of the episode helps us to understand it better.)

The scene of the cleansing was the Court of the Gentiles, the only place in the temple area assigned to the Gentiles for prayer. But what Jesus beheld was a place not of prayer but of profiteering, a holy market where animals and birds were being sold for sacrifice and pilgrims were changing their foreign coinage, no doubt at a dear rate of exchange, for the half-shekel of temple-tax which the law prescribed. In the temple of God, with the approval of the priests, behold the altar of Mammon, with all the sweltering of a dirty cattlemarket and the higgling of a dirtier money one! So Jesus swept the court clean of its holy hucksters—using a whip, John says, to drive out the animals—and stopped the porters from using it as a short-cut through the sacred precincts.

It was a very bold act when we remember that the Jews had their temple police and in the Antonia Tower north-west of the temple were Roman soldiers at the ready to quell any disturbance. Was it

[1] P. T. Forsyth, *The Expositor*, July 1915.
[2] The disciples 'reflected that it was written in scripture that the Servant of the Lord would fall a victim to his zeal for the Temple' (Dodd, *Historical Tradition in the Fourth Gospel*, p. 158).

simply the indignant gesture of a religious reformer whose soul was shocked at the desecration of holy things? Hardly, for Jesus cannot have supposed that his single act would put an end to the profanation. Next day the traders would be back. . . . Nor can it have been an attempted political *coup d'état*, with Jesus playing the role of another Judas Maccabaeus and striking the first blow for Jewish independence; for he did not follow up his act with others of the same sort. 'Do not turn my Father's house into a market,' St John reports him as saying. His act had rather the character of a religious manifesto proclaiming that the original purpose of God in ordaining worship in his house should be honoured. But if we recall how a prophecy from Zechariah had inspired the entry of the previous day, we may find in the same prophet a clue to the meaning of the cleansing. The seer had envisioned the coming age as a time when all nations would flock to Jerusalem to worship God, adding that on that day 'there would no longer be a trader in the house of the Lord of hosts' (Zech. 14.21). That prophecy Jesus now enacted in drastic symbol, showing, to those who had eyes to see and ears to hear, that the day of the Lord and his Messiah were now upon them.

According to Mark, Jesus accused the traders and their priestly patrons of turning the place God had intended as 'a house of prayer for all nations' (Isa. 56.7) into 'a robbers' den' (Jer. 7.11), that is, the stronghold of a powerful and ruthless faction. Now it was part of the popular messianic hope (see *The Psalms of Solomon*, ch. xvii) that 'great David's greater Son', when he came, would clear the Gentiles bag and baggage out of holy city and temple. Yet here was Jesus doing precisely the opposite. Instead of purging the temple from the Gentiles, he was actually clearing a space for them in it, and asserting their divine right to be there.

According to John, when Jesus was challenged by the authorities to justify his act, he replied, 'Destroy this sanctuary, and in three days I will raise it up.' That Jesus did utter some such saying is unquestionable (see Mark 14.58; 15.29). What did he mean by it? When we recall that Jesus knew himself called to create a new people of God, the words become a veiled forecast that out of the corruption of old Israel would arise a new one in which Gentile as well as Jew would have his place. His act in the Court of the Gentiles was picture and pledge of what would come to pass, but, as the 'three days' imply (reminding us of the passion prophecies), only through his own death and victory could it be accomplished. The cleansing therefore was a link in that chain of events which took Jesus to the cross and issued in the rise of the new people of God. Meanwhile, Jesus' act was a serious challenge to the Jewish authorities, for it threatened not only their prestige and their pockets but their whole future. As quickly and as quietly as possible he must be removed from the scene.

The betrayal and an anointing (Mark 14.1–11; Matt. 26.1–16; Luke 22.1–6; John 12.1–8)

'Now the festival of Passover and Unleavened Bread was only two days off.' With Mark 14.1 we come to the passion proper and the last Wednesday of Jesus' earthly life. According to Mark, in the events of this day the leading roles were played by an unnamed woman and Judas. But Mark has hardly begun to tell of the priests' plot to kill Jesus when he inserts the story of Jesus' anointing in Bethany. Of this we have an independent account in John, who dates it 'six days before the Passover' and names the woman as Mary sister of Martha. Since Mark's narrative is an insertion, John's dating may be right, and conceivably the woman was Mary of Bethany. (Is it possible that Simon the (cured) leper, in whose house the anointing took place (Mark 14.3), was the father of Lazarus and his two sisters?)

While Jesus was at a meal in the Bethany house, the woman broke a valuable flask of perfumed oil and poured the contents over his head (Mark 14.3; cf. John 12.3). When the disciples (though John says it was Judas) demurred at the waste, Jesus sprang to the woman's defence and pronounced hers 'a beautiful deed'. Clearly the woman was showing her personal devotion to Jesus. But can we read her mind further? Jesus himself said she had anointed his body in advance for the burial. Was he thinking of that criminal's death, without anointing, which now seemed his certain fate, and declaring that, wittingly or unwittingly, the woman had decided that he should not die without the last customary token of respect to his corpse? Or is it possible that the woman (if indeed it was Mary) had really seen into the secret of the Servant Messiah who must die, and by her action was affirming her faith in him and his purpose?

How to get rid of Jesus without causing a riot at the Passover had been the priests' problem when, like some *diabolus ex machina*, appeared one of the man's own disciples with the solution. No wonder they promised Judas that he would not go unrewarded.

'Then Judas Iscariot, one of the Twelve . . .'—in that phrase the enormity of his act is epitomized; but the 'why' and the 'what' of his act are not so easy to explain.

About the 'why' the evangelists have two theories. One is diabolical agency, the other avarice; and if 'the love of money is the root of all evil', perhaps they are not unconnected. De Quincey conjectured that Judas thought Jesus too unworldly and wished by his act to force Jesus into a position where he would be compelled to display his supernatural power, yet with no thought that he would allow himself to be executed. George Eliot evidently thought this another of the Opium-eater's dreams. 'I refuse,' she said, 'to accept a man who has the stomach for such treachery as a hero impatient for the redemption of mankind.' We may agree. Likelier is it that Judas' act was born of disillusionment. Jesus' conception of Messiahship bitterly disappointed him, and sensing the peril in which Jesus and his men now stood, he grasped the last chance of extricating himself from the *débacle*—as well as the chance of making some money—by 'turning king's evidence'.

What did Judas betray to the priests? We cannot rule out Schweitzer's suggestions that it was the Messianic secret and the fact that he had been secretly anointed in Bethany. If the story of the anointing had leaked out, even in garbled form, we have reason enough for the decision of the authorities to compass his death. Yet this does not exclude the old answer that what Judas told the priests was where and when Jesus could be quietly arrested.

The name of Judas has become a byword for treachery. If the evangelists are content to call him the devil's tool and a lover of money, at the last supper Jesus himself, while knowing he was divinely appointed to die, declared that this necessity in no way absolved the man who chose freely to betray him. Better for him, he said, if he had never been born (Mark 14.21). Here we come face to face with a problem which, lacking omniscience, we cannot solve. Side by side are set the factors of divine sovereignty and human responsibility in a way which simply states the mystery of their juxtaposition and affirms the reality of both.

The last supper (Mark 14.12-31; Matt. 26.17-35; Luke 22.7-38; John 13-17)

After sunset, on the Thursday of what we call Holy Week, Jesus held the last supper with the Twelve. Earlier he had made careful plans in order to ensure secrecy. The two disciples sent ahead to execute them were bidden to follow a man bearing a pitcher of water (an unusual sight in a land where women normally carry the water) and on reaching the house to say to its owner, 'The master says, Where is the room reserved for me to eat the Passover with my disciples?' Thereupon they would be shown 'a large room upstairs, set in readiness' and could prepare accordingly.

From this account of Mark's we should infer that Jesus kept the Passover on its official date, viz. Nisan 15 (the day of the Spring full moon). But later details in his narrative of what followed the supper on Nisan 15 (which began at sunset and did not end till sundown next day) consist very ill with this. Thus it is very strange to find the disciples and the arresting posse carrying arms on a holy day; and it is hard to explain how on the following day, without violation of the Jewish law, there could be trials, flogging, men coming in from the fields, a crucifixion, etc.

On the other hand, John states clearly that when Jesus appeared before Pilate the Passover had not yet been celebrated. 'The Jews,' he says, 'stayed outside headquarters (Pilate's, probably in the Antonia Tower) to avoid defilement, so that they could eat the Passover meal' (John 18.28; cf. 19.14).

There is thus a conflict between Mark and John about the date of the supper. Attempts to reconcile them, like that of Mlle Jaubert,[1] have not succeeded. Compelled to choose, we conclude that on this matter of date John is right.

Yet not in Mark alone but in John also the last supper has Passover features, one of the clearest being the dipping of the sop in the dish. Accordingly, the most satisfactory solution of this ancient problem seems to be that of an anticipated Passover. If this is so, why did Jesus anticipate the official date? Whether or not he had learned of Judas' bargain with the priests, the unexpectedly swift march of events compelled him to hold the supper before the official day, and he was dead before orthodox Jews assembled to keep the feast. Was it Jesus' prescience of all this which made him plan to hold the supper in secrecy?

---

[1] In *Le Date de la Cène*, Paris 1957, she argued that Jesus held the supper on the date for Passover in the old solar calendar used, for example, by the Essenes of Qumran. But Jesus was not an Essene, and Mlle Jaubert's arguments have not convinced the experts.

According to John, during the supper—and perhaps because of a dispute among the disciples about precedence at table (cf. Luke 22.24f. L)–Jesus laid aside his garments and taking water and a towel washed the disciples' feet. An echo of that incident seems to be preserved in Luke 22.37, 'Here am I among you like a servant', and we need not doubt that in the upper room Jesus performed some such action. If it was a lesson in humility, the footwashing was some-thing more. When Peter demurred at Jesus' action, 'You, Lord, washing my feet?', Jesus replied, 'If I do not wash you, you are not in fellowship with me'. Thus his symbolic act foreshadowed the cross, hinting that there could be no place in his fellowship for those unwilling to be cleansed by his atoning death.

So we come to the high point in the last supper.

The liturgy of the Passover looked both back to the Exodus from Egypt and forward to the eschatological Exodus of which the Egyp-tian deliverance was a type. 'On this night they were saved,' said the Jewish proverb, 'and on this night they will be saved.' When there-fore Jesus met with the Twelve to keep the Passover, the thought of the new and greater Exodus (cf. Luke 9.31) must have formed a background to what was said and done.

The usual 'order of service' at a Passover meal was this. First, an inaugural blessing and prayer was followed by a dish of herbs, and the first of four cups of wine were drunk. Next, the story of the first Passover was recounted. Thirdly, after a grace they ate the main course of roast Passover lamb with unleavened bread and bitter herbs and drank a third cup of wine. Finally, Psalms 114–118 were sung, and the fourth cup of wine drunk.

It was probably during 'the main course' that Jesus gave the bread and wine the new meaning which transformed the Jewish Passover into the Christian Lord's supper. Breaking the bread he handed it to the disciples with the words: 'Take, this is (represents) my body (myself).' By this symbolic act he was likening himself to the Passover lamb offered in sacrifice. (In Paul's tradition the words were, 'This is my body which is for you', I Cor. 11.24; cf. I Cor. 5.7: 'Our Passover has begun; the sacrifice is offered, Christ himself' NEB.)

Even more explicit were the words with which he handed the Passover cup, with the red wine gleaming in it, to the disciples: 'This is my blood of the covenant (Exod. 24.8) which is poured out for many' (Isa. 53.11f.). (Paul's tradition gives the words as, 'This cup is the new covenant in my blood.')[1] His sacrificial death, thus symbolically prophesied, Jesus believed to be fraught with atoning power (Mark 10.45), as his 'blood' would seal God's new covenant with his people and avail 'for many'.

By setting apart the bread and the wine, Jesus was offering his disciples (and those who should afterwards believe in him) a pledge of life in the kingdom of God soon to come 'with power' through his death. By describing the broken bread and the outpoured wine as his 'body' and 'blood', he was effecting, in moving symbol, that sacrifice of himself soon to be accomplished in fact. And by inviting the Twelve to partake of the bread and wine (so interpreted) he was making over to them that sacrifice of himself which he was making once for all to God—giving them a share in the power of the broken Christ. Finally, with a vow (Mark 14.25) Jesus declared that he would never again drink wine till he drank the 'new' (*kainon*) wine of the consummated kingdom of God. (Compare Paul's comment in I Cor. 11.26: 'For as often as you eat this bread and drink this cup, you proclaim the Lord's death until he comes.')

The story of the last supper has been well called a window into the mind of Jesus as he faced death. So far from regarding it as a judicial murder, he saw it as a means whereby a new order of relations between God and man would be established. Like Isaiah's Servant of the Lord, in obedience to his Father's will, he would 'pour out his life for the many' (i.e. for all), and 'by his stripes they would be healed'.

After the supper followed farewell discourse with his disciples. Though what is recorded in John 13–17 comes to us across the soul of the Fourth Evangelist, John is probably reaching back to early tradition which he magnificently interprets for his readers. Fragments of Jesus' table-talk after supper also survive in Luke 22.24–38 L: the saying about service, the promise to the Twelve of rule in the New Israel soon to arise, the prediction of Peter's denial and his 'conversion' to 'strengthen his brethren', and a warning to all that they were going out into a world where everyman's hand would be against them. 'Sell your coats and buy a sword', said Jesus. Taking him *au pied de la lettre*, they forthwith produced two weapons. 'Enough, enough!' he replied, rather sadly foreclosing the

---

[1] The Lucan text (Luke 22.19f.) poses problems on which there is no general agreement. Some prefer the shorter text which omits 19b and 20; others the longer text which resembles Paul's account of I Cor. 11.23f.

discussion. This was the world's way; for himself there could be only
one end to his ministry, that mapped out for the Servant of the
Lord (Luke 22.37 L).

The agony and the arrest (Mark 14.32–52; Matt. 26.36–56; Luke 22.
39–53; John 18.1–11)

After the supper Jesus and his disciples left the upper room and
crossed 'the Kedron ravine' (John 18.1) to the Mount of Olives. On
the way he lingered to pray in an olive grove. Leaving eight disciples
on its fringe, he took with him Peter, James and John to share his
vigil, 'seeking comfort,' as Luther put it, 'from his disciples whom
previously he had comforted'; for a deadly desolation had fallen on
his spirit. 'Horror and dismay came over him', Mark tells us, as he
said to them in words which echo Ps. 42.5; 43.5, 'My heart is ready
to break with grief; stop here and stay awake' (NEB). What caused
this horror and dismay? 'For the hurt of my people I am hurt' the
prophet had said (Jer. 8.21). Was Jesus again feeling the whole
tragedy of his own people so that the burden of their coming doom
almost broke his heart? Or did he now feel himself exposed to the
final assault of the powers of evil with whom he had wrestled from
the outset of his ministry (cf. Luke 22.53 L: 'This is your hour, and
the power of darkness')?

Advancing a few paces (yet not so far that the three could not
catch the drift of his prayer) and throwing himself on the ground, he
besought God that, if it might be, the hour might never come to him.
'*Abba*, Father, all things are possible to thee; take this cup away
from me. Yet not what I will, but what thou wilt.' The cup was the
cup of God's judgment on human sin which he must drink on sinners'
behalf, as it was the old temptation—Messiahship without a cross—
which now met him with redoubled force. But he had scarcely
prayed for the cup's removal when he was setting it to his lips,
embracing his Father's will. Twice the experience was repeated, as
if to underline the intensity of it. Hardly was the agony of his prayer
over when the silence was broken by the sound of the approaching
posse—a company armed with swords and clubs sent by the chief
priests and backed, John says; John 18.12), by a detachment of
Roman soldiers. 'Up, let us go forward,' said Jesus to his drowsy disciples, 'My betrayer is upon us.' With this came the posse guided to

the spot by Judas who identified his master with a kiss. After a futile attempt at resistance, in which, John says (John 18.10; cf. Luke 22.50f.), Peter cut off the ear of the high priest's servant Malchus, 'the disciples all deserted him and ran away'. Sharing their flight (Mark 14.51f.) was 'a young man with nothing on him but a linen cloth' which he slipped off in order to escape. It may have been Mark himself.

The trial (Mark 14.53–15.20; Matt. 26.57–27.31; Luke 22.54–23.25; John 18.12–19.16)

The trial falls into two parts: the Jewish trial before the Sanhedrin, and the Roman trial before Pilate (probably in the Antonia fortress).

Was it a fair trial? Reading the records, we gain the impression that the whole affair was rushed through with unholy haste, the Jewish authorities trying to give a show of legality to a course of action which would issue in a verdict on which they had already decided. Nor can the proceedings before Pilate be called a proper trial. What they amount to is a few false or garbled charges, a question from Pilate about Jesus' claim to kingship, the rising temper of the mob whipped up by the priests, a perplexed governor trying to act with some semblance of justice and at last weakly capitulating to the crowd's clamour for crucifixion.

In reconstructing what happened we may virtually ignore Matthew and supplement Mark's record from the special traditions preserved in Luke and John.

The probable sequence of events seems to have been this:

(a) *The Jewish trial: on the charge of blasphemy*

1. After arrest Jesus was at once informally examined in the high priest's house by Annas, father-in-law of Caiaphas, and was abused by the police who held him.

2. At daybreak there was a formal meeting of the Sanhedrin at which Caiaphas, the reigning high priest, elicited from Jesus a confession of Messiahship plus some words which, all agreed, amounted to blasphemy and were therefore worthy of death.

But the Sanhedrin had no power to inflict a capital sentence (cf. John 18.31: 'It is not lawful for us to put anyone to death.' The truth of this has been disputed, but the evidence we have from other sources seems to support John[1]). On the other hand, like Gallio (Acts 18.14–17), Pilate would certainly not listen to a charge of 'blasphemy'. So there followed:

(b) *The Roman trial: on the charge of high treason*

Before Pilate who, though he got a qualified claim to kingship from Jesus, was loth to condemn one he really thought innocent. Seeking to save Jesus by the use of a Passover custom, he found that the people, instigated by the priests, preferred the 'bandit' Barabbas, and finally yielding to their wishes, he handed Jesus over to be crucified.[2]

This outline assumes that St John rightly relates an informal examination of Jesus by Annas (i.e. something resembling police investigation of a newly-arrested criminal before the trial begins) and that Luke correctly says that the Sanhedrin met formally at day-break. (Nocturnal sessions were illegal.)

The Jewish trial was really a preliminary investigation to decide what charge the priests would later prefer against Jesus in the Roman court. If their plan were to succeed, they had not only to discredit Jesus in Jewish eyes by showing him guilty of a grave *religious* offence, but also to get him found guilty by the Roman court as a dangerous *political* trouble-maker.

Jesus was brought first before Annas who, though the ex-high priest, was still very much 'the power behind the throne'. Annas asked him about his disciples and his teaching (John 18.13–23). (Doubtless this information came from the disciple who was a 'familiar friend' of the high priest and had gained entry to his house.)

Meanwhile the Sanhedrin were being hurriedly summoned, and at dawn they met in formal assembly. Various charges were brought against the prisoner including his reported threat to 'destroy the temple', but when his accusers could make none or them stand (or, as we say, 'stick'), Caiaphas asked bluntly, 'Are you the Messiah?' 'I am,' replied Jesus[3] (Mark 14.62), adding, 'And you will see the

---

[1] For a summary see R. E. Brown, *The Gospel according to John*, Geoffrey Chapman 1971, pp. 849f. and A. N. Sherwin-White, *Roman Law and Roman Society in the New Testament*, Oxford University Press 1963, pp. 36f.

[2] Luke's story of Pilate's referral of Jesus' case to Herod Antipas is dubiously historical (Luke 23.6–12 L). 1. It occurs only in Luke. 2. If the crucifixion occurred at 9 a.m., there was scarcely time for it. 3. Possibly the story was inspired by Ps. 2.2 which, in Acts 4.25ff., is applied to Herod and Pilate.

[3] As we have seen in the discussion of Jesus' Messiahship, his reply, according to Matt. 26.64 and Luke 22.67, amounted to 'Have it so, if you choose'.

Son of man sitting at the right hand of Power and coming with the clouds of heaven.'

The added words echo Ps. 110.1 and Dan. 7.13 and express (as we have seen) Jesus' conviction that, despite the apparent ruin of his cause, he would yet be vindicated and exalted to 'the highest place that heaven affords'. This the high priest construed as blasphemy, a view with which his colleagues agreed, because it was a claim to share the throne of God. And blasphemy was punishable with death. But the high priest's questioning had also drawn from Jesus the admission that, in some sense, he was the Messiah. This was what Caiaphas sought, for 'Messiah' could easily be translated, for Roman ears, into 'King of the Jews' when the Sanhedrin came to put their case to Pilate.

The terms of the charge made by the Jews before the governor are probably best preserved by Luke: 'We found this man subverting our nation, opposing the payment of taxes to Caesar, and claiming to be Messiah, a king' (Luke 23.2 L NEB). This threefold charge was a deliberate and malicious inversion of the truth. When Jesus did not answer, Pilate asked him point-blank, 'Are you the King of the Jews?' To this question, as all the evangelists agree, Jesus gave a non-committal reply, 'You say so', i.e. the words are yours.

When Jesus refused to say more, Pilate would probably have been glad to wash his hands of the whole affair, as Matt. 27.24–26 M says he literally did. From bitter experience he knew how easy it was to fall foul of these intractable Jews. But if the priests stuck to their charge, he had no alternative but to proceed with it. Then an idea occurred to him. At the Passover season it was the governor's custom (a custom attested in a first-century papyrus from Egypt) to release a prisoner chosen by the people. At that time there were in custody three 'bandits' who had committed murder in a recent uprising, including the ringleader, who bore the name of Barabbas ('son of the father' or, to give him his full name, 'Jesus Barabbas': see Matt. 27.16ff. NEB). Supposing Jesus to be a popular figure with the crowds, Pilate therefore suggested: 'Would you like me to release to you the King of the Jews?' But he had quite miscalculated the temper of the crowd. 'Not this man,' they shouted, 'Barabbas!' While the governor still hesitated, the Jews, according to John 19.12, played their trump card: 'If you let this man go, you are no friend to Caesar.' So Pilate, fearing for his own future, let this travesty of a trial take its course. Technically, Jesus had made a treasonable claim which he had not retracted when given the chance. Besides, the sacrifice of one provincial was a cheap price to pay for preserving the *Pax Romana*. To placate the people, Pilate therefore released Barabbas and condemned Jesus to crucifixion.

How do we explain the *volte face* in the crowd's attitude? Why did the hosannas turn to howls for his death? Mark says that the priests incited the crowd. Doubtless they did, but there is more to it than this. Jesus had refused to play the Messianic role they had cast for him. There is no fury like that of a mob whose dearest wishes have been rudely disappointed. This was why they now cried, 'Away with him! Crucify him!'

The crucifixion (Mark 15.21–47; Matt. 27.32–66; Luke 23.26–56; John 19.17–42)

'Every malefactor,' wrote Plutarch, 'carries his own cross' or, rather, the cross-bar (*patibulum*) to which the condemned man was fastened with nails, or ropes, before being lifted on to an upright post. So Jesus set out for the place of execution with the cross-bar on his back (John 19.17); but, when he sank under its weight, the Romans commandeered a man 'coming from the country' to carry it for him. Mark calls him 'Simon of Cyrene, the father of Alexander and Rufus'. Here is a piece of authentic personal reminiscence. (Compare Mark 15.21 with Rom. 16.13. Alexander and Rufus must have been known to Mark's readers in Rome: otherwise their naming is pointless.)

As he made his way to Calvary (the Vulgate Latin for Golgotha) the women of Jerusalem set up a death-wail for Jesus (Luke 23.27–31 L). His response to their keening shows how deeply the fate of Jerusalem was in his mind. 'Weep not for me,' he said, 'but weep for yourselves and your children.' Grim days lay in store for their city and themselves. 'If these things are done when the wood is green,' he said, 'what will happen when it is dry?' (NEB). Old Testament prophets had likened a nation's man-power to a forest consumed by the fire of God's judgment. Now Israel has kindled the flame of Rome's fury, and if it is fierce enough to consume one whom Rome has declared innocent, what must be the fate of the guilty in the coming days!

Golgotha was a low eminence outside the city wall (either 'Gordon's Calvary' 250 yards NE of the Damascus Gate or, perhaps more likely, the present site of the Church of the Holy Sepulchre). Before crucifixion Jesus was offered drugged wine—a merciful ano- dyne provided by charitable women in Jerusalem. He refused it, possibly because he wished to die with his senses undulled, probably because he had sworn to drink no more wine this side of eternity. At 'the third hour', i.e. 9 a.m., he was lifted up on the cross between the two malefactors to one of whom, in his penitence, Jesus promised, 'Today you will be with me in paradise' (Luke 23.43 L).

A crucified man's clothes were the perquisites of his executioners who, on this occasion, formed a quaternion (John 19.23). If their gambling for his garments recalled to the evangelist Ps. 22—'the Psalm of the Righteous Sufferer', which was a famous early Christian 'testimony', or Messianic proof-text—the incident probably inspired the scripture, not the reverse. On the other hand, the taunts of the chief priests, phrased also in words from the same psalm, may be dramatization rather than history. Yet it is altogether credible that bystanders should have taunted him with his saying about destroying the temple.

The inscription which Pilate had affixed on a chalked board (*titulus*) above Jesus' cross bore the words, 'The King of the Jews'. That it was trilingual—in Hebrew, Latin and Greek (John 19.20)— need not be doubted: polyglot notices in Palestine must have been as common then as they now are on continental railways. St John adds that the Jews demurred at its wording; and the governor's 'What I have written I have written' (John 19.22) suggests the final obstinacy of a weak man who has given way on the main issue.

The strange darkness which descended on the scene at noon was probably due to a sirocco wind laden with thick dust from the desert. (Those of us who live in northern climes know how a 'haar' or 'sea fret' can suddenly mar the brightness of a summer day.) But what are we to make of the statement in Mark 15.38 that, when Jesus died, the temple curtain which separated the holy place from the holy of holies was torn in two? Did it really happen so, or is this Mark's version of what is said in Heb. 10.19f., that by his death Jesus has opened up a way for sinful men into the very presence of God?

'Seven times he spoke.' Three of the words from the cross are peculiar to Luke; three to John. In Mark we have only the cry of dereliction—that cry that runs out into ineffable mystery but is beyond any doubt authentic. The suggestion that, because the words come from Ps. 22.1, it is a cry of faith, beggars belief. Were it so, how odd that Jesus should have chosen the verse least suited to his purpose! If we are to take the cry seriously, we must hear in it 'a *cri de coeur* as the burden of the world's sin which he was carrying walled him off from God for the time of his Passion'.[1] Yet 'never was an utterance that reveals more amazingly the difference between feeling and fact'.[1] The prayer, 'Father, forgive them, for they know not what they are doing' (Luke 23.34), though omitted by some good MSS, is also probably genuine. According to John 19.23, Jesus' last word from the cross was, 'It is finished' (*tetelestai*). Whether this was an actual word of Jesus or not, it has 'the mind of Christ'. He had finished the work his Father had given him to do; he had fulfilled, even unto death, his vocation as the Servant of the Lord.

At 'three in the afternoon' on Friday, Nisan 14, in the year AD 30, Jesus died. 'Truly this man was a son of God,' said the centurion standing by (Mark 15.39), whom tradition names Longinus. He may have meant no more than 'This was a righteous man'. But Mark himself must have read into his words the deepest secret of Jesus' person, that Sonhood which was the mainspring of his life. The last glimpse we get (Mark 15.40) is of a pathetic little group of women 'watching from a distance'. Their loyalty put the Twelve to shame.

Jewish law (Lev. 21.23) ordained that the bodies of executed criminals should be buried the same day, and the task was the more urgent now because in a very few hours the Sabbath would begin. So Joseph of Arimathea, a member of the Sanhedrin and possibly a secret disciple of Jesus, gained Pilate's permission to remove Jesus' body from the cross. Shrouding it (helped, says St John, by Nicodemus), he laid it in a new tomb (Luke 23.53; John 19.41). The curtain seemed to have fallen on unrelieved tragedy . . .

[1] H. E. W. Turner, *Jesus Master and Lord*, Mowbray 1953, p. 210.
[1] T. R. Glover, *The Jesus of History*, Student Christian Movement 1917, p. 192.

15

THE RESURRECTION

'The Resurrection is the land where the great mists lie,' said David S. Cairns, 'but it is also the land where the great rivers spring.' Mystery surrounds events between the crucifixion and the first Easter day: no human eye saw Christ rise. Yet it was the invincible conviction of the men of the New Testament that God raised Jesus from the dead; and out of that conviction was born the greatest society on earth. Is the message of the resurrection history's most influential error or its most tremendous fact? This is the issue.

To begin with, it is not open to dispute that Jesus predicted triumph for himself and his cause. Not only did Isaiah foretell resurrection for the Servant of the Lord:

He shall see his offspring, he shall prolong his days;
The will of the Lord shall prosper in his hand (Isa. 53.10),

but the gospels testify that Jesus, who knew himself to be that Servant, foresaw beyond death victory and life. This conviction he expressed variously. Besides his 'formal' predictions of resurrection 'after three days' (Mark 8.31; 9.31; 10.34), he speaks of 'the day of the Son of man' (Luke 17.26ff.; Matt. 24.27ff.) and of his 'coming with the clouds of heaven', i.e. his enthronement (Mark 14.62) and predicts that the kingdom of God will come 'with power' (Mark 9.1) and a new Israel will arise (Mark 14.58; John 2.18f.). Conceivably these various images describe the same event, a coming of the reign of God defying exact description. But the main thing is clear enough: Jesus expected himself and his cause to be gloriously vindicated. Was he right? Did the kingdom come with power? Did God raise his Son from the dead?

The evidence of faith

It has often been said, with truth, that the primary evidence for the resurrection is the existence of the Christian church. How did the frightened followers of a crucified 'Messianic Pretender' become the nucleus of a militant church, a church which, through countless vicissitudes, has now endured for nineteen centuries? The New Testament attributes this astonishing change in Jesus' disciples to their conviction that God had taken their Master out of the grave and that they had seen him alive and talked with him after he had risen. They may of course, one and all, have been mistaken, the pitiable victims of a mass hallucination. But it must be said that if 'probability is the guide of life', the probabilities are on their side. For besides the existence of the Christian church we may set, secondly, the institution of the Lord's day (Rev. 1.10; Acts 20.7; I Cor. 16.2). Why did the early Christians, who were mostly Jews, change their sacred day (as we would say) from Saturday to Sunday? They did so because it was on that day they believed Jesus had risen from the dead; and we may add that every Sunday, as it comes round, is a new argument for the resurrection. Thirdly, we have to reckon with the New Testament documents themselves. Belief in the risen Christ fills the pages of the New Testament. Certain it is that every book in it—even the Epistle of James which never mentions it, though it implies it—is a resurrection document in the sense that but for belief in the risen Christ it would never have been written.

This whole argument has been memorably summarized thus:[1]

'We live in a real world, not in a fairy tale, and in the real world you can argue back from effects to causes. Water does not rise above the level of its own source; when a tidal wave strikes the shore, we can guess at the power of the disturbance that started it on its course. We do this because the real world is a rational order in which great effects require the existence of commensurate causes. Now the Church and the New Testament rest absolutely and entirely on the Resurrection of Jesus. If there had not been men who could say "We have seen the Lord", and whose lives had been transformed thereby, it is certain that the Christian way of life and the Christian Church would never have existed. What kind of event brought them into existence? What kind of upheaval started that tidal wave?'

There are therefore three great witnesses to the truth of the resurrection—the church, the Lord's day and the New Testament. In other words, belief in the resurrection does not primarily depend on

[1] Sir T. M. Taylor, *Where one man stands*, St. Andrew Press 1960, pp. 66ff.

the verdict we pass on this or that story of the risen Christ recorded in the gospels. Yet the documentary evidence is important, and we must study it before we consider the significance of the event to which it testifies.

The evidence of the documents

The earliest documentary evidence occurs not in the gospels but in I Cor. 15.3ff. There Paul cites a piece of Christian 'tradition' which he had 'received' probably from the apostles during his first visit to Jerusalem after he had become a Christian. (See Gal. 1.18f. describing 'the fortnight's visit'. Since in I Cor. 15.3ff. Paul mentions by name only two apostles, Peter and James, and since these are precisely the two he says he saw during that visit to Jerusalem, we may surmise that he got his 'tradition' from them. Confirmatory of this is the fact that the Greek of the 'tradition' is full of 'Semitisms', that is, Hebrew or Aramaic idioms glimmering through the Greek.)[1]

The 'tradition' therefore goes back to within a very few years of the resurrection, and was rightly pronounced by the great German historian Eduard Meyer (himself a thorough-going 'rationalist') 'the oldest document of the Christian church we possess'.[2] Independent of the gospels, it reads like a guaranteed statement of the sources of evidence used by the first preachers of the gospel:

'For I delivered to you as of first importance what I also received, that Christ died for our sins in accordance with the scriptures, that he was buried, that he was raised on the third day in accordance with the scriptures, and that he appeared to Cephas, then to the twelve. Then he appeared to more than five hundred brethren at one time, most of who are still alive, though some have fallen asleep. Then he appeared to James, then to all the apostles. Last of all, as to one untimely born, he appeared also to me.'

We may note that it implies belief in the empty tomb—'Died, buried, raised', the words are unintelligible unless they mean that what was buried was raised—and that it records six appearances of the risen Christ (to Peter, the Twelve, five hundred brethren, James, all the apostles, Paul himself). Two of these appearances—those to James and the 'five hundred brethren'—are not recorded in the

---

[1] See J. Jeremias, *The Eucharistic Words of Jesus*, SCM Press [2] 1966, pp. 101-3.
[2] *Ursprung und Anfänge des Christentums*, Stuttgart and Berlin 1921-3, I, p. 210.

gospels. The parenthesis in v. 6—'most of whom are still alive, though some have fallen asleep'—though probably no part of the tradition, is interesting; for it is Paul's way of saying to doubters in Corinth, 'Most of the witnesses are still alive to be questioned'. Let there then be no mistake about the value of this 'tradition'. 'It fulfils all the requirements of historical reliability,' says an eminent historian.[1] 'Anyone who doubts it might just as well doubt everything that the new Testament contains—and more.'

To this piece of 'tradition' we may add the references to the resurrection (of which perhaps the most striking is that in Acts 10.40–42) contained in the Jewish-Christian *kērygma* of the early chapters in Acts. These are important because in various ways they seem to rest back on early tradition.

We may now turn to the gospels. Many people have an uneasy feeling that the stories about the risen Christ in the gospels, being somehow different from the stories about Jesus' earthly ministry, are less worthy of credence. A 'form-critical' study of them[2] shows, however, that they are no different from the other stories, that they can be similarly classified, and that therefore they merit the same consideration, not only as testimonies to the faith of the first Christians but as records of things that actually happened.

We may now summarize them.

Mark 16.1–8 tells how, on the first Easter morning, the women found the tomb empty, how a 'young man' told them that Jesus was risen, and how they fled in 'numinous' fear. Though the end of Mark has probably been lost (for we find it incredible that the evangelist's last words were, 'for they were afraid'), enough survives to show what the climax of the story was—an empty tomb.

Matthew 28.1–20, after describing the empty tomb, records an appearance of the risen Lord to the women and an appearance to eleven disciples on a mountain in Galilee where, after giving them their 'marching orders', Jesus promises them his abiding presence to the end of time. (Peculiar to Matthew are the references to the guard at the tomb, the descending angel and the earthquake.)

Luke 24.1–53 tells how the women, after finding the tomb empty, brought the news to the incredulous Eleven. He then records three appearances of the risen Lord: to Cleopas and another on the road

[1] H. von Campenhausen, *Tradition and Life in the Church*, Collins 1968, pp. 44f.
[1] C. H. Dodd, in *Studies in the Gospels*, ed. D. E. Nineham, Blackwell 1955, pp. 9–35.

to Emmaus, to Peter (Luke 24.34), and to the Eleven and others in Jerusalem before Jesus led them out 'as far as Bethany' and 'parted from them'. (The words in Luke 24.51, 'and was carried up to heaven', are probably a later insertion.)

John 20–21 tells how Mary Magdalene found the tomb empty, and how Peter and the Beloved Disciple (John?) visited it to verify her news. He then records four appearances: to Mary in the garden, to ten disciples the same day behind closed doors in Jerusalem, to the same ten plus Thomas in the same place a week later, and to seven disciples in the grey of a Galilean dawn.

How shall we evaluate these narratives? In Matthew we find some embroidering of the miraculous (Matt. 28.2–4) and in Luke what some think is a tendency to materialize (Luke 24.42f.; cf. Luke 3.22). But, if we take them as a whole, they are not only notably free of apocalyptic features but, for the most part, vivid, lifelike and self-authenticating. Different men find different stories more convincing and self-authenticating. For Ruskin[1] it was John's story of Christ by the Lake of Galilee which he found 'pre-eminently open, natural, full fronting our disbelief'. For Malcolm Muggeridge[2] it is the story of the walk to Emmaus: 'There is something in the very language and manner of it which breathes truth.' For the historian Campenhausen[3] it is Mark's story of the finding of the empty tomb which is most impressive: 'It does not give the least impression of the marvellous or fantastic or of being in any way incredible.' For Dodd,[4] the New Testament scholar, it is the 'Rabboni' story which strikes him 'as indefinably first-hand'. 'There is nothing quite like it in the Gospels. Is there anything quite like it in ancient literature?'

That all these narratives cannot be woven into a single consistent harmony hardly needs saying. For example, we cannot be sure when and where Jesus first appeared. Was it to the women (Matthew and John)? Or was it to Peter, as I Cor. 15.5 and Luke 24.34 imply? Again, Matthew and John locate the appearances in both Jerusalem and Galilee, Luke in Jerusalem only. But these uncertainties and inconsistencies, so far from discrediting the stories, show that no harmonizing instinct has been busy on them, no attempt made to fabricate or tell an agreed story. Besides, as every student of history

[1] *Modern Painters*, iii, ch. iv.
[2] *Another King*, St. Andrew Press 1968, p. 14.
[3] Op. cit., pp. 59, 75.
[4] Op. cit., p. 20.

knows, discrepancies in several accounts of an event are far from proving that an event did not occur. Thus, to take one example, there are startling discrepancies in the accounts of Waterloo as given by Wellington, Marshal Ney and Napoleon. Yet no one dreams of denying that a great battle was fought there in 1815. (Lessing, the German 'rationalist', once pleaded for justice in handling the gospels. If, he said, Livy, Polybius, Dionysius and Tacitus describe the same event in discrepant ways, we do not deny that the event occurred. Why should we treat the four evangelists differently?)

On what then do our accounts of the resurrection agree? On two things:

1.   That the tomb was empty. The pre-Pauline tradition of I Cor. 15.3ff. implies this. So does the preaching of the apostles (Acts 2.31; 13.29f.). The four evangelists declare it. The silence of the Jews confirms it.

2.   That the resurrection occurred 'on the third day', and that Jesus appeared to many of his followers, both men and women, on this and succeeding days.

If we are faithful to the evidence, we must start from the fact of the empty tomb, which is not a later embellishment. The theory that the body of Jesus was stolen or hidden is frankly incredible. Had the Romans or the Jews removed it secretly, it would have been easy to refute the Christians' claim by producing it. We may be sure that they did not because they could not. Equally incredible is the suggestion that the disciples hid their Master's body and then went forth to declare that he had risen from the dead. Even a Jew like Klausner admits this: 'The nineteen-hundred years' faith is not founded on deception.'[1]

If then we accept the empty tomb, one of two explanations is open to us. Either we say that Jesus was resuscitated from the grave in his former body—in which case we must face the problem of what eventually happened to it after 'the forty days' (Acts 1.3)[2] or we may agree with a long line of Christians from the apostle Paul to Bishop

---

[1] *Jesus of Nazareth*, Allen and Unwin 1925, p. 359.
[2] In the New Testament, only in Luke–Acts does the Ascension figure as a separate event. The earliest Christians evidently believed the risen Lord was already in heaven before he appeared. For them resurrection and exaltation were one event, so that sometimes, as in Phil. 2.6–11, only the exaltation is mentioned and the resurrection is quietly assumed. See U. Wilckens, *Auferstehung*, Stuttgart 1970, pp. 89ff.

Westcott, that the physical body of Jesus was transformed in the grave into a spiritual body, a body no longer subject to the ordinary limitations of space and time.[1]

It is worth noting here how evangelists like St Luke and St John, despite all differences, agree about the nature of the Lord's risen body. On the one hand, what they tell us suggests something quite unearthly, since Jesus can come and go through closed doors and appear and disappear at will. On the other hand, the risen body has earthly features, since Jesus is said to have eaten and invited Thomas to touch him. This combination of unearthly and earthly features, the evangelists suggest, characterized the reality of the resurrection. In trying to fathom the mystery of the first Easter day, we should therefore think of something essentially other-worldly—a piece of heavenly reality—invading this world of sense and time and manifesting itself to those with 'eyes of faith'. We are concerned with an unmistakably divine event which yet occurred in this world of ours, on an April day in AD 30, while Pontius Pilate was Roman governor in Judea . . .

There we may wisely leave the matter; for the chief thing in the gospels is the disciples' inexpugnable conviction that Jesus had survived death in the fullness of his personal life and had made his presence known to them by appearances which compelled them to say, 'We have seen the Lord'. Only on this basis can we explain the astounding change which came over the disciples—before the resurrection like frightened sheep, after it as bold as lions—the converting power of the message they went forth to proclaim, and that experience of fellowship with a living Lord which has been the vital nerve of true Christianity for nineteen centuries.

The meaning of the resurrection

Most orthodox 'Lives' of Christ leave the matter there. But if it is

[1] In I Cor. 15 Paul declares that a change from a natural to a spiritual body is the appointed destiny of the Christian believer. Since he speaks of Christ as 'the first fruits of those who have fallen asleep', we infer that he believed the same wonderful change to have occurred in Christ's body. In his own phrasing, Christ's 'lowly body' had become 'a body of glory'. Even Lake (*The Historical Evidence for the Resurrection of Jesus Christ*, London 1907, p. 23) admits this. 'An examination of Paul's teaching points to the fact that he believed that at the resurrection the body of Jesus was changed from one of flesh and blood into one that was spiritual, incorruptible and immortal, in such a way that there was no trace left of the corruptible body that had been laid in the grave.'

true that 'Christ in the apostles interpreted his finished work as truly as in his life-time he interpreted his unfinished work',[1] we cannot. We must, however briefly, explore the significance of the resurrection for the rest of the New Testament, since it needs not merely the four gospels but the whole of the New Testament to show who Christ is.

What then did the resurrection mean for the first Christians? And what sort of event is postulated by the preaching of the apostles? We cannot rest content with the vague statement that 'something happened' which persuaded them that Jesus still lived on. Any account we give must be such as to explain the theology of the resurrection which runs through the New Testament and the gospel of the risen Christ by which uncounted millions have lived and died.

We may begin by saying that the resurrection meant *the vindication of righteousness*. For consider: if the story of Jesus ended at the cross, it is stark, unmitigated tragedy and, what is more, the proof that there is no spiritual rhyme and reason in this mysterious universe. Here (to put it in the lowest terms) was a man with an unclouded vision of moral truth, a man who not merely trusted God utterly but 'hazarded all at a clap' on his faith in him. He made the final experiment of faith, *experimentum crucis*. If that life went out in utter darkness, there is no 'friend behind phenomena', as he believed (though he called him *Abba*) but only, in Thomas Hardy's phrase, 'a vast Imbecility'. Quite otherwise speaks the New Testament, from its first book to its last. It declares that when Jesus laid down his life on God, nature echoed and rang to his venture of faith. God raised him from the dead, God vindicated his Son, and in vindicating Jesus, vindicated his own righteousness.

But in an even more specific way, divine righteousness was vindicated by the resurrection. In the Bible (e.g. the Psalms, II Isaiah and St Paul, e.g. Rom. 1.17), 'the righteousness of God' has a dynamic meaning—expresses the saving purpose of him whose property it is to 'put things right' for his people—describes God's vindicating activity. Now the man who made 'the experiment of the cross' was one who uniquely embodied that saving purpose of God in himself. He was the Son of man come, in God's name, to seek and to save the lost. If 'the many' were to be 'ransomed', he believed that he must lay down his life for them as the Servant Messiah. So, embodying in himself that purpose and making himself utterly at one with sinners,

[1] P. T. Forsyth, *The Person and Place of Jesus Christ*, p. 60.

Jesus went down to death. Was he deluded? On the third day, says
the tradition in its oldest form (I Cor. 15.4), God raised Jesus—and
all he represented—from the grave. Thus the resurrection is the
making manifest by miracle of the victory of God's saving purpose
which took Jesus to Calvary.

Next, the resurrection signified *the defeat of death* (or, as II Tim.
1.10 puts it, 'Our Saviour Jesus Christ broke the power of death and
brought life and immortality to light').

This needs careful defining. Let us clarify it by saying that the
first Christians did not regard the resurrection as a dramatic verifica-
tion of the truth of human survival of death: one more stone, so to
speak, added to the cairn of proof of the immortality of the soul (a
doctrine which in any case is Greek, not Jewish). They said that
Jesus had *overcome* death, not merely survived it. They spoke of
resurrection. Now, resurrection, a characteristically Jewish doctrine,
means various things: first, that Jesus was truly dead; second, that
he came to life again not merely as a disembodied spirit but in the
fullness of his personality so that, as the records say, he was, though
different, still recognizably the same person; and that, above all,
what had happened was a great act of God. (Notice in the New
Testament that the writers say 'he was raised' rather than 'he rose'.)
But the resurrection of Jesus meant even more. It implied, as we
have seen, that the cause which he embodied had also triumphed
over the grave, that in the risen Christ the reign of God had come
'in power'. In short, for the first Christians the resurrection was an
eschatological act of God as new as the primal act of creation: an
act in which the strong Son of God had vanquished sin and death
and miraculously inaugurated the new age. The apostles knew that
by the resurrection of Christ a new world had come into being and
that they were themselves living in its power (Heb. 6.5).

As the resurrection meant a new mode of life for Jesus, so it carried
the promise of life for all who were his. He had given his life to
'ransom' men from their ancient enemies, sin and death and the
devil, and in his resurrection triumph was the promise of victory for
all who trusted in him (Rom. 8.37: 'We are more than conquerors
through him who loved us'). This is the basic meaning of Paul's
argument in I Cor. 15 and of Peter's in the opening doxology of his
Epistle (I Peter 1.3ff.). If one, and that one he who carried in his
own person the whole destiny of God's people, had shattered the
myth of death's invincibility, there was life in prospect for all who

were his. This is what Paul is saying in I Cor. 15.22 which means, 'As all that are in Adam die, so all that are in Christ will be made alive'. And the power which took Christ from the grave was available for all his, not merely at the end of their earthly pilgrimage, but here and now.

Lastly, as the book of Acts shows, the resurrection meant *the ongoing ministry*. During his earthly mission Jesus had described his blood-baptism as a means of initiation into a fuller and freer activity (Luke 12.49f.), as though visualizing a time when he would be 'let loose in the world where neither Roman nor Jew could stop his truth'. And so, as a mere matter of history, it proved to be.

If we ask what precisely it was that Caiaphas, Pilate and the rest were trying to do on the first Good Friday, the answer is that they were trying to stop what we call the ministry of Jesus. Now, in the story of the wonderful sequel, this or that point may be doubtful; but one thing is quite certain—the ministry of Jesus was *not* stopped. On the contrary, it went on, went forward, so that the book of Acts has been well called 'The Acts of Christ continued'.

St Luke was right when he summarized all that led up to the resurrection thus: 'All that Jesus *began* to do and to teach' (Acts 1.1). The resurrection was the end of the beginning or (as the first Christians saw it) the beginning of the end. In any case, in the light of the resurrection the ministry of Jesus found its climax, as the cross found its interpretation, and the future, its path to power and victory. *Vexilla Regis prodeunt!* And, as Paul says (I Cor. 15.25ff.), Christ must be king—must reign—till he has put all enemies under his feet. 'Then the Son himself will also be made subordinate to God who made all things subject to him, and thus God will be all in all.'

Appendices

THE GOSPEL SOURCES

I. THE TEXT OF Q

The symbol Q designates the sayings-source used by the first and the third evangelists. Existing originally in Aramaic and possibly compiled by the Apostle Matthew, it was put together, probably in Antioch, about A.D. 50, to serve as a moral handbook for catechumens.

Q has often been reconstructed. Though scholars disagree about some items, there is substantial agreement about the main portions of it. Reconstructed, it amounts to roughly 250 verses. It is generally admitted that the order in which Q appears in Luke is superior to that in Matthew; for Matthew likes to group his materials and to conflate his sources. Moreover, in most passages the Lucan wording seems demonstrably more primitive, i.e. nearer the original, than the Matthaean. Therefore it is customary nowadays to reconstruct Q in terms of Luke. When we thus reconstruct it, Q seems to fall into four sections which (following T. W. Manson) we may entitle:

A. Jesus and John: iii. 7–9, 16–17, 21–22; iv. 1–13; vi. 20–49; vii. 1–10, 18f., 22–35.
B. Jesus and His Disciples: ix. 57–62; x. 2–16, 21–24; xi. 9–13.
C. Jesus and His Opponents: xi. 14–52; xii. 2–12, 22–34.
D. Jesus and the Future: xii. 35–59; xiii. 18–30, 34–35; xiv. 11, 15–27, 34–35; xvi. 13, 16–18; xvii. 1–6, 22–37.

N.B. In the text of Q we have given the Matthaean parallels in footnotes. The sign (=), used to indicate parallels, does not mean that there is exact verbal equivalence: very often is it only approximate.

A. JESUS AND JOHN

The Preaching of John
iii. 7–9, 16–17=Mt. iii. 7–10, 11–12. Cf. Mk. i. 7–8.

7. He said therefore to the multitudes that went out to be baptised of him, Ye offspring of vipers, who warned you to flee from the wrath to come? 8. Bring forth therefore fruits worthy of repentance, and begin not to say within yourselves, We have Abraham to our father: for I say unto you, that God is able of these stones to raise up children unto Abraham. 9. And even now is the axe also laid unto the root of the trees: every tree therefore that bringeth not forth good fruit is hewn down, and cast into the fire.

16. John answered, saying unto them all, I indeed baptise you with water; but there cometh he that is mightier than I, the latchet of whose shoes I am not worthy to unloose: he shall baptise you with

the Holy Ghost and with fire: 17. whose fan is in his hand, throughly to cleanse his threshing-floor, and to gather the wheat into his garner; but the chaff he will burn up with unquenchable fire.

The Baptism of Jesus
21–22=Mt. iii. 16–17. Cf. Mk. i. 9–11

21. Now it came to pass, when all the people were baptised, that, Jesus also having been baptised, and praying, the heaven was opened, 22. and the Holy Ghost descended in a bodily form, as a dove, upon him, and a voice came out of heaven, Thou art my beloved Son; in thee I am well pleased.

The Temptation
iv. 1–13=Mt. iv. 1–11. Cf. Mk. i. 12–13.

1. And Jesus, full of the Holy Spirit, returned from the Jordan, and was led by the Spirit in the wilderness during forty days, 2. being tempted of the devil. And he did eat nothing in those days: and when they were completed, he hungered. 3. And the devil said unto him, If thou art the Son of God, command this stone that it become bread. 4. And Jesus answered unto him, It is written, Man shall not live by bread alone (Deut. viii. 3). 5. And he led him up, and shewed him all the kingdoms of the world in a moment of time. 6. And the devil said unto him, To thee will I give all this authority, and the glory of them: for it hath been delivered unto me; and to whomsoever I will I give it. 7. If thou therefore wilt worship before me, it shall all be thine. 8. And Jesus answered and said unto him, It is written, Thou shalt worship the Lord thy God, and him only shalt thou serve (Deut. vi. 13). 9. And he led him to Jerusalem, and set him on the pinnacle of the temple, and said unto him, If thou art the Son of God, cast thyself down from hence: 10. for it is written,

He shall give his angels concerning thee, to guard thee,

and, On their hands they shall bear thee up,

Lest haply thou dash thy foot against a stone (Ps. xci. 11f.).

12. And Jesus answering said unto him, It is said, Thou shalt not tempt the Lord thy God (Deut. vi. 16).

13. And when the devil had completed every temptation, he departed from him for a season.

The Sermon
vi. 20–49.

20.[1] And he lifted up his eyes on his disciples, and said, Blessed are ye poor: for yours is the kingdom of God. 21. Blessed are ye that hunger now: for ye shall be filled. Blessed are ye that weep now:

[1]=Mt. v. 3, 4, 6, 11f.

for ye shall laugh. 22. Blessed are ye, when men shall hate you, and when they shall separate you from their company, and reproach you, and cast out your name as evil, for the Son of man's sake. 23. Rejoice in that day, and leap for joy: for behold, your reward is great in heaven: for in the same manner did their fathers unto the prophets. 24.[1] But woe unto you that are rich! for ye have received your consolation. 25. Woe unto you, ye that are full now! for ye shall hunger. Woe unto you, ye that laugh now! for ye shall mourn and weep. 26. Woe unto you, when all men shall speak well of you! for in the same manner did their fathers to the false prophets.

27.[2] But I say unto you which hear, Love your enemies, do good to them that hate you, 28. bless them that curse you, pray for them that despitefully use you. 29.[3] To him that smiteth thee on the one cheek offer also the other; and from him that taketh away thy cloke withhold not thy coat also. 30.[4] Give to everyone that asketh thee; and of him that taketh away thy goods ask them not again. 31.[5] And as ye would that men should do to you, do ye also to them likewise. 32.[6] And if ye love them that love you, what thank have ye? for even sinners love those that love them. 33. And if ye do good to them that do good to you, what thank have ye? for even sinners do the same. 34. And if ye lend to them of whom ye hope to receive, what thank have ye? even sinners lend to sinners, to receive again as much. 35.[7] But love your enemies, and do them good, and lend, never despairing; and your reward shall be great, and ye shall be sons of the Most High: for he is kind toward the unthankful and evil. 36.[8] Be ye merciful, even as your Father is merciful. 37.[9] And judge not, and ye shall not be judged: and condemn not, and ye shall not be condemned: release, and ye shall be released: 38. give, and it shall be given unto you; good measure, pressed down, shaken together, running over, shall they give into your bosom. For with what measure ye mete, it shall be measured to you again.

39.[10] And he spake also a parable unto them, Can the blind guide the blind? shall they not both fall into a pit? 40.[11] The disciple is not above his master: but everyone when he is perfected shall be as his master. 41.[12] And why beholdest thou the mote that is in thy brother's eye, but considerest not the beam that is in thine own eye? 42. Or how canst thou say to thy brother, Brother, let me cast out the mote that is in thine eye, when thou thyself beholdest not the beam that

[1] The four 'woes' are not in Mt.   [2] =Mt. v. 44.
[3] =Mt. v. 39f.   [4] =Mt. v. 42.   [5] =Mt. vii. 12.
[6] =Mt. v. 46f.   [7] Cf. Mt. v. 45, M.   [8] Cf. Mt. v. 48, M.
[9] =Mt. vii. 1f.   [10] =Mt. xv. 14.   [11] Cf. Mt. x. 24f., M.
[12] =Mt. vii. 3-5.

is in thine own eye? Thou hypocrite, cast out first the beam out of thine own eye, and then shalt thou see clearly to cast out the mote that is in thy brother's eye. 43.[1] For there is no good tree that bringeth forth corrupt fruit; nor again a corrupt tree that bringeth forth good fruit. 44. For each tree is known by its own fruit. For of thorns men do not gather figs, nor of a bramble bush gather they grapes. 45. The good man out of the good treasure of his heart bringeth forth that which is good; and the evil man out of the evil treasure bringeth forth that which is evil: for out of the abundance of the heart his mouth speaketh.

46.[2] And why call ye me, Lord, Lord, and do not the things which I say? 47.[3] Everyone that cometh unto me, and heareth my words, and doeth them, I will shew you to whom he is like: 48. he is like a man building a house, who digged and went deep, and laid a foundation upon the rock; and when a flood arose, the stream brake against that house, and could not shake it: because it had been well builded. 49. But he that heareth, and doeth not, is like a man that built a house upon the earth without a foundation; against which the stream brake, and straightway it fell in; and the ruin of that house was great.

The Centurion's Servant[4]
vii. 1*b*–10=Mt. viii. 5–10, 13.

1*b*. He entered into Capernaum.

2. And a certain centurion's servant, who was dear unto him, was sick and at the point of death. 3. And when he heard concerning Jesus, he sent unto him elders of the Jews, asking him that he would come and save his servant. 4. And they, when they came to Jesus, besought him earnestly, saying, He is worthy that thou shouldest do this for him: 5. for he loveth our nation, and himself built us our synagogue. 6. And Jesus went with them. And when he was now not far from the house, the centurion sent friends to him, saying unto him, Lord, trouble not thyself: for I am not worthy that thou shouldest come under my roof: 7. wherefore neither thought I myself worthy to come unto thee: but say the word, and my servant shall be healed. 8. For I also am a man set under authority, having under myself soldiers: and I say to this one, Go, and he goeth; and to another, Come, and he cometh; and to my servant, Do this, and he doeth it. 9. And when Jesus heard these things, he marvelled at him, and turned and said unto the multitude that followed him, I say unto you, I have not found so great faith, no, not in Israel. 10. And they that were sent, returning to the house, found the servant whole.

---

[1] =Mt. vii. 16-20 and xii. 33-35.   [2] Cf. Mt. vii. 21, M.

[3] =Mt. vii. 24-27.   [4] Some think only the dialogue stood in Q.

John and Jesus
   vii. 18f., 22–35=Mt. xi. 2–11, 16–19.

18. And the disciples of John told him of all these things. 19. And
John calling unto him two of his disciples sent them to the Lord,
saying, Art thou he that cometh, or look we for another? 22. And
he answered and said unto them, Go your way, and tell John what
thing ye have seen and heard; the blind receive their sight, the lame
walk, the lepers are cleansed, and the deaf hear, the dead are raised
up, the poor have good tidings preached to them. 23. And blessed
is he, whosoever shall find none occasion of stumbling in me.

24. And when the messengers of John were departed, he began to
say unto the multitudes concerning John, What went ye out into
the wilderness to behold? a reed shaken with the wind? 25. But what
went ye out to see? a man clothed in soft raiment? Behold, they which
are gorgeously apparelled, and live delicately, are in kings' courts.
26. But what went ye out to see? A prophet? Yea, I say unto you,
and much more than a prophet. 27. This is he of whom it is written;

   Behold, I send my messenger before thy face
   Who shall prepare thy way before thee (Mal. iii. 1).

28. I say unto you, Among them that are born of women there
is none greater than John: yet he that is but little in the kingdom
of God is greater than he. 29.[1] And all the people when they heard,
and the publicans, justified God, being baptised with the baptism
of John. 30. But the Pharisees and the lawyers rejected for themselves
the counsel of God, being not baptised of him. 31. Whereunto then
shall I liken the men of this generation, and to what are they like?
32. They are like unto children that sit in the marketplace, and call
one to another; which say, We piped unto you, and ye did not dance;
we wailed, and ye did not weep. 33. For John the Baptist is come
eating no bread nor drinking wine; and ye say, He hath a devil.
34. The Son of man is come eating and drinking; and ye say, Behold,
a gluttonous man, and a winebibber, a friend of publicans and
sinners! 35. And wisdom is justified of all her children.

B. JESUS AND HIS DISCIPLES

Prospective Disciples
   ix. 57–62=Mt. viii. 19–22.

And as they went in the way, a certain man said unto him, I will
follow thee whithersoever thou goest. 58. And Jesus said unto him,
The foxes have holes, and the birds of the heaven have nests; but the
Son of man hath not where to lay his head. 59. And he said unto

[1] 29-30. Not in Mt.

another, Follow me. But he said, Lord, suffer me first to go and bury
my father. 60. But he said unto him, Leave the dead to bury their
own dead; but go thou and publish abroad the kingdom of God.
61.[1] And another also said, I will follow thee, Lord; but first suffer
me to bid farewell to them that are at my house. 62. But Jesus said
unto him, No man, having put his hand to the plough, and looking
back, is fit for the kingdom of God.

The Mission Charge
x. 2–16.

2.[2] And he said unto them, The harvest is plenteous, but the
labourers are few: pray ye therefore the Lord of the harvest, that he
send forth labourers into his harvest. 3.[3] Go your ways: behold, I send
you forth as lambs in the midst of wolves. 4.[4] Carry no purse, no
wallet, no shoes: and salute no man on the way. 5. And into whatsoever house ye shall enter, first say, Peace be to this house. 6. And
if a son of peace be there, your peace shall rest upon him: but if not,
it shall turn to you again. 7. And in that same house remain, eating
and drinking such things as they give: for the labourer is worthy of
his hire. Go not from house to house. 8.[5] And into whatsoever city
ye enter, and they receive you, eat such things as are set before you:
9. and heal the sick that are therein, and say unto them, The kingdom
of God is come nigh unto you. 10.[6] But into whatsoever city ye shall
enter, and they receive you not, go out into the streets thereof and
say, 11. Even the dust from your city, that cleaveth unto our feet,
we do wipe off against you: howbeit know this, that the kingdom of
God is come nigh. 12.[7] I say unto you, It shall be more tolerable in
that day for Sodom, than for that city. 13.[8] Woe unto thee, Chorazin!
woe unto thee, Bethsaida! for if the mighty works had been done in
Tyre and Sidon, which were done in you, they would have repented
long ago, sitting in sackcloth and ashes. 14. Howbeit it shall be more
tolerable for Tyre and Sidon in the judgement, than for you. 15. And
thou, Capernaum, shalt thou be exalted unto heaven? thou shalt be
brought down unto Hades. 16.[9] He that heareth you heareth me;
and he that rejecteth you rejecteth me; and he that rejecteth me
rejecteth him that sent me.

The Great Thanksgiving
x. 21–24=Mt. xi. 25–27; xiii. 16–17.

21. In that same hour he rejoiced in the Holy Spirit, and said, I thank
thee, O Father, Lord of heaven and earth, that thou didst hide

---

[1] 61-62 not in Mt.   [2] =Mt. ix. 37-38.   [3] =Mt. x. 16.
[4] Cf. Mt. x. 9-13.   [5] Cf. Mt. x. 7-8, M.   [6] Cf. Mt. x. 14.
[7] =Mt. x. 15.   [8] =Mt. xi. 21-23.   [9] Cf. Mt. x. 40, M, also Mk. ix. 37.

these things from the wise and understanding, and didst reveal them unto babes: yea, Father; for so it was well-pleasing in thy sight. 22. All things have been delivered unto me of my Father: and no one knoweth who the Son is, save the Father; and who the Father is, save the Son, and he to whomsoever the Son willeth to reveal him. 23. And turning to the disciples, he said privately, Blessed are the eyes which see the things that ye see: 24. for I say unto you, that many prophets and kings desired to see the things which ye see, and saw them not; and to hear the things which ye hear, and heard them not.

Asking and Receiving
    xi. 9–13=Mt. vii. 7–11.
9. And I say unto you, Ask, and it shall be given you; seek, and ye shall find; knock, and it shall be opened unto you. 10. For everyone that asketh receiveth; and he that seeketh findeth; and to him that knocketh it shall be opened. 11. And of which of you that is a father shall his son ask a loaf, and he give him a stone? or a fish, and he for a fish give him a serpent? 12. Or if he shall ask an egg, will he give him a scorpion? 13. If ye then, being evil, know how to give good gifts unto your children, how much more shall your heavenly Father give the Holy Spirit[1] to them that ask him?

C. JESUS AND HIS OPPONENTS

The Beelzebub Controversy
    xi. 14–26=Mt. xii. 22–30, 43–45. Cf. Mk. iii. 22–27.

14. And he was casting out a devil which was dumb. And it came to pass, when the devil was gone out, the dumb man spake; and the multitudes marvelled. 15. But some of them said, By Beelzebub the prince of the devils casteth he out devils. 16. And others, tempting him, sought of him a sign from heaven. 17. But he, knowing their thoughts, said unto them, Every kingdom divided against itself is brought to desolation; and a house divided against a house falleth. 18. And if Satan also is divided against himself, how shall his kingdom stand? because ye say that I cast out devils by Beelzebub. 19. And if I by Beelzebub cast out devils, by whom do your sons cast them out? therefore shall they be your judges. 20. But if I by the finger of God[2] cast out devils, then is the kingdom of God come upon you. 21. When the strong man fully armed guardeth his own court his goods are in peace: 22. but when a stronger than he shall come upon him, and overcome him, he taketh from him his whole armour wherein he trusted, and divideth his spoils. 23. He that is not with

[1] Mt. has 'good things.'   [2] Mt. has 'the Spirit of God.'

me is against me; and he that gathereth not with me scattereth.
24. The unclean spirit when he is gone out of the man, passeth through
waterless places, seeking rest; and finding none, he saith, I will
turn back unto my house whence I came out. 25. And when he is
come, he findeth it swept and garnished. 26. Then goeth he, and
taketh to him seven other spirits more evil than himself; and they
enter in and dwell there: and the last state of that man becometh
worse than the first.

The Blessedness of Christ's Mother
xi. 27–28. (No parallel in Mt. Possibly L. Cf. Mk. iii. 31–35.)

27. And it came to pass, as he said these things, a certain woman
out of the multitude lifted up her voice, and said unto him, Blessed
is the womb that bare thee, and the breasts which thou didst suck.
28. But he said, Yea rather, blessed are they that hear the word of
God, and keep it.

Sign of Jonah
xi. 29–32=Mt. xii. 38–42. Cf. Mk. viii. 11f.

29. And when the multitudes were gathering together unto him,
he began to say, This generation is an evil generation: it seeketh
after a sign; and there shall no sign be given to it but the sign of
Jonah. 30. For even as Jonah became a sign unto the Ninevites, so
shall also the Son of man be to this generation. 31. The queen of
the south shall rise up in the judgement with the men of this generation, and shall condemn them: for she came from the ends of the earth
to hear the wisdom of Solomon; and behold, a greater[1] than Solomon
is here. 32. The men of Nineveh shall stand up in the judgement
with this generation, and shall condemn it: for they repented at the
preaching of Jonah; and behold, a greater[1] than Jonah is here.

Lamp and Bushel
xi. 33–36.

33.[2] No man, when he hath lighted a lamp, putteth it in a cellar,
neither under the bushel, but on the stand, that they which enter
in may see the light. 34.[3] The lamp of thy body is thine eye: when
thine eye is single, thy whole body also is full of light; but when it is
evil, thy body also is full of darkness. 35. Look therefore whether the
light that is in thee be not darkness. 36. If therefore thy whole body
be full of light, having no part dark, it shall be wholly full of light,
as when the lamp with its bright shining doth give thee light.

---

[1] Lit. 'something greater,' i.e. the kingdom of God.

[2] Cf. Mt. v. 15 and Mk. iv. 21.   [3] =Mt. vi. 22f.

Against Pharisees and Scribes
xi. 37–52.

37. Now as he spake, a Pharisee asketh him to dine with him: and he went in, and sat down to meat. 38. And when the Pharisee saw it, he marvelled that he had not first washed before dinner. 39.[1] And the Lord said unto him, Now do ye Pharisees cleanse the outside of the cup and of the platter; but your inward part is full of extortion and wickedness. 40. Ye foolish ones, did not he that made the outside make the inside also? 41. Howbeit give for alms[2] those things which are within; and behold, all things are clean unto you.

42.[3] But woe unto you Pharisees! for ye tithe mint and rue and every herb, and pass over judgement and the love of God: but these ought ye to have done, and not to leave the other undone. 43.[4] Woe unto you Pharisees! for ye love the chief seats in the synagogues, and the salutations in the marketplaces. 44.[5] Woe unto you! for ye are as the tombs which appear not, and the men that walk over them know it not.

45. And one of the lawyers answering saith unto him, Master, in saying this thou reproachest us also. 46.[6] And he said, Woe unto you lawyers also! for ye lade men with burdens grievous to be borne, and ye yourselves touch not the burdens with one of your fingers. 47.[7] Woe unto you! for ye build the tombs of the prophets, and your fathers killed them. 48. So ye are witnesses and consent unto the works of your fathers: for they killed them, and ye build their tombs. 49.[8] Therefore also said the wisdom of God,[9] I will send unto them prophets and apostles; and some of them they shall kill and persecute; 50. that the blood of all the prophets which was shed from the foundation of the world, may be required of this generation; 51. from the blood of Abel unto the blood of Zachariah,[10] who perished between the altar and the sanctuary: yea, I say unto you, it shall be required of this generation. 52.[11] Woe unto you lawyers! for ye took away the key of knowledge: ye entered not in yourselves, and them that were entering in ye hindered.

[1] Cf. Mt. xxiii. 25f., M.

[2] 'Give for alms' probably renders the Aramaic *zakki*. Probably Luke has confused *zakki* with *dakki*='cleanse,' which is Matthew's version (xxiii. 26).

[3] Cf. Mt. xxiii. 23.   [4] Cf. Mt. xxiii. 6f., M.   [5] Cf. Mt. xxiii. 27, M.

[6] Cf. Mt. xxiii. 4, M.   [7] Cf. Mt. xxiii. 29ff., M.   [8] =Mt. xxiii. 34ff.

[9] I.e. God in His wisdom.

[10] 2 Chron. xxiv. 20f. 2 Chron., the last book in the Hebrew Bible, records the death of Zacharias, as Genesis, the first book, records the death of Abel.

[11] Cf. Mt. xxiii. 13, M.

Disciples in Persecution
xii. 2–12.

2.[1] But there is nothing covered up, that shall not be revealed: and hid, that shall not be known. 3. Wherefore whatsoever ye have said in the darkness shall be heard in the light; and what ye have spoken in the ear in the inner chambers shall be proclaimed upon the house-tops. 4.[2] And I say unto you my friends, Be not afraid of them which kill the body, and after that have no more that they can do. 5. But I will warn you whom ye shall fear: Fear him, which after he hath killed hath power to cast into hell; yea, I say unto you, Fear him. 6. Are not five sparrows sold for two farthings? and not one of them is forgotten in the sight of God. 7. But the very hairs of your head are all numbered. Fear not: ye are of more value than many sparrows. 8.[3] And I say unto you, Every one who shall confess me before men, him shall the Son of man also confess before the angels of God: 9. but he that denieth me in the presence of men shall be denied in the presence of the angels of God. 10.[4] And everyone who shall speak a word against the Son of man, it shall be forgiven him: but unto him that blasphemeth against the Holy Spirit it shall not be forgiven. 11.[5] And when they bring you before the synagogues, and the rulers, and the authorities, be not anxious how or what ye shall answer, or what ye shall say: 12. for the Holy Spirit shall teach you in that very hour what ye ought to say.

Trust in God
xii. 22–34

22.[6] And he said unto his disciples, Therefore I say unto you, Be not anxious for your life, what ye shall eat; nor yet for your body, what ye shall put on. 23. For the life is more than the food, and the body than the raiment. 24. Consider the ravens, that they sow not, neither reap; which have no store-chamber nor barn; and God feedeth them: of how much more value are ye than the birds! 25. And which of you by being anxious can add a cubit unto his stature? 26. If ye then are not able to do even that which is least, why are ye anxious concerning the rest? 27. Consider the lilies, how they grow: they toil not, neither do they spin; yet I say unto you, Even Solomon in all his glory was not arrayed like one of these. 28. But if God doth so clothe the grass in the field, which to-day is, and to-morrow is cast into the oven; how much more shall he clothe you, O ye of little faith? 29. And seek not ye what ye shall eat, and what ye shall drink,

---

[1] =Mt. x. 26f.; cf. Mk. iv. 22.   [2] =Mt. x. 28-33.

[3] Cf. Mk. viii. 38.   [4] =Mt. xii. 32; cf. Mk. iii. 28f.

[5] =Mt. x. 19f.; cf. Mk. xiii. 11 and Lk. xxi. 14f.   [6] =Mt. vi. 25-33.

neither be ye of doubtful mind. 30. For all these things do the nations
of the world seek after: but your Father knoweth that ye have need
of these things. 31. Howbeit seek ye his kingdom, and these things
shall be added unto you. 32.[1] Fear not, little flock; for it is your
Father's good pleasure to give you the kingdom. 33.[2] Sell that ye
have, and give alms; make for yourselves purses which wax not old,
a treasure in the heavens that faileth not, where no thief draweth
near, neither moth destroyeth. 34.[3] For where your treasure is, there
will your heart be also.

D. JESUS AND THE FUTURE

Watchfulness and Faithfulness
    xii. 35–48.

35.[4] Let your loins be girded about, and your lamps burning; 36. and
be ye yourselves like unto men looking for their lord, when he shall
return from the marriage feast; that, when he cometh and knocketh,
they may straightway open unto him. 37. Blessed are those servants,
whom the lord when he cometh shall find watching: verily I say unto
you, that he shall gird himself, and make them sit down to meat, and
shall come and serve them. 38. And if he shall come in the second
watch, and if in the third, and find them so, blessed are those servants.
39.[5] But know this, that if the master of the house had known in
what hour the thief was coming, he would have watched, and not
have left his house to be broken through. 40. Be ye also ready; for
in an hour that ye think not the Son of man cometh.

41. And Peter said, Lord, speaketh thou this parable unto us,
or even unto all? 42. And the Lord said, Who then is the faithful
and wise steward, whom his lord shall set over his household, to
give them their portion of food in due season? 43. Blessed is that
servant, whom his lord when he cometh shall find so doing. 44. Of
a truth I say unto you, that he will set him over all that he hath.
45. But if that servant shall say in his heart, My lord delayeth his
coming; and shall begin to beat the menservants and the maid-
servants, and to eat and drink, and to be drunken; 46. the lord of
that servant shall come in a day when he expecteth not, and in an
hour when he knoweth not, and shall cut him asunder,[6] and appoint
his portion with the unfaithful. 47.[7] And that servant, which knew
his lord's will, and made not ready, nor did according to his will,
shall be beaten with many stripes; 48. but he that knew not, and
did things worthy of stripes, shall be beaten with few stripes. And to

[1] No parallel in Mt.   [2] Cf. Mt. vi. 19-20, M.   [3] =Mt. vi. 21.
[4] Cf. Mt. xxv. 1-13, M.   [5] =Mt. xxiv. 43-51; cf. Mk. xiii. 35f.
[6] The Aramaic possibly meant 'shall separate him' (from the rest).
[7] 47-48 not in Mt.

whomsoever much is given, of him shall much be required: and to
whom they commit much, of him will they ask the more.

Fire upon the Earth—Weather Signs—The Parable of the Defendant
  xii. 49–59.

49.[1] I came to cast fire upon the earth; and what will I, if it is already
kindled?[2] 50. But I have a baptism to be baptised with; and how am
I straitened till it be accomplished! 51.[3] Think ye that I am come to
give peace in the earth? I tell you, Nay; but rather division: 52. for
there shall be from henceforth five in one house divided, three
against two, and two against three. 53. They shall be divided, father
against son, and son against father; mother against daughter, and
daughter against her mother; mother in law against her daughter
in law, and daughter in law against her mother in law.

54.[4] And he said to the multitudes also, When ye see a cloud
rising in the west, straightway ye say, There cometh a shower; and
so it cometh to pass. 55. And when ye see a south wind blowing, ye
say, There will be a scorching heat; and it cometh to pass. 56. Ye
hypocrites, ye know how to interpret the face of the earth and the
heaven; but how is it that ye know not how to interpret this time?
57. And why even of yourselves judge ye not what is right?

58.[5] For as thou art going with thine adversary before the
magistrate, on the way give diligence to be quit of him; lest haply
he hale thee unto the judge, and the judge shall deliver thee to the
officer, and the officer shall cast thee into prison. 59. I say unto thee,
Thou shalt by no means come out thence, till thou have paid the very
last mite.

The Mustard Seed and the Leaven
  xiii. 18–21: Mt. xiii. 31–33. Cf. Mk. iv. 30–32.

18. He said therefore, Unto what is the kingdom of God like? and
whereunto shall I liken it? 19. It is like unto a grain of mustard seed,
which a man took, and cast into his own garden; and it grew, and
became a tree; and the birds of the heaven lodged in the branches
thereof. 20. And again he said, Whereunto shall I liken the kingdom
of God? 21. It is like unto leaven, which a woman took and hid in
three measures of meal, till it was all leavened.

The Narrow Door
  xiii. 22–30.

22. And he went on his way through cities and villages, teaching,

---

[1] 49-50 not in Mt.

[2] The probable meaning is: 'How I wish that it were already kindled!'

[3] =Mt. x. 34-36.   [4] 54-57 have no parallel in Mt.   [5] =Mt. v. 25-26.

and journeying on unto Jerusalem. 23. And one said unto him, Lord, are they few that be saved? And he said unto them, 24.[1] Strive to enter in by the narrow door: for many, I say unto you, shall seek to enter in, and shall not be able. 25.[2] When once the master of the house is risen up, and hath shut to the door, and ye begin to stand without, and to knock at the door, saying, Lord, open to us; and he shall answer and say to you, I know you not whence ye are; 26.[3] then shall ye begin to say, We did eat and drink in thy presence, and thou didst teach in our streets; 27. and he shall say, I tell you, I know not whence ye are; depart from me, all ye workers of iniquity. 28.[4] There shall be the weeping and gnashing of teeth, when ye shall see Abraham, and Isaac, and Jacob, and all the prophets, in the kingdom of God, and yourselves cast forth without. 29. And they shall come from the east and west, and from the north and south, and shall sit down in the kingdom of God. 30.[5] And behold, there are last which shall be first, and there are first which shall be last.

Lament over Jerusalem
xiii. 34–35=Mt. xxiii. 37–39.

34. O Jerusalem, Jerusalem, which killeth the prophets, and stoneth them that are sent unto her! how often would I have gathered thy children together, even as a hen gathereth her own brood under her wings, and ye would not! 35. Behold, your house is left unto you desolate: and I say unto you, Ye shall not see me, until ye shall say, Blessed is he that cometh in the name of the Lord.

xiv. 11=Mt. xxiii. 12. Everyone that exalteth himself shall be humbled; and he that humbleth himself shall be exalted.

The Great Supper
xiv. 15–24. Cf. Mt. xxii. 1–10 (the M version of the parable).

15. And when one of them that sat at meat with him heard these things, he said unto him, Blessed is he that shall eat bread in the kingdom of God. 16. But he said unto him, A certain man made a great supper; and he bade many: 17. and he sent forth his servant at supper time to say to them that were bidden, Come; for all things are now ready. 18. And they all with one consent began to make excuse. The first said unto him, I have bought a field, and I must needs go out and see it: I pray thee have me excused. 19. And another said, I have bought five yoke of oxen, and I go to prove them: I pray thee have me excused. 20. And another said, I have married a wife, and therefore I cannot come. 21. And the servant came, and told

[1] Cf. Mt. vii. 13f., M. [2] Cf. Mt. xxv. 10-12, M. [3] Cf. Mt. vii. 22f., M.
[4] =Mt. viii. 11f. [5] Cf. Mt. xix. 30 and Mk. x. 31.

his lord these things. Then the master of the house being angry said to his servant, Go out quickly into the streets and lanes of the city, and bring in hither the poor and maimed and blind and lame. 22. And the servant said, Lord, what thou didst command is done, and yet there is room. 23. And the lord said unto the servant, Go out into the highways and hedges, and constrain them to come in, that my house may be filled. 24. For I say unto you, that none of those men which were bidden shall taste of my supper.

Cross-bearing
xiv. 25–27=Mt. x. 37–38.

25. Now there went with him great multitudes: and he turned, and said unto them, 26. If any man cometh unto me, and hateth[1] not his own father, and mother, and wife, and children, and brethren, and sisters, yea, and his own life also, he cannot be my disciple. 27.[2] Whosoever doth not bear his own cross, and come after me, cannot be my disciple.

The Parable of the Salt
xiv. 34–35 = Mt. v. 13. Cf. Mk. ix. 50.

34. Salt therefore is good: but if even the salt have lost its savour, wherewith shall it be seasoned? 35. It is fit neither for the land nor for the dunghill: men cast it out. He that hath ears to hear, let him hear.

God and Mammon
xvi. 13=Mt. vi. 24.

13. No servant can serve two masters: for either he will hate the one, and love the other; or else he will hold to one, and despise the other. Ye cannot serve God and mammon.

Old and New
xvi. 16–18.

16.[3] The law and the prophets were until John: from that time the gospel of the kingdom of God is preached, and every man entereth violently into it.

17.[4] But it is easier for heaven and earth to pass away, than for one tittle of the law to fall.[5]

18.[6] Everyone that putteth away his wife, and marrieth another, committeth adultery: and he that marrieth one that is put away from a husband committeth adultery.

[1] 'hate'=love less.   [2] Cf. Mk. viii. 34.
[3] =Mt. xi. 12f.   [4] Cf. Mt. v. 18, M.
[5] Probably an ironic comment on the rigid conservatism of the scribes.
[6] Cf. Mt. v. 32, M; also Mk. x. 11f.

Stumbling-blocks, etc.
    xvii. 1–6.

1.[1] And he said unto his disciples, It is impossible but that occasions of stumbling should come: but woe unto him, through whom they come! 2. It were well for him if a millstone were hanged about his neck, and he were thrown into the sea, rather than that he should cause one of these little ones to stumble. 3.[2] Take heed to yourselves: if thy brother sin, rebuke him; and if he repent, forgive him. 4. And if he sin against thee seven times in the day, and seven times turn again to thee, saying, I repent; thou shalt forgive him.

    5.[3] And the apostles said unto the Lord, Increase our faith. 6. And the Lord said, If ye have faith as a grain of mustard seed, ye would say unto this sycamine tree, Be thou rooted up, and be thou planted in the sea; and it would have obeyed you.

The Day of the Son of Man
    xvii. 22–37.

22. And he said unto the disciples, The days will come, when ye shall desire to see one of the days of the Son of man, and ye shall not see it. 23.[4] And they shall say to you, Lo, there! Lo, here! go not away, nor follow after them: 24. for as the lightning, when it lighteneth out of the one part under the heaven, shineth unto the other part under heaven: so shall the Son of man be in his day. 25. But first must he suffer many things and be rejected of this generation. 26.[5] And as it came to pass in the days of Noah, even so shall it be also in the days of the Son of man. 27. They ate, they drank, they married, they were given in marriage, until the day that Noah entered into the ark, and the flood came, and destroyed them all. 28. Likewise even as it came to pass in the days of Lot; they ate, they drank, they bought, they sold, they planted, they builded; 29. but in the day that Lot went out from Sodom it rained fire and brimstone from heaven, and destroyed them all: 30. after the same manner shall it be in the day that the Son of man is revealed. 31.[6] In that day, he which shall be on the housetop, and his goods in the house, let him not go down to take them away: and let him that is in the field likewise not return back. 32. Remember Lot's wife. 33.[7] Whosoever shall seek to gain his life shall lose it: but whosoever shall lose his life shall preserve it. 34.[8] I say unto you, In that night there shall be two men on one bed; the one shall be taken, and the other shall

---

[1] =Mt. xviii. 6-7; cf. Mk. ix. 42.   [2] Cf. Mt. xviii. 15, 21, 22, M.
[3] Cf. Mt. xvii. 20, M; also Mk. xi. 23 and 1 Cor. xiii. 2.   [4] =Mt. xxiv. 26ff.
[5] =Mt. xxiv. 37-41.   [6] Cf. Mk. xiii. 15f.
[7] =Mt. x. 39; cf. Mk. viii. 35.   [8] =Mt. xxiv. 40f.

be left. 35. There shall be two women grinding together; the one shall be taken, and the other shall be left.[1] 37.[2] And they answering say unto him, Where, Lord? And he said unto them, Where the body is, thither will the eagles also be gathered together.

[1] 36 of the A.V. is not found in our best MSS.　　　　[2] =Mt. xxiv. 28.

II. THE TEXT OF M

We use the symbol M to denote the Gospel tradition peculiar to Matthew—'Special Matthew.'

Apart from editorial insertions, it consists of (a) about a dozen O.T. proof-texts, which we shall not print; (b) some dozen narratives: The Nativity Narrative (i–ii), Peter's Walking on the Water, the Coin in the Fish's Mouth, and stories connected with the Passion and Resurrection (the death of Judas, Pilate's Wife's Dream, the Handwashing, the resurrection of the Jewish Saints, the Watch at the Tomb, the Earthquake, the Appearance to the Women, the Bribing of the Guard, and the Final Commission); and (c) many sayings and parables in chap. v–xxv, of which the chief are:

> three-fifths of the Sermon on the Mount (v–vii),
> more than twelve verses of the Mission Charge (x),
> five parables of the Kingdom (xiii),
> most of xviii,
> almost all the speech against the Pharisees (xxiii),
> the three eschatological parables of xxv,

plus such sayings as 'Come unto me,' the two 'ecclesiastical' sayings (xvi. 17–19 and xviii. 15–20) and such parables as the Labourers in the Vineyard, the Two Sons, the Marriage Feast and the Wedding Garment.

Many of the narratives in (b) sound like Jerusalem gossip and 'rarely rise above the level of edifying stories to that of historicity' (Moffatt). This is the least valuable bit of the Synoptic tradition.

It is to (c) the teaching peculiar to Matthew that Streeter and others apply the symbol M. Some portions of it are 'divergent versions' of sayings in Q. Did it all reach 'Matthew' orally, or did he derive it from some hypothetical document M? Scholars are divided between these two views. What is certain is that it represents a distinct cycle of tradition with a clear Jewish tincture. Its respect for the law, coupled with its hatred of the lawyers, its Palestinian Jewish atmosphere, sayings like x. 6 and its strong Church interest suggest that it emanated from the Churches of Judaea, which were centred in the Jerusalem Mother Church; and that it belongs to the years just before the Fall of Jerusalem.

M undoubtedly contains much genuine teaching of Jesus; but since it has suffered adulteration from the Jewish side, we must use it with considerable caution.

The Birth Stories
i–ii.

John the Baptist's Hesitation
iii. 14–15.

14. But John would have hindered him, saying, I have need to be

baptised of thee, and comest thou to me? 15. But Jesus answering said unto him, Suffer it now: for thus it becometh us to fulfil all righteousness. Then he suffereth him.

The Sermon on the Mount
v–vii. (Verses probably derived from Q are bracketed.)

1. And seeing the multitudes, Jesus went up into the mountain: and when he had sat down, his disciples came unto him: 2. and he opened his mouth and taught them, saying,

[3. Blessed are the poor in spirit: for theirs is the kingdom of heaven.]

[4. Blessed are they that mourn: for they shall be comforted.]

5. Blessed are the meek: for they shall inherit the earth.

[6. Blessed are they that hunger and thirst after righteousness: for they shall be filled.]

7. Blessed are the merciful: for they shall obtain mercy.

8. Blessed are the pure in heart: for they shall see God.

9. Blessed are the peacemakers: for they shall be called sons of God.

10. Blessed are they that have been persecuted for righteousness' sake: for theirs in the kingdom of heaven.

[11. Blessed are ye when men shall reproach you, and persecute you, and say all manner of evil against you falsely, for my sake.]

[12. Rejoice, and be exceeding glad: for great is your reward in heaven: for so persecuted they the prophets which were before you.]

Salt and Light
13–16.

13. Ye are the salt of the earth: [but if the salt have lost its savour, wherewith shall it be salted? it is thenceforth good for nothing, but to be cast out and trodden under foot of men.] 14. Ye are the light of the world. A city set on a hill cannot be hid. [15. Neither do men light a lamp, and put it under the bushel, but on the stand; and it shineth unto all that are in the house.] 16. Even so let your light shine before men, that they may see your good works, and glorify your Father which is in heaven.

Jesus and the Law
17–20.

17. Think not that I came to destroy the law or the prophets: I came not to destroy, but to fulfil. 18. For verily I say unto you, Till heaven or earth pass away, one jot or one tittle shall in no wise pass away from the law, till all things be accomplished. 19. Whosoever therefore shall break one of these least commandments, and shall

teach men so, shall be called least in the kingdom of heaven: but whosoever shall do and teach them, he shall be called great in the kingdom of heaven. 20. For I say unto you, that except your right-eousness shall exceed the righteousness of the scribes and Pharisees, ye shall in no wise enter into the kingdom of heaven.

On Murder
21–26.

21. Ye have heard that it was said to them of old time, Thou shalt not kill; and whosoever shall kill shall be in danger of the judgement: 22. but I say unto you, that every one who is angry with his brother shall be in danger of the judgement; and whosoever shall say to his brother, Raca, shall be in danger of the council; and whosoever shall say, Thou fool, shall be in danger of the hell of fire. 23. If therefore thou art offering thy gift at the altar, and there rememberest that thy brother hath aught against thee, 24. leave there thy gift before the altar, and go thy way, first be reconciled to thy brother, and then come and offer thy gift. [25. Agree with thine adversary quickly, whiles thou art with him in the way; lest haply the adversary deliver thee to the judge, and the judge deliver thee to the officer, and thou be cast into prison. 26. Verily, I say unto thee, Thou shalt by no means come out thence, till thou have paid the last farthing.]

On Adultery
27–30.

27. Ye have heard that it was said, Thou shalt not commit adultery: 28. but I say unto you, that everyone that looketh on a woman to lust after her hath committed adultery with her already in his heart. 29.[1] And if thy right eye causeth thee to stumble, pluck it out, and cast it from thee: for it is profitable for thee that one of thy members should perish, and not thy whole body be cast into hell. 30. And if thy right hand causeth thee to stumble, cut it off, and cast it from thee: for it is profitable for thee that one of thy members should perish, and not thy whole body go into hell.

On Divorce
31–32. Cf. Lk. xvi. 18 and Mk. x. 11–12.

31. It was said also, Whosoever shall put away his wife, let him give her a writing of divorcement: 32. but I say unto you, that every one that putteth away his wife, saving for the cause of fornication, maketh her an adulteress: and whosoever shall marry her when she is put away committeth adultery.

[1] Cf. Mk. ix. 43-48.

On Vows and Oaths

33–37.

33. Again, ye have heard that it was said to them of old time, Thou shalt not forswear thyself, but shalt perform unto the Lord thine oaths: 34. but I say unto you, Swear not at all; neither by the heaven, for it is the throne of God; 35. nor by the earth, for it is the footstool of his feet; nor by Jerusalem, for it is the city of the great King. 36. Neither shalt thou swear by thy head, for thou canst not make one hair white or black. 37. But let your speech be, Yea, yea; Nay, nay: and whatsoever is more than these is of the evil one.

On Retribution

38–42

38. Ye have heard that it was said, An eye for an eye, and a tooth for a tooth: 39. but I say unto you, Resist not him that is evil: [but whosoever smiteth thee on thy right cheek, turn to him the other also.] [40. And if any man would go to law with thee, and take away thy coat, let him have thy cloke also.] 41. And whosoever shall compel thee to go one mile, go with him twain. [42. Give to him that asketh thee, and from him that would borrow of thee, turn not thou away.]

On Love of Neighbour

43–48.

43. Ye have heard that it was said, Thou shalt love thy neighbour, and hate thine enemy: [44. but I say unto you, Love your enemies, and pray for them that persecute you] 45. that ye may be sons of your Father which is in heaven: for he maketh his sun to rise on the evil and the good, and sendeth rain on the just and the unjust. [46. For if ye love them that love you, what reward have ye? do not even the publicans the same?] 47. And if ye salute your brethren only, what do ye more than others? do not even the Gentiles the same? 48. Ye therefore shall be perfect, as your heavenly Father is perfect.

On Almsgiving

vi. 1–4.

1. Take heed that ye do not your righteousness before men, to be seen of them: else ye have no reward with your Father which is in heaven.

2. When therefore thou doest alms, sound not a trumpet before thee, as the hypocrites do in the synagogues and in the streets, that they may have glory of men. Verily I say unto you, They have received their reward. 3. But when thou doest alms, let not thy left hand know what thy right hand doeth: 4. that thine alms may be

in secret: and thy Father which seeth in secret shall recompense thee.

On Prayer
5–15. Cf. Lk. xi. 2–4.

5. And when ye pray, ye shall not be as the hypocrites: for they love to stand and pray in the synagogues and in the corners of the streets, that they may be seen of men. Verily I say unto you, They have received their reward. 6. But thou, when thou prayest, enter into thine inner chamber, and having shut thy door, pray to thy Father which is in secret, and thy Father which seeth in secret shall recompense thee. 7. And in praying use not vain repetitions, as the Gentiles do: for they think that they shall be heard for their much speaking. 8. Be not therefore like unto them: for your Father knoweth what things ye have need of, before ye ask him. 9. After this manner therefore pray ye: Our Father which art in heaven, Hallowed be thy name. 10. Thy kingdom come. Thy will be done, as in heaven, so on earth. 11. Give us this day our daily bread. 12. And forgive us our debts, as we also have forgiven our debtors. 13. And bring us not into temptation, but deliver us from the evil one. 14. For if ye forgive men their trespasses, your heavenly Father will also forgive you. 15. But if ye forgive not men their trespasses, neither will your Father forgive your trespasses.

On Fasting
16–18.

16. Moreover, when ye fast, be not, as the hypocrites, of a sad countenance: for they disfigure their faces, that they may be seen of men to fast. Verily I say unto you, They have received their reward. 17. But thou, when thou fastest, anoint thy head, and wash thy face; 18. that thou be not seen of men to fast, but of thy Father which is in secret: and thy Father, which seeth in secret, shall recompense thee.

Treasures
19–21. Cf. Lk. xii. 33.

19. Lay not up for yourselves treasures upon the earth, where moth and rust doth consume, and where thieves break through and steal: 20. but lay up for yourselves treasures in heaven, where neither moth nor rust doth consume, and where thieves do not break through nor steal: [21. for where thy treasure is, there will thy heart be also.]

Light
22–23.

[22. The lamp of the body is the eye: if therefore thine eye be single, ·

thy whole body shall be full of light. But if thine eye be evil, thy whole body shall be full of darkness. 23. If therefore the light that is in thee be darkness, how great is the darkness!]

Loyalty
24.

[No man can serve two masters: for either he will hate the one, and love the other; or else he will hold to one, and despise the other. Ye cannot serve God and mammon.]

Freedom from Worry
25–34.

[25. Therefore I say unto you, Be not anxious for your life, what ye shall eat, or what ye shall drink; nor yet for your body, what ye shall put on. Is not the life more than the food, and the body than the raiment? 26. Behold the birds of the heaven, that they sow not, neither do they reap, nor gather into barns; and your heavenly Father feedeth them. Are not ye of much more value than they? 27. And which of you by being anxious can add one cubit unto his stature? 28. And why are ye anxious concerning raiment? Consider the lilies of the field, how they grow; they toil not, neither do they spin: 29. yet I say unto you, that even Solomon in all his glory was not arrayed like one of these. 30. But if God so clothe the grass of the field, which to-day is, and to-morrow is cast into the oven, shall he not much more clothe you, O ye of little faith? 31. Be not therefore anxious, saying, What shall we eat? or, What shall we drink? or, Wherewithal shall we be clothed? 32. For after all these things do the Gentiles seek; for your heavenly Father knoweth that ye have need of all these things. 33. But seek ye first his kingdom, and his righteousness; and all these things shall be added unto you.] 34. Be not therefore anxious for the morrow: for the morrow will be anxious for itself. Sufficient unto the day is the evil thereof.

Against Judging
vii. 1–5.

[1. Judge not, that ye be not judged. 2. For with what judgement ye judge, ye shall be judged: and with what measure ye mete, it shall be measured unto you. 3. And why beholdest thou the mote that is in thy brother's eye, but considerest not the beam that is in thine own eye? 4. Or how wilt thou say to thy brother, Let me cast out the mote out of thine eye; and lo, the beam is in thine own eye? 5. Thou hypocrite, cast out first the beam out of thine own eye; and then shalt thou see clearly to cast out the mote out of thy brother's eye.]

On Discrimination
6.

Give not that which is holy unto the dogs, neither cast your pearls before the swine, lest haply they trample them under their feet, and turn and rend you.

On asking God
7–11.

[7. Ask, and it shall be given you; seek, and ye shall find; knock, and it shall be opened unto you: 8. for every one that asketh receiveth; and he that seeketh findeth; and to him that knocketh it shall be opened. 9. Or what man is there of you, who, if his son shall ask him for a loaf, will give him a stone; 10. or if he shall ask for a fish, will give him a serpent? 11. If ye then, being evil, know how to give good gifts unto your children, how much more shall your Father which is in heaven give good things to them that ask him?]

The Golden Rule
12.

[All things therefore whatsoever ye would that men should do unto you, even so do ye also unto them]: for this is the law and the prophets.

The Two Ways
13–14. Cf. Lk. xiii. 23–24.

13. Enter ye in by the narrow gate: for wide is the gate, and broad is the way, that leadeth to destruction, and many be they that enter in thereby. 14. For narrow is the gate, and straitened the way, that leadeth unto life, and few be they that find it.

False Prophets
15–20.

15. Beware of false prophets, which come to you in sheep's clothing, but inwardly are ravening wolves. 16. By their fruits ye shall know them. [Do men gather grapes of thorns, or figs of thistles? 17. Even so every good tree bringeth forth good fruit; but the corrupt tree bringeth forth evil fruit. 18. A good tree cannot bring forth evil fruit, neither can a corrupt tree bring forth good fruit. 19. Every tree that bringeth not forth good fruit is hewn down, and cast into the fire.[1]] 20. Therefore by their fruits ye shall know them.

Exorcists
21–23. Cf. Lk. vi. 46 and xiii. 26–27.

21. Not every one that saith unto me, Lord, Lord, shall enter into

[1] This verse belongs to the Q report of the Baptist's teaching. See Lk. iii. 9.

the kingdom of heaven; but he that doeth the will of my Father which is in heaven. 22. Many will say to me in that day, Lord, Lord, did we not prophesy by thy name, and by thy name cast out devils, and by thy name do many mighty works? 23. And then will I profess unto them, I never knew you: depart from me, ye that work iniquity.

Parable of the Two Houses
24–27.

24. [Every one therefore which heareth these words of mine, and doeth them, shall be likened unto a wise man, which built his house upon the rock: 25. and the rain descended, and the floods came, and the winds blew, and beat upon that house; and it fell not; for it was founded upon the rock. 26. And every one that heareth these words of mine, and doeth them not, shall be likened unto a foolish man, which built his house upon the sand: 27. and the rain descended, and the floods came, and the winds blew, and smote upon that house; and it fell: and great was the fall thereof.]

ix. 13a.

But go ye and learn what this meaneth, I desire mercy, and not sacrifice.

The Mission Charge
x. 5–8.

5. Go not into any way of the Gentiles, and enter not into any city of the Samaritans: 6. but go rather to the lost sheep of the house of Israel. 7. And as ye go, preach, saying, The kingdom of heaven is at hand. 8. Heal the sick, raise the dead, cleanse the lepers, cast out devils: freely ye received, freely give.

9–13,[1] 16b.

9. Get you no gold, nor silver, nor brass in your purses; no wallet for your journey, neither two coats, nor shoes, nor staff: for the labourer is worthy of his food. 11. And into whatsoever city or village ye shall enter, search out who in it is worthy; and there abide till ye go forth. 12. And as ye enter into the house, salute it. 13. And if the house be worthy, let your peace come upon it: but if it be not worthy, let your peace return to you . . . be ye therefore wise as serpents, and harmless as doves.

23.

But when they persecute you in this city, flee into the next: for verily I say unto you, Ye shall not have gone through the cities of Israel, till the Son of man be come.

[1] 9-13 are a mixture of Mk. and M.

24–25.

24. A disciple is not above his master, nor a servant above his lord.
25. It is enough for the disciple that he be as his master, and the servant as his lord. If they have called the master of the house Beelzebub, how much more shall they call them of his household!

40–42.

40. He that receiveth you receiveth me, and he that receiveth me receiveth him that sent me. 41. He that receiveth a prophet in the name of a prophet shall receive a prophet's reward; and he that receiveth a righteous man in the name of a righteous man shall receive a righteous man's reward. 42. And whosoever shall give to drink unto one of these little ones a cup of cold water only, in the name of a disciple, verily I say unto you, he shall in no wise lose his reward.

xi. 14f.

14. And if ye are willing to receive it, this is Elijah which is to come.
15. He that hath ears to hear, let him hear.

The Great Invitation
28–30

28. Come unto me, all ye that labour and are heavy laden, and I will give you rest. 29. Take my yoke upon you, and learn of me; for I am meek and lowly in heart: and ye shall find rest unto your souls. 30. For my yoke is easy, and my burden is light.

On the Sabbath
xii. 5–7.

5. Or have ye not read in the law, how that on the sabbath day the priests in the temple profane the sabbath, and are guiltless? 6. But I say unto you, that one greater than the temple is here. 7. But if ye had known what this meaneth, I desire mercy, and not sacrifice, ye would not have condemned the guiltless.

11–12*a*.

11. And he said unto them, What man shall there be of you, that shall have one sheep, and if this fall into a pit on the sabbath day, will he not lay hold of it, and lift it out? 12. How much then is a man of more value than a sheep!

Idle Words
36–37.

36. And I say unto you, that every idle word that men shall speak,

they shall give account thereof in the day of judgement. 37. For by thy words thou shalt be justified, and by thy words thou shalt be condemned.

Parable of the Tares
xiii. 24–30, 36–43.

24. Another parable set he before them, saying, The kingdom of heaven is likened unto a man that sowed good seed in his field: 25. but while men slept, his enemy came and sowed tares also among the wheat, and went away. 26. But when the blade sprang up, and brought forth fruit, then appeared the tares also. 27. And the servants of the householder came and said unto him, Sir, didst thou not sow good seed in thy field? whence then hath it tares? 28. And he said unto them, An enemy hath done this. And the servants say unto him, Wilt thou then that we go and gather them up? 29. But he saith, Nay: lest haply while ye gather up the tares, ye root up the wheat with them. 30. Let both grow together until the harvest: and in the time of the harvest I will say to the reapers, Gather up first the tares, and bind them in bundles to burn them: but gather the wheat into my barn.

36. Then he left the multitudes, and went into the house: and his disciples came unto him, saying, Explain unto us the parable of the tares of the field. 37. And he answered and said, He that soweth the good seed is the Son of man, 38. and the field is the world; and the good seed, these are the sons of the kingdom; and the tares are the sons of the evil one; 39. and the enemy that sowed them is the devil: and the harvest is the end of the world; and the reapers are angels. 40. As therefore the tares are gathered up and burned with fire; so shall it be in the end of the world. 41. The Son of man shall send forth his angels, and they shall gather out of his kingdom all things that cause stumbling, and them that do iniquity, 42. and shall cast them into the furnace of fire: there shall be the weeping and gnashing of teeth. 43. Then shall the righteous shine forth as the sun in the kingdom of their Father. He that hath ears, let him hear.

Parables of Hid Treasure and Costly Pearl
44–46.

44. The kingdom of heaven is like unto a treasure hidden in the field; which a man found, and hid; and in his joy he goeth and selleth all that he hath, and buyeth that field.

45. Again, the kingdom of heaven is like unto a man that is a merchant seeking goodly pearls: 46. and having found one pearl of great price, he went and sold all that he had, and bought it.

Parable of the Drag-net, etc.
47–52.

47. Again, the kingdom of heaven is like unto a net, that was cast into the sea, and gathered of every kind: 48. which, when it was filled, they drew up on the beach; and they sat down, and gathered the good into vessels, but the bad they cast away. 49. So shall it be in the end of the world: the angels shall come forth, and sever the wicked from among the righteous, 50. and shall cast them into the furnace of fire: there shall be the weeping and gnashing of teeth.

51. Have ye understood all these things? They say unto him, Yea. 52. And he said unto them, Therefore every scribe who hath been made a disciple to the kingdom of heaven, is like unto a man that is a householder, which bringeth forth out of his treasure things new and old.

Peter's Walking on the Water
xiv. 28–33.

28. And Peter answered him and said, Lord, if it be thou, bid me come unto thee upon the waters. And he said, Come. 29. And Peter went down from the boat, and walked upon the waters, to come to Jesus. 30. But when he saw the wind, he was afraid; and beginning to sink, he cried out, saying, Lord, save me. 31. And immediately Jesus stretched forth his hand, and took hold of him, and saith unto him, O thou of little faith, wherefore didst thou doubt? 32. And when they were gone up into the boat, the wind ceased. 33. And they that were in the boat worshipped him, saying, Of a truth thou art the Son of God.

xv. 12–13.

12. Then came the disciples, and said unto him, Knowest thou that the Pharisees were offended, when they heard this saying? 13. But he answered and said, Every plant which my heavenly Father planted not, shall be rooted up.

The Canaanitish Woman
22–25

22. And behold, a Canaanitish woman came out from those borders, and cried, saying, Have mercy on me, O Lord, thou son of David; my daughter is grievously vexed with a devil. 23. But he answered her not a word. And his disciples came and besought him, saying, Send her away; for she crieth after us. 24. But he answered and said, I was not sent but unto the lost sheep of the house of Israel. 25. But she came and worshipped him, saying, Lord, help me.

The Promise to Peter
xvi. 17–19.

17. And Jesus answered and said unto him, Blessed art thou, Simon Bar-Jonah: for flesh and blood hath not revealed it unto thee, but my Father which is in heaven. 18. And I also say unto thee, that thou art Peter, and upon this rock I will build my church; and the gates of Hades shall not prevail against it. 19. I will give unto thee the keys of the kingdom of heaven: and whatsoever thou shalt bind on earth shall be bound in heaven: and whatsoever thou shalt loose on earth shall be loosed in heaven.

A Saying about Faith
xvii. 20. Cf. Lk. xvii. 6, Q; Mk. xi. 23; 1 Cor. xiii. 2.

20. And he saith unto them, Because of your little faith: for verily I say unto you, If ye have faith as a grain of mustard seed, ye shall say unto this mountain, Remove hence to yonder place; and it shall remove; and nothing shall be impossible unto you.

Coin in the Fish's Mouth
24–27.

24. And when they were come to Capernaum, they that received the half-shekel came to Peter, and said, Doth not your master pay the half-shekel? 25. He saith, Yea. And when he came into the house, Jesus spake first to him, saying, What thinkest thou, Simon? the kings of the earth, from whom do they receive toll or tribute? from their sons, or from strangers? 26. And when he said, From strangers, Jesus said unto him, Therefore the sons are free. 27. But, lest we cause them to stumble, go thou to the sea, and cast a hook, and take up the fish that first cometh up; and when thou hast opened his mouth, thou shalt find a shekel: that take, and give unto them for me and thee.

Parable of the Lost Sheep
xviii. 10, 12–14. Cf. Lk. xv. 3–7, L.

10. See that ye despise not one of these little ones; for I say unto you, that in heaven their angels do always behold the face of my Father which is in heaven.
12. How think ye? if any man have a hundred sheep, and one of them be gone astray, doth he not leave the ninety and nine, and go unto the mountains, and seek that which goeth astray? 13. And if so be that he find it, verily I say unto you, he rejoiceth over it more than over the ninety and nine which have not gone astray. 14. Even so it is not the will of your Father which is in heaven, that one of these little ones should perish.

Life within the Church
    15–20.

15. And if thy brother sin against thee, go shew him his fault between thee and him alone; if he hear thee, thou hast gained thy brother. 16. But if he hear thee not, take with thee one or two more, that at the mouth of two witnesses or three every word may be established. 17. And if he refuse to hear them, tell it unto the church: and if he refuse to hear the church also, let him be unto thee as the Gentile and the publican. 18. Verily I say unto you, What things soever ye shall bind on earth shall be bound in heaven: and what things soever ye shall loose on earth shall be loosed in heaven. 19. Again I say unto you, that if two of you shall agree on earth as touching anything that they shall ask, it shall be done for them of my Father which is in heaven. 20. For where two or three are gathered together in my name, there am I in the midst of them.

On Forgiveness: the Unmerciful Servant
    21–35.

21. Then came Peter, and said to him, Lord, how oft shall my brother sin against me, and I forgive him? until seven times? 22. Jesus saith unto him, I say not unto thee, Until seven times; but, Until seventy times seven.

23. Therefore is the kingdom of heaven likened unto a certain king, which would make a reckoning with his servants. 24. And when he had begun to reckon, one was brought unto him, which owed him ten thousand talents. 25. But forasmuch as he had not wherewith to pay, his lord commanded him to be sold, and his wife, and children, and all that he had, and payment to be made. 26. The servant therefore fell down and worshipped him, saying, Lord, have patience with me, and I will pay thee all. 27. And the lord of that servant, being moved with compassion, released him, and forgave him the debt. 28. But that servant went out, and found one of his fellow-servants, which owed him a hundred pence: and he laid hold on him, and took him by the throat, saying, Pay what thou owest. 29. So his fellow-servant fell down and besought him, saying, Have patience with me, and I will pay thee. 30. And he would not: but went and cast him into prison, till he should pay that which was due. 31. So when his fellow-servants saw what was done, they were exceeding sorry, and came and told unto their lord all that was done. 32. Then his lord called him unto him, and saith to him, Thou wicked servant, I forgave thee all that debt, because thou besoughtest me: 33. shouldest not thou also have had mercy on thy fellow-servant, even as I had mercy on thee? 34. And his lord was wroth, and delivered him to the tormentors, till he should pay all that was due.

35. So shall also my heavenly Father do unto you, if ye forgive not every one his brother from your hearts.

Celibacy and the Kingdom
xix. 10–12.

10. The disciples say unto him, If the case of the man is so with his wife, it is not expedient to marry. 11. But he said unto them, All men cannot receive this saying, but they to whom it is given. 12. For there are eunuchs, which were so born from their mother's womb: and there are eunuchs, which were made eunuchs by men: and there are eunuchs, which made themselves eunuchs[1] for the kingdom of heaven's sake. He that is able to receive it, let him receive it.

The Twelve Thrones
28. Cf. Lk. xxii. 28–30, L.

28. And Jesus said unto them, Verily I say unto you, that ye which have followed me, in the regeneration when the Son of man shall sit on the throne of his glory, ye also shall sit upon twelve thrones, judging the twelve tribes of Israel.

Parable of the Labourers in the Vineyard
xx. 1–16.

1. For the kingdom of heaven is like unto a man that is a householder, which went out early in the morning to hire labourers into his vineyard. 2. And when he had agreed with the labourers for a penny a day, he sent them into his vineyard. 3. And he went out about the third hour, and saw others standing in the marketplace idle; 4. and to them he said, Go ye also into the vineyard, and whatsoever is right I will give you. And they went their way. 5. Again he went out about the sixth and ninth hour, and did likewise. 6. And about the eleventh hour he went out, and found others standing; and he saith unto them, Why stand ye here all the day idle? 7. They say unto him, Because no man hath hired us. He saith unto them, Go ye also into the vineyard. 8. And when even was come, the lord of the vineyard saith unto his steward, Call the labourers, and pay them their hire, beginning from the last unto the first. 9. And when they came that were hired about the eleventh hour, they received every man a penny. 10. And when the first came, they supposed that they would receive more; and they likewise received every man a penny. 11. And when they received it, they murmured against the householder, saying, 12. These last have spent but one hour, and thou hast made them equal unto us, which have borne the burden of the day and the scorching heat. 13. But he answered and said to

---

[1] I.e. remained celibate.

one of them, Friend, I do thee no wrong: didst not thou agree with me for a penny? 14. Take up that which is thine, and go thy way; it is my will to give unto this last, even as unto thee. 15. Is it not lawful for me to do what I will with mine own? or is thine eye evil, because I am good? 16. So the last shall be first, and the first last.

Who is this?
xxi. 10–11.

10. And when he was come into Jerusalem, all the city was stirred, saying, Who is this? 11. And the multitude said, This is the prophet, Jesus, from Nazareth of Galilee.

The Children's Hosannas
14–16.

14. And the blind and the lame came to him in the temple: and he healed them. 15. But when the chief priests and the scribes saw the wonderful things that he did, and the children that were crying in the temple and saying, Hosanna to the son of David; 16. they were moved with indignation, and said unto him, Hearest thou what these are saying? And Jesus saith unto them, Yea: did ye never read, Out of the mouth of babes and sucklings thou hast perfected praise?

The Parable of the Two Sons
28–32.

28. But what think ye? A man had two sons; and he came to the first, and said, 29. Son, go work to-day in the vineyard. And he answered and said, I will not: but afterward he repented himself, and went. 30. And he came to the second, and said likewise. And he answered and said, I go, sir: and went not. 31. Whether of the twain did the will of his father? They say, The first. Jesus saith unto them, Verily I say unto you, that the publicans and the harlots go into the kingdom of God before you. 32.[1] For John came unto you in the way of righteousness, and ye believed him not: but the publicans and the harlots believed him: and ye, when ye saw it, did not even repent yourselves afterward, that ye might believe him.

The Parables of the Marriage Feast and the Wedding Garment
xxii. 1–14.

1. And Jesus answered and spake again in parables unto them, saying, 2. The kingdom of heaven is likened unto a certain king, which made a marriage feast for his son, 3. and sent forth his servants to call them that were bidden to the marriage feast: and they would not come. 4. Again he sent forth other servants, saying, Tell them

[1] Cf. Lk. vii. 29.

that are bidden, Behold, I have made ready my dinner: my oxen and my fatlings are killed, and all things are ready: come to the marriage feast. 5. But they made light of it, and went their ways, one to his own farm, another to his merchandise: 6. and the rest laid hold on his servants, and entreated them shamefully, and killed them. 7. But the king was wroth; and he sent his armies, and destroyed those murderers, and burned their city. 8. Then saith he to his servants, The wedding is ready, but they that were bidden were not worthy. 9. Go ye therefore unto the partings of the highways, and as many as ye shall find, bid to the marriage feast. 10. And those servants went out into the highways, and gathered together all as many as they found, both bad and good: and the wedding was filled with guests. 11. But when the king came in to behold the guests, he saw there a man which had not on a wedding-garment: 12. and he saith unto him, Friend, how camest thou in hither not having a wedding-garment? 13. And he was speechless. Then the king said to the servants, Bind him hand and foot, and cast him out into the outer darkness; there shall be the weeping and gnashing of teeth. 14. For many are called, but few chosen.

Woes on Scribes and Pharisees[1]
xxiii. 1–39.

1. Then spake Jesus to the multitudes and to his disciples, 2. saying, The scribes and the Pharisees sit on Moses' seat: 3. all things therefore whatsoever they bid you, these do and observe: but do not ye after their works; for they say, and do not. 4. Yea, they bind heavy burdens and grievous to be borne, and lay them on men's shoulders; but they themselves will not move them with their finger. 5.[2] But all their works they do for to be seen of men: for they make broad their phylacteries, and enlarge the borders of their garments, 6. and love the chief place at feasts, and chief seats in the synagogues, 7. and the salutations in the marketplaces, and to be called of men, Rabbi. 8. But be not ye called Rabbi: for one is your teacher, and all ye are brethren. 9. And call no man your father on the earth: for one is your Father, which is in heaven. 10. Neither be ye called masters: for one is your master, even the Christ. 11. But he that is greatest among you shall be your servant. [12. And whosoever shall exalt himself shall be humbled; and whosoever shall humble himself shall be exalted.]

13. But woe unto you, scribes and Pharisees, hypocrites! because ye shut the kingdom of heaven against men: for ye enter not in yourselves, neither suffer ye them that are entering in to enter.

[1] Verses assignable to Q are bracketed. But most of the chapter is M.
[2] With 5-7 cf. Mk. xii. 38-40.

15. Woe unto you, scribes and Pharisees, hypocrites! for ye compass sea and land to make one proselyte; and when he is become so, ye make him twofold more a son of hell than yourselves.

16. Woe unto you, ye blind guides, which say, Whosoever shall swear by the temple, it is nothing; but whosoever shall swear by the gold of the temple, he is a debtor. 17. Ye fools and blind; for whether is greater, the gold, or the temple that hath sanctified the gold? 18. And, whosoever shall swear by the altar, it is nothing; but whosoever shall swear by the gift that is upon it, he is a debtor. 19. Ye blind: for whether is greater, the gift, or the altar that sanctifieth the gift? 20. He therefore that sweareth by the altar, sweareth by it, and by all things thereon. 21. And he that sweareth by the temple, sweareth by it, and by him that dwelleth therein. 22. And he that sweareth by the heaven, sweareth by the throne of God, and by him that sitteth thereon.

[23. Woe unto you, scribes and Pharisees, hypocrites! for ye tithe mint and anise and cummin, and have left undone the weightier matters of the law, judgement, and mercy, and faith: but these ye ought to have done, and not to have left the other undone.] 24. Ye blind guides, which strain out the gnat, and swallow the camel!

25. Woe unto you, scribes and Pharisees, hypocrites! for ye cleanse the outside of the cup and of the platter, but within they are full from extortion and excess. 26. Thou blind Pharisee, cleanse first the inside of the cup and of the platter, that the outside thereof may become clean also.

27. Woe unto you, scribes and Pharisees, hypocrites! for ye are like unto whited sepulchres, which outwardly appear beautiful, but inwardly are full of dead men's bones, and of all uncleanness. 28. Even so ye also outwardly appear righteous unto men, but inwardly ye are full of hypocrisy and iniquity.

29. Woe unto you, scribes and Pharisees, hypocrites! for ye build the sepulchres of the prophets, and garnish the tombs of the righteous, 30. and say, If we had been in the days of our fathers, we should not have been partakers with them in the blood of the prophets. 31. Wherefore ye witness to yourselves, that ye are sons of them that slew the prophets. 32. Fill ye up then the measure of your fathers. 33. Ye serpents, ye offspring of vipers, how shall ye escape the judgement of hell?[1]

[34.[2] Therefore, behold, I send unto you prophets, and wise men, and scribes: some of them shall ye kill and crucify; and some of them shall ye scourge in your synagogues, and persecute from city to city: 35. that upon you may come all the righteous blood shed on the earth, from the blood of Abel the righteous unto the blood of

[1] Probably a saying of the Baptist; cf. Lk. iii. 7, Q.   [2] Cf. Lk. xi. 49-51.

Zachariah son of Barachiah, whom ye slew between the sanctuary and the altar. 36. Verily I say unto you, All these things shall come upon this generation.]

[37. O Jerusalem, Jerusalem, which killeth the prophets, and stoneth them that are sent unto her! how often would I have gathered thy children together, even as a hen gathereth her chickens under her wings, and ye would not! 38. Behold, your house is left unto you desolate. 39. For I say unto you, Ye shall not see me henceforth, till ye shall say, Blessed is he that cometh in the name of the Lord.]

Apocalyptic Sayings
   xxiv. 10–12, 30.

10. And then shall many stumble, and shall deliver up one another, and shall hate one another. 11. And many false prophets shall arise, and shall lead many astray. 12. And because iniquity shall be multiplied, the love of the many shall wax cold. 30. And then shall appear the sign of the Son of man in heaven: and then shall all the tribes of the earth mourn.

Parable of the Ten Virgins
   xxv. 1–13.

1. Then shall the kingdom of heaven be likened unto ten virgins, which took their lamps, and went forth to meet the bridegroom. 2. And five of them were foolish, and five were wise. 3. For the foolish, when they took their lamps, took no oil with them: 4. but the wise took oil in their vessels with their lamps. 5. Now while the bridegroom tarried, they all slumbered and slept. 6. But at midnight there is a cry, Behold, the bridegroom! Come ye forth to meet him. 7. Then all those virgins arose, and trimmed their lamps. 8. And the foolish said unto the wise, Give us of your oil; for our lamps are going out. 9. But the wise answered, saying, Peradventure there will not be enough for us and you: go ye rather to them that sell, and buy for yourselves. 10. And while they went away to buy, the bridegroom came; and they that were ready went in with him to the marriage feast: and the door was shut. 11. ·Afterward come also the other virgins, saying, Lord, Lord, open to us. 12. But he answered and said, Verily I say unto you, I know you not. 13. Watch therefore, for ye know not the day nor the hour.

Parable of the Talents
   14–30. Cf. Lk. xix. 11–27, L.

14. For it is as when a man, going into another country, called his own servants, and delivered unto them his goods. 15. And unto one he gave five talents, to another two, to another one; to each according

to his several ability; and he went on his journey. 16. Straightway he that received the five talents went and traded with them, and made other five talents. 17. In like manner he also that received the two gained other two. 18. But he that received the one went away and digged in the earth, and hid his lord's money. 19. Now after a long time the lord of those servants cometh, and maketh a reckoning with them. 20. And he that received the five talents came and brought other five talents, saying, Lord, thou deliveredst unto me five talents: lo, I have gained other five talents. 21. His lord said unto him, Well done, good and faithful servant: thou hast been faithful over a few things, I will set thee over many things: enter thou into the joy of thy lord. 22. And he also that received the two talents came and said, Lord, thou deliveredst unto me two talents: lo, I have gained other two talents. 23. His lord said unto him, Well done, good and faithful servant; thou hast been faithful over a few things, I will set thee over many things: enter thou into the joy of thy lord. 24. And he also that had received the one talent came and said, Lord, I knew thee that thou art a hard man, reaping where thou didst not sow, and gathering where thou didst not scatter: 25. and I was afraid, and went away and hid thy talent in the earth: lo, thou hast thine own. 26. But his lord answered and said unto him, Thou wicked and slothful servant, thou knewest that I reap where I sowed not, and gather where I did not scatter; 27. thou oughtest therefore to have put my money to the bankers, and at my coming I should have received back mine own with interest. 28. Take ye away therefore the talent from him, and give it unto him that hath the ten talents. 29. For unto every one that hath shall be given, and he shall have abundance: but from him that hath not, even that which he hath shall be taken away. 30. And cast ye out the unprofitable servant into the outer darkness: there shall be the weeping and gnashing of teeth.

Parable of the Sheep and the Goats
  31–46.

31. But when the Son of man shall come in his glory, and all the angels with him, then shall he sit on the throne of his glory: 32. and before him shall be gathered all the nations: and he shall separate them one from another, as the shepherd separateth the sheep from the goats: 33. and he shall set the sheep on his right hand, but the goats on the left. 34. Then shall the King say unto them on his right hand, Come, ye blessed of my Father, inherit the kingdom prepared for you from the foundation of the world: 35. for I was an hungred, and ye gave me meat: I was thirsty, and ye gave me drink: I was a stranger, and ye took me in; 36. naked, and ye clothed me: I was sick, and

ye visited me: I was in prison, and ye came unto me. 37. Then shall the righteous answer him, saying, Lord, when saw we thee an hungred, and fed thee? or athirst, and gave thee drink? 38. And when saw we thee a stranger, and took thee in? or naked, and clothed thee? 39. And when saw we thee sick, or in prison, and came unto thee? 40. And the King shall answer and say unto them, Verily I say unto you, Inasmuch as ye did it unto one of these my brethren, even these least, ye did it unto me. 41. Then shall he say also unto them on the left hand, Depart from me, ye cursed, into the eternal fire which is prepared for the devil and his angels: 42. for I was an hungred, and ye gave me no meat: I was thirsty, and ye gave me no drink: 43. I was a stranger, and ye took me not in; naked, and ye clothed me not; sick, and in prison, and ye visited me not. 44. Then shall they also answer, saying, Lord, when saw we thee an hungred, or athirst, or a stranger, or naked, or sick, or in prison, and did not minister unto thee? 45. Then shall he answer them, saying, Verily I say unto you, Inasmuch as ye did it not unto one of these least, ye did it not unto me. 46. And these shall go away into eternal punishment: but the righteous into eternal life.

Sayings to the Traitor
xxvi. 25, 50a.

25. And Judas, which betrayed him, answered and said, Is it I, Rabbi? He saith unto him, Thou hast said. 50a. And Jesus said unto him, Friend, do that for which thou art come.

Twelve Legions of Angels
52–54.

52. Then Jesus saith unto him, Put up again thy sword into its place: for all they that take the sword shall perish with the sword. 53. Or thinkest thou that I cannot beseech my Father, and he shall even now send me more than twelve legions of angels? 54. How then should the scriptures be fulfilled, that thus it must be?

The Death of Judas
xxvii. 3–8.

3. Then Judas, which betrayed him, when he saw that he was condemned, repented himself, and brought back the thirty pieces of silver to the chief priests and elders, 4. saying, I have sinned in that I betrayed innocent blood. But they said, What is that to us? see thou to it. 5. And he cast down the pieces of silver into the sanctuary, and departed; and he went away and hanged himself. 6. And the chief priests took the pieces of silver, and said, It is not lawful to put them into the treasury, since it is the price of blood.

7. And they took counsel, and bought with them the potter's field, to bury strangers in. 8. Wherefore that field was called, The field of blood, unto this day.

Pilate's Wife
19.

19. And while he was sitting on the judgement-seat, his wife sent unto him, saying, Have thou nothing to do with that righteous man: for I have suffered many things this day in a dream because of him.

Pilate's Hand-washing
24–25.

24. So when Pilate saw that he prevailed nothing, but rather that a tumult was arising, he took water, and washed his hands before the multitude, saying, I am innocent of the blood of this righteous man: see ye to it. 25. And all the people answered and said, His blood be on us, and on our children.

The Resurrection of the Jewish Saints
51*b*–53.

51*b*. And the earth did quake; and the rocks were rent; 52. and the tombs were opened; and many bodies of the saints that had fallen asleep were raised; 53. and coming forth out of the tombs after his resurrection they entered into the holy city and appeared unto many.

The Watch at the Tomb
62–66.

62. Now on the morrow, which is the day after the Preparation, the chief priests and the Pharisees were gathered together unto Pilate, 63. saying, Sir, we remember that that deceiver said, while he was yet alive, After three days I rise again. 64. Command therefore that the sepulchre be made sure until the third day, lest haply his disciples come and steal him away, and say unto the people, He is risen from the dead: and the last error will be worse than the first. 65. Pilate said unto them, Ye have a guard: go your way, make it as sure as ye can. 66. So they went, and made the sepulchre sure, sealing the stone, the guard being with them.

The Earthquake
xxviii. 2–4.

2. And behold, there was a great earthquake; for an angel of the Lord descended from heaven, and came and rolled away the stone, and sat upon it. 3. His appearance was as lightning, and his raiment

white as snow: 4. and for fear of him the watchers did quake, and became as dead men.

Appearance to the Women
9–10.

9. And behold, Jesus met them, saying, All hail. And they came and took hold of his feet, and worshipped him. 10. Then saith Jesus unto them, Fear not: go tell my brethren that they depart into Galilee, and there shall they see me.

The Bribing of the Guard
11–15.

11. Now while they were going, behold, some of the guard came into the city, and told unto the chief priests all the things that were come to pass. 12. And when they were assembled with the elders, and had taken counsel, they gave large money unto the soldiers, 13. saying, Say ye, His disciples came by night, and stole him away while we slept. 14. And if this come to the governor's ears, we will persuade him, and rid you of care. 15. So they took the money, and did as they were taught: and this saying was spread abroad among the Jews, and continueth until this day.

The Final Commission
16–20.

16. But the eleven disciples went into Galilee, unto the mountain where Jesus had appointed them. 17. And when they saw him, they worshipped him: but some doubted. 18. And Jesus came to them and spake unto them, saying, All authority hath been given unto me in heaven and on earth. 19. Go ye therefore, and make disciples of all the nations, baptising them into the name of the Father and of the Son and of the Holy Ghost: 20. teaching them to observe all things whatsoever I commanded you: and lo, I am with you alway, even unto the end of the world.

III. THE TEXT OF L

The symbol L denotes the Gospel tradition peculiar to St. Luke's Gospel. It comprises narrative and teaching matter, and adds much to our knowledge of the Passion Story. L probably represents the oral tradition about Jesus which Luke gathered at Caesarea when staying there during Paul's imprisonment, A.D. 57–59. As a source, it is much superior in historical value to M. In the list of contents which follows we do not include the Birth Stories (i–ii) which stand apart and possibly depend on Hebrew or Aramaic sources.

I. John and Jesus:

    (a) The Mission of John: iii. 1–6, 10–14, 18–20.
    (b) The Genealogy of Jesus: iii. 23–38.

II. The Rejection at Nazareth: iv. 16–30.

III. Mighty Works:

    (a) The Wonderful Draught: v. 1–11.
    (b) The Widow of Nain's Son: vii. 11–17.
    (c) The Woman who was a Sinner: vii. 36–viii. 3.

IV. Lessons:

    (a) To the Disciples in Samaria: ix. 51–56.
    (b) To the Seventy: x. 1, 17–20.
    (c) To a Rabbi—the Good Samaritan: x. 25–37.
    (d) To Martha—the Good Part: x. 38–42.
    (e) How to Pray—the Friend·at Midnight: xi. 1–8, 53f.; xii. 1.

V. Warnings:

    (a) Against Greed—the Rich Fool: xii. 13–21.
    (b) On Repentance—the Barren Fig Tree: xiii. 1–9.
    (c) Sabbath Observance—(1) the Hunch-backed Woman: xiii. 10–17.
    (d) To Herod Antipas: xiii. 31–33.
    (e) Sabbath Observance—(2) the Man with Dropsy: xiv. 1–6.
    (f) On Precedence and Hospitality: xiv. 7–14.
    (g) On Counting the Cost: xiv. 28–33.

VI. Parables of the Lost (Lost Sheep, Lost Coin, Lost Son): xv.

VII. Parables, etc., of Responsibility:

    (a) Foresight—the Unjust Steward: xvi. 1–12.
    (b) Money—Dives and Lazarus: xvi. 14–15, 19–31.
    (c) On Serving God—Master and Servant: xvii. 7–10.
    (d) On Gratitude—the Ten Lepers: xvii. 11–21.
    (e) On Perseverance—the Importunate Widow: xviii. 1–8.
    (f) On Prayer—the Pharisee and the Publican: xviii. 9–14.

(g) On Opportunities—Zaccheus: the Parable of the Pounds: xix. 1–27.

VIII. Jerusalem:

(a) Approach to the City: xix. 37–44.
(b) Apocalyptic Sayings: xxi. 11b, 18, 25b, 26a, 28, 34–36.
(c) The Passion and the Resurrection: xxii. 14–xxiv (less Marcan passages).

I. JOHN AND JESUS

(a) *The Mission of John*
iii. 1–6, 10–14, 18–20.

1. Now in the fifteenth year of the reign of Tiberius Caesar, Pontius Pilate being governor of Judaea, and Herod being tetrarch of Galilee, and his brother Philip tetrarch of the region of Ituraea and Trachonitis, and Lysanias tetrarch of Abilene, 2. in the high-priesthood of Annas and Caiaphas, the word of God came unto John the son of Zacharias in the wilderness. 3. And he came into all the region round about Jordan, preaching the baptism of repentance unto remission of sins; 4. as it is written in the book of the words of Isaiah the prophet,

> The voice of one crying in the wilderness,
> Make ye ready the way of the Lord,
> Make his paths straight.
> 5. Every valley shall be filled,
> And every mountain and hill shall be brought low;
> And the crooked shall become straight,
> And the rough ways smooth;
> 6. And all flesh shall see the salvation of God (Isa. xl. 3ff.).

10. And the multitudes asked him, saying, What then must we do? 11. And he answered and said unto them, He that hath two coats, let him impart to him that hath none; and he that hath food, let him do likewise. 12. And there came also publicans to be baptised, and they said unto him, Master, what must we do? 13. And he said unto them, Extort no more than that which is appointed you. 14. And soldiers also asked him, saying, And we, what must we do? And he said unto them, Do violence to no man, neither exact anything wrongfully; and be content with your wages.

18. With many other exhortations therefore preached he good tidings unto the people; 19. but Herod the tetrarch, being reproved by him for Herodias his brother's wife, and for all the evil things which Herod had done, 20. added yet this above all, that he shut up John in prison.

(b) *The Genealogy of Jesus*
   iii. 23–28. Cf. Mt. i. 1–17.

23. And Jesus himself, when he began to teach, was about thirty
years of age, being the son (as was supposed) of Joseph, the son of
Heli. (Here follows the genealogy.)

II. THE REJECTION AT NAZARETH
(iv. 16–30)

16. And he came to Nazareth, where he had been brought up: and
he entered, as his custom was, into the synagogue on the sabbath day,
and stood up to read. 17. And there was delivered unto him the book
of the prophet Isaiah. And he opened the book, and found the place
where it was written,

> 18. The Spirit of the Lord is upon me,
>   Because he anointed me to preach good tidings to the poor:
>   He hath sent me to proclaim release to the captives,
>   And recovering of sight to the blind,
>   To set at liberty them that are bruised,
> 19. To proclaim the acceptable year of the Lord (Isa. lxi. 1f.).

20. And he closed the book, and gave it back to the attendant,
and sat down: and the eyes of all in the synagogue were fastened on
him. 21. And he began to say unto them, To-day hath this scripture
been fulfilled in your ears. 22. And all bare him witness, and wondered
at the words of grace which proceeded out of his mouth: and they
said, Is not this Joseph's son? 23. And he said unto them, Doubtless
ye will say unto me this parable, Physician, heal thyself: whatsoever
we have heard done at Capernaum, do also here in thine own country.
24. And he said, Verily I say unto you, No prophet is acceptable in
his own country. 25. But of a truth I say unto you, There were many
widows in Israel in the days of Elijah, when the heaven was shut up
three years and six months, when there came a great famine over all
the land; 26. and unto none of them was Elijah sent, but only to
Zarephath, in the land of Sidon, unto a woman that was a widow.
27. And there were many lepers in Israel in the time of Elisha the
prophet; and none of them was cleansed, but only Naaman the
Syrian. 28. And they were all filled with wrath in the synagogue, as
they heard these things; 29. and they rose up, and cast him forth out
of the city, and led him unto the brow of the hill whereon their city
was built, that they might throw him down headlong. 30. But he
passing through the midst of them went his way.

III. MIGHTY WORKS

(a) *The Wonderful Draught*
   v. 1–11. Cf. Mk. i. 16–20 and Jn. xxi. 1–14.

1. Now it came to pass, while the multitude pressed upon him and heard the word of God, that he was standing by the lake of Gennesaret; 2. and he saw two boats standing by the lake: but the fishermen had gone out of them, and were washing their nets. 3. And he entered into one of the boats, which was Simon's, and asked him to put out a little from the land. And he sat down and taught the multitudes out of the boat. 4. And when he had left speaking, he said unto Simon, Put out into the deep, and let down your nets for a draught. 5. And Simon answered and said, Master, we toiled all night, and took nothing: but at thy word I will let down the nets. 6. And when they had this done, they inclosed a great multitude of fishes; and their nets were breaking; 7. and they beckoned unto their partners in the other boat, that they should come and help them. And they came, and filled both the boats, so that they began to sink. 8. But Simon Peter, when he saw it, fell down at Jesus' knees, saying, Depart from me; for I am a sinful man, O Lord. 9. For he was amazed, and all that were with him, at the draught of the fishes which they had taken; 10. and so were also James and John, sons of Zebedee, which were partners with Simon. And Jesus said unto Simon, Fear not; from henceforth thou shalt catch men. 11. And when they had brought their boats to land, they left all, and followed him.

(b) *The Widow of Nain's Son*
   vii. 11–17.

11. And it came to pass soon afterwards, that he went to a city called Nain; and his disciples went with him, and a great multitude. 12. Now when he drew near to the gate of the city, behold, there was carried out one that was dead, the only son of his mother, and she was a widow: and much people of the city was with her. 13. And when the Lord saw her, he had compassion on her, and said unto her, Weep not. 14. And he came nigh and touched the bier: and the bearers stood still. And he said, Young man, I say unto thee, Arise. 15. And he that was dead sat up, and began to speak. And he gave him to his mother. 16. And fear took hold on all: and they glorified God, saying, A great prophet is arisen among us: and, God hath visited his people. 17. And this report went forth concerning him in the whole of Judaea, and all the region round about.

(c) *The Woman who was a Sinner*
   vii. 36–viii. 3. Cf. Mk. xiv. 3f.

36. And one of the Pharisees desired him that he would eat with

him. And he entered into the Pharisee's house, and sat down to meat. 37. And behold, a woman which was in the city, a sinner; and when she knew that he was sitting at meat in the Pharisee's house, she brought an alabaster cruse of ointment, 38. and standing behind at his feet, weeping, she began to wet his feet with her tears, and wiped them with the hair of her head, and kissed his feet, and anointed them with the ointment. 39. Now when the Pharisee which had bidden him saw it, he spake within himself, saying, This man, if he were a prophet, would have perceived who and what manner of woman this is which toucheth him, that she is a sinner. 40. And Jesus answering said unto him, Simon, I have somewhat to say unto thee. And he saith, Master, say on. 41. A certain lender had two debtors: the one owed five hundred pence, and the other fifty. 42. When they had not wherewith to pay, he forgave them both. Which of them therefore will love him most? 43. Simon answered and said, He, I suppose, to whom he forgave the most. And he said unto him, Thou hast rightly judged. 44. And turning to the woman, he said unto Simon, Seest thou this woman? I entered into thine house, thou gavest me no water for my feet: but she hath wetted my feet with her tears, and wiped them with her hair. 45. Thou gavest me no kiss: but she, since the time I came in, hath not ceased to kiss my feet. 46. My head with oil thou didst not anoint: but she hath anointed my feet with ointment. 47. Wherefore I say unto thee, Her sins, which are many, are forgiven; for she loved much: but to whom little is forgiven, the same loveth little. 48. And he said unto her, Thy sins are forgiven. 49. And they that sat at meat with him began to say within themselves, Who is this that even forgiveth sins? 50. And he said unto the woman, Thy faith hath saved thee; go in peace.

viii. 1. And it came to pass soon afterwards, that he went about through cities and villages, preaching and bringing the good tidings of the kingdom of God, and with him the twelve, 2. and certain women which had been healed of evil spirits and infirmities, Mary that was called Magdalene, from whom seven devils had gone out, 3. and Joanna the wife of Chuza Herod's steward, and Susanna, and many others, which ministered unto them of their substance.

IV. LESSONS

(a) *To the Disciples in Samaria*
    ix. 51–56.

51. And it came to pass, when the days were well-nigh come that he should be received up, he stedfastly set his face to go to Jerusalem, 52. and sent messengers before his face: and they went, and entered

into a village of the Samaritans, to make ready for him. 53. And they did not receive him, because his face was as though he were going to Jerusalem. 54. And when his disciples James and John saw this, they said, Lord, wilt thou that we bid fire to come down from heaven, and consume them? 55. But he turned, and rebuked them. 56. And they went to another village.

(b) To the Seventy
x. 1, 17–20.

1. Now after these things the Lord appointed seventy others, and sent them two and two before his face into every city and place, whither he himself was about to come.

17. And the seventy returned with joy, saying, Lord, even the devils are subject unto us in thy name. 18. And he said unto them, I beheld Satan fallen as lightning from heaven. 19. Behold, I have given you authority to tread upon serpents and scorpions, and over all the power of the enemy: and nothing shall in any wise hurt you, 20. Howbeit in this rejoice not, that the spirits are subject unto you; but rejoice that your names are written in heaven.

(c) To a Rabbi—the Good Samaritan
x. 25–37.

25. And behold, a certain lawyer stood up and tempted him, saying, Master, what shall I do to inherit eternal life? 26. And he said unto him, What is written in the law? how readest thou? 27. And he answering said, Thou shalt love the Lord thy God with all thy heart, and with all thy soul, and with all thy strength, and with all thy mind; and thy neighbour as thyself. 28. And he said unto him, Thou hast answered right: this do, and thou shalt live. 29. But he, desiring to justify himself, said unto Jesus, And who is my neighbour? 30. Jesus made answer and said, A certain man was going down from Jerusalem to Jericho; and he fell among robbers, which both stripped him and beat him, and departed, leaving him half dead. 31. And by chance a certain priest was going down that way: and when he saw him, he passed by on the other side. 32. And in like manner a Levite also, when he came to the place, and saw him, passed by on the other side. 33. But a certain Samaritan, as he journeyed, came where he was: and when he saw him, he was moved with compassion, 34. and came to him, and bound up his wounds, pouring on them oil and wine; and he set him on his own beast, and brought him to an inn, and took care of him. 35. And on the morrow he took out two pence, and gave them to the host, and said, Take care of him; and whatsoever thou spendest more, I, when I come back again, will repay

thee. 36. Which of these three, thinkest thou, proved neighbour unto him that fell among the robbers? 37. And he said, He that shewed mercy on him. And Jesus said unto him, Go, and do thou likewise.

(d) To Martha—the Good Part
x. 38–42.

38. Now as they went on their way, he entered into a certain village: and a certain woman named Martha received him into her house. 39. And she had a sister called Mary, which also sat at the Lord's feet, and heard his word. 40. But Martha was cumbered about much serving; and she came up to him, and said, Lord, dost thou not care that my sister did leave me to serve alone? bid her therefore that she help me. 41. But the Lord answered and said unto her, Martha, Martha, thou art anxious and troubled about many things: 42. but one thing is needful: for Mary hath chosen the good part, which shall not be taken away from her.

(e) How to Pray—the Friend at Midnight
xi. 1–8, 53f., xii. 1.

1. And it came to pass, as he was praying in a certain place, that when he ceased, one of his disciples said unto him, Lord, teach us to pray, even as John also taught his disciples. 2. And he said unto them, When ye pray, say, Father, Hallowed be thy name. Thy kingdom come. 3. Give us day by day our daily bread. 4. And forgive us our sins; for we ourselves also forgive every one that is indebted to us. And bring us not into temptation.

5. And he said unto them, Which of you shall have a friend, and shall go unto him at midnight, and say to him, Friend, lend me three loaves; 6. for a friend of mine is come to me from a journey, and I have nothing to set before him; 7. and he from within shall answer and say, Trouble me not: the door is now shut, and my children are with me in bed; I cannot rise and give thee? 8. I say unto you, Though he will not rise and give him, because he is his friend, yet because of his importunity he will arise and give him as many as he needeth.

53. And when he was come out from thence, the scribes and the Pharisees began to press upon him vehemently, and to provoke him to speak of many things; 54. laying wait for him, to catch something out of his mouth.

xii. 1. In the mean time, when the many thousands of the multitude were gathered together, insomuch that they trode one upon another, he began to say unto his disciples first of all, Beware ye of the leaven of the Pharisees, which is hypocrisy.

V. WARNINGS

(a) Against Greed—the Rich Fool
xii. 13-21.

13. And one out of the multitude said unto him, Master, bid my brother divide the inheritance with me. 14. But he said unto him, Man, who made me a judge or a divider over you? 15. And he said unto them, Take heed, and keep yourselves from all covetousness: for a man's life consisteth not in the abundance of the things which he possesseth. 16. And he spake a parable unto them, saying, The ground of a certain rich man brought forth plentifully: 17. and he reasoned within himself, saying, What shall I do, because I have not where to bestow my fruits? 18. And he said, This will I do: I will pull down my barns, and build greater; and there will I bestow all my corn and my goods. 19. And I will say to my soul, Soul, thou hast much goods laid up for many years; take thine ease, eat, drink, be merry. 20. But God said unto him, Thou foolish one, this night is thy soul required of thee; and the things which thou hast prepared, whose shall they be? 21. So is he that layeth up treasure for himself, and is not rich toward God.

(b) On Repentance—the Barren Fig Tree
xiii. 1-9.

1. Now there were some present at that very season which told him of the Galilaeans, whose blood Pilate had mingled with their sacrifices. 2. And he answered and said unto them, Think ye that these Galilaeans were sinners above all the Galilaeans, because they have suffered these things? 3. I tell you, Nay: but, except ye repent, ye shall all in like manner perish. 4. Or those eighteen, upon whom the tower in Siloam fell, and killed them, think ye that they were offenders above all the men that dwell in Jerusalem? 5. I tell you, Nay: but, except ye repent, ye shall all likewise perish.

6. And he spake this parable; A certain man had a fig tree planted in his vineyard; and he came seeking fruit thereon, and found none. 7. And he said unto the vine-dresser, Behold, these three years I come seeking fruit on this fig tree, and find none: cut it down; why doth it also cumber the ground? 8. And he answering saith unto him, Lord, let it alone this year also, till I shall dig about it, and dung it: 9. and if it bear fruit thenceforth, well; but if not, thou shalt cut it down.

(c) Sabbath Observance—(1) The Hunch-backed Woman
xiii. 10-17.

10. And he was teaching in one of the synagogues on the sabbath day. 11. And behold, a woman which had a spirit of infirmity eighteen

years; and she was bowed together, and could in no wise lift herself up. 12. And when Jesus saw her, he called her, and said to her, Woman, thou art loosed from thine infirmity. 13. And he laid his hands upon her: and immediately she was made straight, and glorified God. 14. And the ruler of the synagogue, being moved with indignation because Jesus had healed on the sabbath, answered and said to the multitude, There are six days in which men ought to work: in them therefore come and be healed, and not on the day of the sabbath. 15. But the Lord answered him, and said, Ye hypocrites, doth not each one of you on the sabbath loose his ox or his ass from the stall, and lead him away to watering? 16. And ought not this woman, being a daughter of Abraham, whom Satan had bound, lo, these eighteen years, to have been loosed from this bond on the day of the sabbath? 17. And as he said these things, all his adversaries were put to shame: and all the multitude rejoiced for all the glorious things that were done by him.

(d) *To Herod Antipas*
     xiii. 31–33.

31. In that very hour there came certain Pharisees, saying to him, Get thee out, and go hence: for Herod would fain kill thee. 32. And he said unto them, Go and say to that fox, Behold, I cast out devils and perform cures to-day and to-morrow, and the third day I am perfected. 33. Howbeit I must go on my way to-day and to-morrow and the day following: for it cannot be that a prophet perish out of Jerusalem.

(e) *Sabbath Observance*—(2) *the Man with Dropsy*
     xiv. 1–6.

1. And it came to pass, when he went into the house of one of the rulers of the Pharisees on a sabbath to eat bread, that they were watching him. 2. And behold, there was before him a certain man which had the dropsy. 3. And Jesus answering spake unto the lawyers and the Pharisees, saying, Is it lawful to heal on the sabbath, or not? 4. But they held their peace. And he took him, and healed him, and let him go. 5. And he said unto them, Which of you shall have an ass or an ox fallen into a well, and will not straightway draw him up on a sabbath day? 6. And they could not answer again unto these things.

(f) *On Precedence and Hospitality*
     xiv. 7–10, 12–14.

7. And he spake a parable unto those which were bidden, when he marked how they chose out the chief seats; saying unto them, 8. When

thou art bidden of any man to a marriage feast, sit not down in the chief seat; lest haply a more honourable man than thou be bidden of him, 9. and he that bade thee and him shall come and say to thee, Give this man place; and then thou shalt begin with shame to take the lowest place. 10. But when thou art bidden, go and sit down in the lowest place; that when he that hath bidden thee cometh, he may say to thee, Friend, go up higher: then shalt thou have glory in the presence of all that sit at meat with thee.

12. And he said to him also that had bidden him, When thou makest a dinner or a supper, call not thy friends, nor thy brethren, nor thy kinsmen, nor rich neighbours; lest haply they also bid thee again, and a recompense be made thee. 13. But when thou makest a feast, bid the poor, the maimed, the lame, the blind: 14. and thou shalt be blessed; because they have not wherewith to recompense thee: for thou shalt be recompensed in the resurrection of the just.

(g) *On Counting the Cost*
    xiv. 28–33.

28. For which of you, desiring to build a tower, doth not first sit down and count the cost, whether he have wherewith to complete it? 29. Lest haply, when he hath laid a foundation, and is not able to finish, all that behold begin to mock him, 30. saying, This man began to build, and was not able to finish. 31. Or what king, as he goeth to encounter another king in war, will not sit down first and take counsel whether he is able with ten thousand to meet him that cometh against him with twenty thousand? 32. Or else, while the other is yet a great way off, he sendeth an ambassage, and asketh conditions of peace. 33. So therefore whosoever he be of you that renounceth not all that he hath, he cannot be my disciple.

VI. PARABLES OF THE LOST

(a) *The Lost Sheep*
    xv. 1–7. Cf. Mt. xviii. 12–14, M.

1. Now all the publicans and sinners were drawing near unto him for to hear him. 2. And both the Pharisees and the scribes murmured, saying, This man receiveth sinners, and eateth with them.

3. And he spake unto them this parable, saying, 4. What man of you, having a hundred sheep, and having lost one of them, doth not leave the ninety and nine in the wilderness, and go after that which is lost, until he find it? 5. And when he hath found it, he layeth it on his shoulders, rejoicing. 6. And when he cometh home, he calleth together his friends and his neighbours, saying unto them, Rejoice with me, for I have found my sheep which was lost. 7. I say unto

you, that even so there shall be joy in heaven over one sinner that repenteth, more than over ninety and nine righteous persons, which need no repentance.

(b) *The Lost Coin*
    xv. 8–10.

8. Or what woman having ten pieces of silver, if she lose one piece, doth not light a lamp, and sweep the house, and seek diligently until she find it? 9. And when she hath found it, she calleth together her friends and neighbours, saying, Rejoice with me, for I have found the piece which I had lost. 10. Even so, I say unto you, there is joy in the presence of the angels of God over one sinner that repenteth.

(c) *The Lost Son*
    xv. 11–32.

11. And he said, A certain man had two sons: 12. and the younger of them said to his father, Father, give me the portion of thy substance that falleth to me. And he divided unto them his living. 13. And not many days after the younger son gathered all together, and took his journey into a far country; and there he wasted his substance with riotous living. 14. And when he had spent all, there arose a mighty famine in that country; and he began to be in want. 15. And he went and joined himself to one of the citizens of that country; and he sent him into his fields to feed swine. 16. And he would fain have been filled with the husks that the swine did eat: and no man gave unto him. 17. But when he came to himself he said, How many hired servants of my father's have bread enough and to spare, and I perish here with hunger! 18. I will arise and go to my father, and will say unto him, Father, I have sinned against heaven, and in thy sight: 19. I am no more worthy to be called thy son: make me as one of thy hired servants. 20. And he arose, and came to his father. But while he was yet afar off, his father saw him, and was moved with compassion, and ran, and fell on his neck, and kissed him. 21. And the son said unto him, Father, I have sinned against heaven, and in thy sight: I am no more worthy to be called thy son. 22. But the father said to his servants, Bring forth quickly the best robe, and put it on him; and put a ring on his hand, and shoes on his feet: 23. and bring the fatted calf, and kill it, and let us eat, and make merry: 24. for this my son was dead, and is alive again; he was lost, and is found. And they began to be merry. 25. Now his elder son was in the field: and as he came and drew nigh to the house, he heard music and dancing. 26. And he called to him one of the servants, and inquired what these things might be. 27. And he said unto him, Thy brother is come; and thy father hath killed the fatted calf, because

*

he hath received him safe and sound. 28. But he was angry, and
would not go in: and his father came out, and intreated him. 29. But
he answered and said to his father, Lo, these many years do I serve
thee, and I never transgressed a commandment of thine: and yet
thou never gavest me a kid, that I might make merry with my friends:
30. but when this thy son came, which hath devoured thy living
with harlots, thou killedst for him the fatted calf. 31. And he said
unto him, Son, thou art ever with me, and all that is mine is thine.
32. But it was meet to make merry and be glad: for this thy brother
was dead, and is alive again; and was lost, and is found.

VII. PARABLES, ETC., OF RESPONSIBILITY

(a) Foresight—the Unjust Steward
xvi. 1–12.

1. And he said also unto the disciples, There was a certain rich man,
which had a steward; and the same was accused unto him that he
was wasting his goods. 2. And he called him, and said unto him,
What is this that I hear of thee? render the account of thy stewardship; for thou canst be no longer steward. 3. And the steward said
within himself, What shall I do, seeing that my lord taketh away the
stewardship from me? I have not strength to dig; to beg I am
ashamed. 4. I am resolved what to do, that, when I am put out of
the stewardship, they may receive me into their houses. 5. And calling
to him each one of his lord's debtors, he said to the first, How much
owest thou unto my lord? 6. And he said, A hundred measures of oil.
And he said unto him, Take thy bond, and sit down quickly and
write fifty. 7. Then said he to another, And how much owest thou?
And he said, A hundred measures of wheat. He saith unto him,
Take thy bond, and write fourscore. 8. And his lord commended
the unrighteous steward because he had done wisely: for the sons
of this world are for their own generation wiser than the sons of the
light. 9. And I say unto you, Make to yourselves friends by means
of the mammon of unrighteousness; that, when it shall fail, they
may receive you in the eternal tabernacles. 10. He that is faithful
in a very little is faithful also in much: and he that is unrighteous in
a very little is unrighteous also in much. 11. If therefore ye have not
been faithful in the unrighteous mammon, who will commit to your
trust the true riches? 12. And if ye have not been faithful in that
which is another's, who will give you that which is your own?

(b) Money—Dives and Lazarus
xvi. 14–15, 19–31.

14. And the Pharisees, who were lovers of money, heard all these

things; and they scoffed at him. 15. And he said unto them, Ye are they that justify yourselves in the sight of men; but God knoweth your hearts: for that which is exalted among men is an abomination in the sight of God. 19. Now there was a certain rich man, and he was clothed in purple and fine linen, faring sumptuously every day: 20. and a certain beggar named Lazarus was laid at his gate, full of sores, 21. and desiring to be fed with the crumbs that fell from the rich man's table; yea, even the dogs came and licked his sores. 22. And it came to pass, that the beggar died, and that he was carried away by the angels into Abraham's bosom: and the rich man also died, and was buried. 23. And in Hades he lifted up his eyes, being in torments, and seeth Abraham afar off, and Lazarus in his bosom. 24. And he cried and said, Father Abraham, have mercy on me, and send Lazarus, that he may dip the tip of his finger in water, and cool my tongue; for I am in anguish in this flame. 25. But Abraham said, Son, remember that thou in thy lifetime receivedst thy good things, and Lazarus in like manner evil things: but now here he is comforted, and thou art in anguish. 26. And beside all this, between us and you there is a great gulf fixed, that they which would pass from hence to you may not be able, and that none may cross over from thence to us. 27. And he said, I pray thee therefore, father, that thou wouldest send him to my father's house; 28. for I have five brethren; that he may testify unto them, lest they also come into this place of torment. 29. But Abraham saith, They have Moses and the prophets; let them hear them. 30. And he said, Nay, father Abraham: but if one go to them from the dead, they will repent. 31. And he said unto him, If they hear not Moses and the prophets, neither will they be persuaded, if one rise from the dead.

(c) *On Serving God—Master and Servant*
    xvii. 7–10.

7. But who is there of you, having a servant plowing or keeping sheep, that will say unto him, when he is come in from the field, Come straightway and sit down to meat: 8. and will not rather say unto him, Make ready wherewith I may sup, and gird thyself, and serve me, till I have eaten and drunken; and afterward thou shalt eat and drink? 9. Doth he thank the servant because he did the things that were commanded? 10. Even so ye also, when ye shall have done all the things that are commanded you, say, We are unprofitable servants; we have done that which it was our duty to do.

(d) *On Gratitude—the Ten Lepers*
    xvii. 11–21.

11. And it came to pass, as they were on the way to Jerusalem, that

he was passing through the midst of Samaria and Galilee. 12. And as he entered into a certain village, there met him ten men that were lepers, which stood afar off: 13. and they lifted up their voices, saying, Jesus, Master, have mercy on us. 14. And when he saw them, he said unto them, Go and shew yourselves unto the priests. And it came to pass, as they went, they were cleansed. 15. And one of them, when he saw that he was healed, turned back, with a loud voice glorifying God; 16. and he fell upon his face at his feet, giving him thanks: and he was a Samaritan. 17. And Jesus answering said, Were not the ten cleansed? but where are the nine? 18. Were there none found that returned to give glory to God, save this stranger? 19. And he said unto him, Arise, and go thy way: thy faith hath made thee whole.

20. And being asked by the Pharisees, when the kingdom of God cometh, he answered them and said, The kingdom of God cometh not with observation: 21. neither shall they say, Lo, here! or, There! for lo, the kingdom of God is within you.

(e) On Perseverance—the Importunate Widow
    xviii. 1–8.

1. And he spake a parable unto them to the end that they ought always to pray, and not to faint; 2. saying, There was in a city a judge, which feared not God, and regarded not man: 3. and there was a widow in that city; and she came oft unto him, saying, Avenge me of mine adversary. 4. And he would not for a while: but afterward he said within himself, Though I fear not God, nor regard man; 5. yet because this widow troubleth me, I will avenge her, lest she wear me out by her continual coming. 6. And the Lord said, Hear what the unrighteous judge saith. 7. And shall not God avenge his elect, which cry to him day and night, and he is longsuffering over them? 8. I say unto you, that he will avenge them speedily. Howbeit when the Son of man cometh, shall he find faith on the earth?

(f) On Prayer—the Pharisee and the Publican
    xviii. 9–14.

9. And he spake also this parable unto certain which trusted in themselves that they were righteous, and set all others at nought: 10. Two men went up into the temple to pray; the one a Pharisee, and the other a publican. 11. The Pharisee stood and prayed thus with himself, God, I thank thee, that I am not as the rest of men, extortioners, unjust, adulterers, or even as this publican. 12. I fast twice in the week; I give tithes of all that I get. 13. But the publican, standing afar off, would not lift up so much as his eyes unto heaven, but smote his breast, saying, God, be merciful to me a sinner. 14. I say

unto you, This man went down to his house justified rather than the other: for every one that exalteth himself shall be humbled; but he that humbleth himself shall be exalted.

(g) On Opportunities—Zaccheus: the Parable of the Pounds
xix. 1–27.

1. And he entered and was passing through Jericho. 2. And behold, a man called by name Zacchaeus; and he was a chief publican, and he was rich. 3. And he sought to see Jesus who he was; and could not for the crowd, because he was little of stature. 4. And he ran on before, and climbed up into a sycomore tree to see him: for he was to pass that way. 5. And when Jesus came to the place, he looked up, and said unto him, Zacchaeus, make haste, and come down; for to-day I must abide at thy house. 6. And he made haste, and came down, and received him joyfully. 7. And when they saw it, they all murmured, saying, He is gone in to lodge with a man that is a sinner. 8. And Zacchaeus stood, and said unto the Lord, Behold, Lord, the half of my goods I give to the poor; and if I have wrongfully exacted aught of any man, I restore fourfold. 9. And Jesus said unto him, To-day is salvation come to this house, forasmuch as he also is a son of Abraham. 10. For the Son of man came to seek and to save that which was lost.

Parable of the Pounds
11–27. Cf. Mt. xxv. 14–30, M.

11. And as they heard these things, he added and spake a parable, because he was nigh to Jerusalem, and because they supposed that the kingdom of God was immediately to appear. 12. He said therefore, A certain nobleman went into a far country, to receive for himself a kingdom, and to return. 13. And he called ten servants of his, and gave them ten pounds, and said unto them, Trade ye herewith till I come. 14. But his citizens hated him, and sent an ambassage after him, saying, We will not that this man reign over us. 15. And it came to pass, when he was come back again, having received the kingdom, that he commanded these servants, unto whom he had given the money, to be called to him, that he might know what they had gained by trading. 16. And the first came before him, saying, Lord, thy pound hath made ten pounds more. 17. And he said unto him, Well done, thou good servant: because thou wast found faithful in a very little, have thou authority over ten cities. 18. And the second came, saying, Thy pound, Lord, hath made five pounds. 19. And he said unto him also, Be thou also over five cities. 20. And another came, saying, Lord, behold, here is thy pound, which I kept laid up in a napkin: 21. for I feared thee, because thou art an

austere man: thou takest up that thou layedst not down, and reapest that thou didst not sow. 22. He saith unto him, Out of thine own mouth will I judge thee, thou wicked servant. Thou knewest that I am an austere man, taking up that I laid not down, and reaping that I did not sow; 23. then wherefore gavest thou not my money into the bank, and I at my coming should have required it with interest? 24. And he said unto them that stood by, Take away from him the pound, and give it unto him that hath the ten pounds. 25. And they said unto him, Lord, he hath ten pounds. 26. I say unto you, that unto every one that hath shall be given; but from him that hath not, even that which he hath shall be taken away from him. 27. Howbeit these mine enemies, which would not that I should reign over them, bring hither, and slay them before me.

VIII. JERUSALEM

(a) *Approach to the City*
    xix. 37–44.

37. And as he was now drawing nigh, even at the descent of the mount of Olives, the whole multitude of the disciples began to rejoice and praise God with a loud voice for all the mighty works which they had seen; 38. saying, Blessed is the King that cometh in the name of the Lord: peace in heaven, and glory in the highest. 39. And some of the Pharisees from the multitude said unto him, Master, rebuke thy disciples. 40. And he answered and said, I tell you that, if these shall hold their peace, the stones will cry out.

41. And when he drew nigh, he saw the city and wept over it, 42. saying, If thou hadst known in this day, even thou, the things which belong unto peace! but now they are hid from thine eyes. 43. For the days shall come upon thee, when thine enemies shall cast up a bank about thee, and compass thee round, and keep thee in on every side, and shall dash thee to the ground, and thy children within thee; 44. and they shall not leave in thee one stone upon another; because thou knewest not the time of thy visitation.

    xx. 18.

Every one that falleth on that stone shall be broken to pieces; but on whomsoever it shall fall, it will scatter him as dust.

(b) *Apocalyptic Sayings*
    xxi. 11b, 18, 25b, 26a, 28, 34–36.

(N.B. The basis of Lk. xxi seems to be Mk. xiii which Luke has revised and, in parts, re-written in the light of A.D. 70, and to which he has added the following sayings.)

11*b*. And there shall be terrors and great signs from heaven.

18. And not a hair of your head shall perish.

25*b*–26*a*. And there shall be . . . upon the earth distress of nations, in perplexity for the roaring of the sea and the billows; men fainting for fear, and for expectation of the things which are coming on the world.

28. But when these things begin to come to pass, look up, and lift up your heads; because your redemption draweth nigh.

34–36. But take heed to yourselves, lest haply your hearts be overcharged with surfeiting, and drunkenness, and cares of this life, and that day come on you suddenly as a snare: 35. for so shall it come upon all them that dwell on the face of all the earth. 36. But watch ye at every season, making supplication, that ye may prevail to escape all these things that shall come to pass, and to stand before the Son of man.

(c) The Passion and the Resurrection
xxii. 14–xxiv.

(Narratives which seem to be based on Mark are bracketed.)

xxii. 14. And when the hour was come, he sat down, and the apostles with him. 15. And he said unto them, With desire I have desired to eat this passover with you before I suffer: 16. for I say unto you, I will not eat it, until it be fulfilled in the kingdom of God. 17. And he received a cup, and when he had given thanks, he said, Take this and divide it among yourselves: [18. for I say unto you, I will not drink from henceforth of the fruit of the vine, until the kingdom of God shall come. 19. And he took bread, and when he had given thanks, he brake it, and gave to them, saying, This is my body][1] which is given for you: this do in remembrance of me. 20. And the cup in like manner after supper, saying, This cup is the new covenant in my blood, even that which is poured out for you [21. But behold, the hand of him that betrayeth me is with me on the table. 22. For the Son of man indeed goeth, as it hath been determined: but woe unto that man through whom he is betrayed! 23. And they began to question among themselves, which of them it was that should do this thing.]

24. And there arose also a contention among them, which of them is accounted to be the greatest. 25. And he said unto them, The kings of the Gentiles have lordship over them; and they that have authority over them are called Benefactors. 26. But ye shall not be so: but he that is the greater among you, let him become as the younger; and he that is chief, as he that doth serve. 27. For whether

[1] 19*b*-20 textually doubtful.

is greater, he that sitteth at meat, or he that serveth? is not he that sitteth at meat? but I am in the midst of you as he that serveth. 28. But ye are they which have continued with me in my temptations; 29. and I appoint unto you a kingdom, even as my Father appointed unto me, 30. that ye may eat and drink at my table in my kingdom; and ye shall sit on thrones judging the twelve tribes of Israel. 31. Simon, Simon, behold, Satan asked to have you, that he might sift you as wheat: 32. but I have made supplication for thee, that thy faith fail not; and do thou, when once thou hast turned again, stablish thy brethren. 33. And he said unto him, Lord, with thee I am ready to go both to prison and to death. [34. And he said, I tell thee, Peter, the cock shall not crow this day, until thou shalt thrice deny that thou knowest me.]

35. And he said unto them, When I sent you forth without purse, and wallet, and shoes, lacked ye anything? And they said, Nothing. 36. And he said unto them, But now, he that hath a purse, let him take it, and likewise a wallet: and he that hath none, let him sell his cloke, and buy a sword. 37. For I say unto you, that this which is written must be fulfilled in me, And he was reckoned with transgressors: for that which concerneth me hath fulfilment. 38. And they said, Lord, behold, here are two swords. And he said unto them, It is enough.

[39. And he came out, and went, as his custom was, unto the mount of Olives; and the disciples also followed him. 40. And when he was at the place, he said unto them, Pray that ye enter not into temptation. 41. And he was parted from them about a stone's cast; and he kneeled down and prayed, 42. saying, Father, if thou be willing, remove this cup from me: nevertheless not my will, but thine, be done.] 43.[1] And there appeared unto him an angel from heaven, strengthening him. 44. And being in an agony he prayed more earnestly: and his sweat became as it were great drops of blood falling down upon the ground. [45. And when he rose up from his prayer, he came unto the disciples, and found them sleeping for sorrow, 46. and said unto them, Why sleep ye? rise and pray, that ye enter not into temptation.]

[47. While he yet spake, behold, a multitude, and he that was called Judas, one of the twelve, went before them; and he drew near unto Jesus to kiss him.] 48. But Jesus said unto him, Judas, betrayest thou the Son of man with a kiss? 49. And when they that were about him saw what would follow, they said, Lord, shall we smite with the sword? [50. And a certain one of them smote the servant of the high priest, and struck off his right ear.] 51. But Jesus answered and said, Suffer ye thus far. And he touched his ear, and healed him. [52. And

[1] 43-44 textually doubtful.

Jesus said unto the chief priests, and captains of the temple, and
elders, which were come against him, Are ye come out, as against a
robber, with swords and staves? 53. When I was daily with you in
the temple, ye stretched not forth your hands against me:] but this
is your hour, and the power of darkness.

[54. And they seized him, and led him away, and brought him
into the high priest's house. But Peter followed afar off. 55. And
when they had kindled a fire in the midst of the court, and had sat
down together, Peter sat in the midst of them. 56. And a certain maid
seeing him as he sat in the light of the fire, and looking stedfastly
upon him, said, This man also was with him. 57. But he denied,
saying, Woman, I know him not. 58. And after a little while another
saw him, and said, Thou also art one of them. But Peter said, Man,
I am not. 59. And after the space of about one hour another confidently affirmed, saying, Of a truth this man also was with him: for
he is a Galilaean. 60. But Peter said, Man, I know not what thou
sayest. And immediately, while he yet spake, the cock crew. 61. And
the Lord turned, and looked upon Peter. And Peter remembered the
word of the Lord, how that he said unto him, Before the cock crow
this day, thou shalt deny me thrice. 62. And he went out, and wept
bitterly.]

63. And the men that held Jesus mocked him, and beat him.
[64. And they blindfolded him, and asked him, saying, Prophesy:
who is he that struck thee?] 65. And many other things spake they
against him, reviling him.

[66. And as soon as it was day, the assembly of the elders of the
people was gathered together, both chief priests and scribes; and they
led him away into their council, saying, 67. If thou art the Christ,
tell us. But he said unto them, If I tell you, ye will not believe: 68. and
if I ask you, ye will not answer. 69. But from henceforth shall the
Son of man be seated at the right hand of the power of God. 70. And
they all said, Art thou then the Son of God? And he said unto them,
Ye say that I am. 71. And they said, What further need have we of
witness? for we ourselves have heard from his own mouth.]

xxiii. 1. And the whole company of them rose up, and brought
him before Pilate. 2. And they began to accuse him, saying, We
found this man perverting our nation, and forbidding to give tribute
to Caesar, and saying that he himself is Christ a king. [3. And Pilate
asked him, saying, Art thou the King of the Jews? And he answered
him and said, Thou sayest.] 4. And Pilate said unto the chief priests
and the multitudes, I find no fault in this man. 5. But they were
the more urgent, saying, He stirreth up the people, teaching throughout all Judaea, and beginning from Galilee even unto this place.
6. But when Pilate heard it, he asked whether the man were a Galilaean.

7. And when he knew that he was of Herod's jurisdiction, he sent him unto Herod, who himself also was at Jerusalem in these days. 8. Now when Herod saw Jesus, he was exceeding glad: for he was of a long time desirous to see him, because he had heard concerning him; and he hoped to see some miracle done by him. 9. And he questioned him in many words; but he answered him nothing. 10. And the chief priests and the scribes stood, vehemently accusing him. 11. And Herod with his soldiers set him at nought, and mocked him, and arraying him in gorgeous apparel sent him back to Pilate. 12. And Herod and Pilate became friends with each other that very day: for before they were at enmity between themselves.

13. And Pilate called together the chief priests and the rulers and the people, 14, and said unto them, Ye brought unto me this man, as one that perverteth the people: and behold, I, having examined him before you, found no fault in this man touching those things whereof ye accuse him: 15. no, nor yet Herod: for he sent him back unto us; and behold, nothing worthy of death hath been done by him. 16. I will therefore chastise him, and release him. [18. But they cried out all together, saying, Away with this man, and release unto us Barabbas: 19. one who for a certain insurrection made in the city, and for murder, was cast into prison. 20. And Pilate spake unto them again, desiring to release Jesus; 21. but they shouted, saying, Crucify, crucify him. 22. And he said unto them the third time, Why, what evil hath this man done? I have found no cause of death in him: I will therefore chastise him and release him. 23. But they were instant with loud voices, asking that he might be crucified. And their voices prevailed. 24. And Pilate gave sentence that what they asked for should be done. 25. And he released him that for insurrection and murder had been cast into prison, whom they asked for; but Jesus he delivered up to their will.]

[26. And when they led him away, they laid hold upon one Simon of Cyrene, coming from the country, and laid on him the cross, to bear it after Jesus.]

27. And there followed him a great multitude of the people, and of women who bewailed and lamented him. 28. But Jesus turning unto them said, Daughters of Jerusalem, weep not for me, but weep for yourselves, and for your children. 29. For behold, the days are coming, in which they shall say, Blessed are the barren, and the wombs that never bare, and the breasts that never gave suck. 30. Then shall they begin to say to the mountains, Fall on us; and to the hills, Cover us. 31. For if they do these things in the green tree, what shall be done in the dry?

[32. And there were also two others, malefactors, led with him to be put to death.]

[33. And when they came unto the place which is called The skull, there they crucified him, and the malefactors, one on the right hand and the other on the left.] 34.[1] And Jesus said, Father, forgive them; for they know not what they do. [And parting his garments among them, they cast lots. 35. And the people stood beholding. And the rulers also scoffed at him, saying, He saved others; let him save himself, if this is the Christ of God, his chosen. 36. And the soldiers also mocked him, coming to him, offering him vinegar, 37. and saying, If thou art the King of the Jews, save thyself. 38. And there was also a superscription over him, THIS IS THE KING OF THE JEWS.]

39. And one of the malefactors which were hanged railed on him, saying, Art not thou the Christ? save thyself and us. 40. But the other answered, and rebuking him said, Dost thou not even fear God, seeing thou art in the same condemnation? 41. And we indeed justly; for we receive the due rewards of our deeds: but this man hath done nothing amiss. 42. And he said, Jesus, remember me when thou comest in thy kingdom. 43. And he said unto him, Verily I say unto thee, To-day shalt thou be with me in Paradise. [44. And it was now about the sixth hour, and a darkness came over the whole land until the ninth hour, 45. the sun's light failing: and the veil of the temple was rent in the midst. 46. And when Jesus had cried with a loud voice] he said, Father, into thy hands I commend my spirit: and having said this, [he gave up the ghost. 47. And when the centurion saw what was done, he glorified God, saying, Certainly this was a righteous man.] 48. And all the multitudes that came together to this sight, when they beheld the things that were done, returned smiting their breasts. [49. And all his acquaintance, and the women that followed with him from Galilee, stood afar off, seeing these things.]

[50. And behold, a man named Joseph, who was a councillor, a good man and a righteous (51. he had not consented to their counsel and deed), a man of Arimathaea, a city of the Jews, who was looking for the kingdom of God: 52. this man went to Pilate, and asked for the body of Jesus. 53. And he took it down, and wrapped it in a linen cloth, and laid him in a tomb, that was hewn in stone, where never man had yet lain. 54. And it was the day of the Preparation, and the sabbath drew on]. 55. And the women, which had come with him out of Galilee, followed after, and beheld the tomb, and how his body was laid. 56. And they returned, and prepared spices and ointments.

56b. And on the sabbath they rested according to the commandment. xxiv. [1. But on the first day of the week, at early dawn, they

[1] 34a textually doubtful.

came unto the tomb, bringing the spices which they had prepared.
2. And they found the stone rolled away from the tomb. 3. And they
entered in, and found not the body of the Lord Jesus. 4. And it came
to pass, while they were perplexed thereabout, behold, two men
stood by them in dazzling apparel: 5. and as they were affrighted,
and bowed down their faces to the earth, they said unto them, Why
seek ye the living among the dead? 6.[1] He is not here, but is risen:
remember how he spake unto you when he was yet in Galilee, 7. saying
that the Son of man must be delivered up into the hands of sinful
men, and be crucified, and the third day rise again.] 8. And they
remembered his words, 9. and returned from the tomb, and told all
these things to the eleven, and to all the rest. 10. Now they were
Mary Magdalene, and Joanna, and Mary the mother of James: and
the other women with them told these things unto the apostles. 11.
And these words appeared in their sight as idle talk; and they disbelieved them. 12.[2] But Peter arose, and ran unto the tomb; and
stooping and looking in, he seeth the linen cloths by themselves; and
he departed to his home, wondering at that which was come to
pass.

13. And behold, two of them were going that very day to a village
named Emmaus, which was threescore furlongs from Jerusalem.
14. And they communed with each other of all these things which
had happened. 15. And it came to pass, while they communed and
questioned together, that Jesus himself drew near, and went with
them. 16. But their eyes were holden that they should not know him.
17. And he said unto them, What communications are these that ye
have one with another, as ye walk? And they stood still, looking sad.
18. And one of them, named Cleopas, answering said unto him, Dost
thou alone sojourn in Jerusalem and not know the things which are
come to pass there in these days? 19. And he said unto them, What
things? And they said unto him, The things concerning Jesus of
Nazareth, which was a prophet mighty in deed and word before
God and all the people: 20. and how the chief priests and our rulers
delivered him up to be condemned to death, and crucified him.
21. But we hoped that it was he which should redeem Israel. Yea
and beside all this, it is now the third day since these things came
to pass. 22. Moreover certain women of our company amazed us,
having been early at the tomb; 23. and when they found not his
body, they came, saying, that they had also seen a vision of angels,
which said that he was alive. 24. And certain of them that were
with us went to the tomb, and found it even so as the women had
said: but him they saw not. 25. And he said unto them, O foolish

[1] 6a textually doubtful.

[2] 12 textually doubtful.

men, and slow of heart to believe in all that the prophets have spoken! 26. Behoved it not the Christ to suffer these things, and to enter into his glory? 27. And beginning from Moses and from all the prophets, he interpreted to them in all the scriptures the things concerning himself. 28. And they drew nigh unto the village, whither they were going: and he made as though he would go further. 29. And they constrained him, saying, Abide with us: for it is toward evening, and the day is now far spent. And he went in to abide with them. 30. And it came to pass, when he had sat down with them to meat, he took the bread, and blessed it, and brake, and gave to them. 31. And their eyes were opened, and they knew him; and he vanished out of their sight. 32. And they said one to another, Was not our heart burning within us, while he spake to us in the way, while he opened to us the scriptures? 33. And they rose up that very hour, and returned to Jerusalem, and found the eleven gathered together, and them that were with them, 34. saying, The Lord is risen indeed, and hath appeared to Simon. 35. And they rehearsed the things that happened in the way, and how he was known of them in the breaking of the bread.

36. And as they spake these things, he himself stood in the midst of them, [1]and saith unto them, Peace be unto you. 37. But they were terrified and affrighted, and supposed that they beheld a spirit. 38. And he said unto them, Why are ye troubled? and wherefore do reasonings arise in your heart? 39. See my hands and my feet, that it is I myself: handle me, and see; for a spirit hath not flesh and bones, as ye behold me having. 40.[2] And when he had said this, he shewed them his hands and his feet. 41. And while they still disbelieved for joy, and wondered, he said unto them, Have ye here anything to eat? 42. And they gave him a piece of a broiled fish. 43. And he took it, and did eat before them.

44. And he said unto them, These are my words which I spake unto you, while I was yet with you, how that all things must needs be fulfilled, which are written in the law of Moses, and the prophets, and the psalms, concerning me. 45. Then opened he their mind, that they might understand the scriptures; 46. and he said unto them, Thus it is written, that the Christ should suffer, and rise again from the dead the third day; 47. and that repentance and remission of sins should be preached in his name unto all the nations, beginning from Jerusalem. 48. Ye are witnesses of these things. 49. And behold, I send forth the promise of my Father upon you: but tarry ye in the city, until ye be clothed with power from on high.

50. And he led them out until they were over against Bethany:

[1] 36b textually doubtful.

[2] 40 textually doubtful.

and he lifted up his hands, and blessed them. 51. And it came to pass, while he blessed them, he parted from them, [1]and was carried up into heaven. 52. And they worshipped him, and returned to Jerusalem with great joy: 53. and were continually in the temple, blessing God.

[1] 51-52 the words 'and . . . into heaven' and 'worshipped him, and' are textually doubtful.

INDEX OF SUBJECTS

INDEX OF AUTHORS